Die Frau ohne Schatten
by Hugo von Hofmannsthal and Richard Strauss
An Analysis of Text, Music, and their Relationship

German Studies in America

Edited by Heinrich Meyer

No. 29

PETER LANG

Bern · Frankfurt am Main · Las Vegas

Sherrill Hahn Pantle

Die Frau ohne Schatten by Hugo von Hofmannsthal and Richard Strauss

An Analysis of Text, Music, and their Relationship

PETER LANG
Bern · Frankfurt am Main · Las Vegas

© Peter Lang Publishers Ltd., Berne (Switzerland) 1978
Successors of Herbert Lang & Co. Ltd., Berne

ISBN 3-261-03073-9

Printed by Lang Druck Ltd., Liebefeld/Berne (Switzerland)

For Celia, Hardin, and David

TABLE OF CONTENTS

TABLE OF CONTENTS

TABLE OF CONTENTS

PREFACE

Many of Richard Strauss's and Hugo von Hofmannsthal's biographers have censured the collaboration in which these two men engaged. The Hofmannsthal scholars express the belief that Strauss's sensual settings inundate the libretti while the Strauss biographers tend to blame the poet for the composer's loss of pre-eminence in the musical avant-garde of his time. The assumption that the poet or the composer would have produced better works had he not collaborated with the other stands behind criticisms of this nature. The study which follows attempts to avoid such prejudicial methodology by basing its conclusions upon an exhaustive analysis of one opera and by confining its discussion to the soluble question of whether or not Strauss was successful in fulfilling Hofmannsthal's desires for the libretto of that opera.

Among the collaborators' disputed works the Frau ohne Schatten, premiered in 1919, has received attention which is remarkable for the diversity of opinion expressed about the libretto's and the opera's worth. This variation in assessments, the high regard which Strauss accorded the work, the central position which it occupies in the works of Hofmannsthal, and the existence of the fairy-tale in the equally valid but differentiated forms of prose and libretto make the opera an especially appropriate subject for analysis. The goal is to provide an objective basis for discussion of Strauss's treatment of Hofmannsthal's text.

The analysis offered here is divided into two separate parts. The first consists of a study of the symbols which Hofmannsthal employed in the libretto and characterizes the principal figures of the opera. The entire body of Hofmannsthal's works, including both versions of the fairy-tale, serves as source material for this part of the analysis. The second section of the analysis examines the music and its relationship to the libretto.

Preceding the second part of the analysis is a discussion which attempts to document Hofmannsthal's desires for the musical setting of his libretto the Frau ohne Schatten: 1) he expected Strauss to develop the musical characterizations of the principal figures in a manner which would be consistent with the characterizations begun in the libretto; 2) he hoped that Strauss would perceive the forms of the speeches and set them with music appropriate for their structure; 3) he desired that the musical setting of the text should allow comprehension of significant verse lines; 4) he perceived an analogy between his Frau ohne Schatten and W. A. Mozart's Zauberflöte, which led him to envision a definite musical style as an appropriate setting for the text.

The second section of the analysis is arranged in the form of a table having three parts. The first of these three parts consists of an analysis of the libretto and treats specific elements of the text, such as assonance and length of verse lines, and distinguishes between verse lines which serve primarily as vehicles for the expression of emotions and those which convey significant information and need to be comprehended by the audience if the plot is to be followed. A second section of this part of the analysis is reserved specifically for visual effects, such as lighting and gestures, which are indispensable for enhancing the libretto and the music. The third section analyzes the music and details both the structurally significant aspects

11

of the music, such as key centers and melodic-harmonic motives, and also the composer's treatment of the verses. Attention is also given here to Hofmannsthal's desires for the text and to whether or not Strauss's treatment of specific passages is an apparent fulfillment of these wishes.

The results of this detailed analysis of both the text and the music of the Frau ohne Schatten reveal that Strauss was most successful in fulfilling Hofmannsthal's expectation that the musical characterizations of the principal figures be consistent with the characterizations begun in the libretto. The musical characterizations of the Empress, the Emperor, and Barak seem to be particularly appropriate developments from the bare text. Less successful perhaps is the characterization of the Wife while the composer's characterization of the Nurse reveals at times a conception of her personality which differs from that of the poet's.

There is both convergence and divergence in Strauss's handling of the structures of the speeches. In most of the cases of divergence an identifiable and probably justifiable musical basis underlies the difference. There are a few instances, however, where the composer obviously differed from the poet in his conception of a speech or situation. The results in these cases, although apparently diverging from the poet's intent, are not necessarily lesser, only different.

As for Hofmannsthal's wish that the musical setting of the text should allow comprehension of significant verse lines, Strauss was sometimes successful in fulfilling this desire and sometimes unsuccessful. The musical fabric reveals frequent attempts to reduce the volume of or even completely silence the orchestral accompaniment in striving after this goal. Complete fulfillment of this desire was, however, not within Strauss's capability. The diction of soloists, the conductor's sense of balance between the orchestral accompaniment and the singers, the acoustics of the theater, even the timbre of the soloists' voices affect too greatly the audience's ability to comprehend the verses. The score and Strauss's testimony that he attempted to revive the secco recitativ for this opera indicate the composer's wish to satisfy this desire of the poet, even though he did not always succeed.

Hofmannsthal hoped that Strauss would find a musical style characterized by lightness and deftness, a style which would reconcile the good and the evil, the somber and the happy aspects of the opera, as he perceived Mozart had done in the Zauberflöte. To judge from Hofmannsthal's reaction to the opera, he found the finished product to be too somber and too heavy. The poet did not, however, blame Strauss entirely for what he perceived was a failing in this respect, but accepted for himself part of the responsibility for what he felt was excessive seriousness.

When the work is judged in its entirety, Strauss may be said to have succeeded most of the time in fulfilling the desires of Hofmannsthal for the libretto. The greatest variation between the poet's conception of the work and the composer's realization of it occurs in the third act, the weakest act of the entire opera. In spite of this weakness, any negative criticism of the work must bear in mind the positive realization of the first two acts. Hofmannsthal apparently made his desires for the text clear to Strauss and the composer was in apparent agreement with the poet's goals.

The current revival of the work has resulted in a more favorable assessment of the work than was the case upon the occasion of its premiere and immediately afterwards. The idealism and optimism inherent in the text seem to express a current widespread desire to experience a world healed of factionalism and dichotomies. The opera thus stands before its audiences as the realization of a lost hope.

This book owes its genesis and completion to many people. Dr. W.V. Blomster of the University of Colorado at Boulder was instrumental in the development of a synthetic view of a text and its musical setting. Dr. Gretchen Hieronymus of the same institution assisted on matters both of content and stylistics. Dr. Robert T. Firestone, also of the University of Colorado, gave many hours to reading and suggesting improvements in the manuscript. The quotations from the music and the libretto of the opera Die Frau ohne Schatten are reproduced by permission of Boosey and Hawkes Music Publishers Ltd., London, in the territory of all countries of the world except Germany, Danzig, Italy, Portugal and th U.S.S.R., and in these territories by Adolph Fürstner. Permission to quote from the collected works (Gesammelte Werke in Einzelausgaben) of Hugo von Hofmannsthal was kindly granted by S. Fischer Verlag of Frankfurt a.M. Atlantis Verlag of Zurich gave permission to quote from their publication of the correspondence between Richard Strauss and Hugo von Hofmannsthal. The assistance of all of these people and publishers has made this book possible. Deep gratitude is hereby expressed to each one.

Denver, Colorado
September 1977   Sherrill Hahn Pantle

CHAPTER I

INTRODUCTION

Early in the year 1906 Strauss contacted Hugo von Hofmannsthal inquiring whether he might have permission to compose Hofmannsthal's Elektra. Strauss had seen the drama performed by Max Reinhardt's theater troupe and was so impressed by it that he desired it as a libretto. (1) Hofmannsthal replied positively to this request:

> . . . und wie steht's mit Ihnen und "Elektra"? Es ist doch die
> Hoffnung auf keine geringe Freude, die Sie in mir so unerwartet
> rege gemacht haben. Wollen Sie mich durch ganz wenige Zeilen
> wissen lassen, ob diese Hoffnung wach bleiben darf oder sich
> schlafen legen soll? (2)

In this manner a relationship began which resulted in the production of several works, among them six operas - Elektra, premiered in 1909, the Rosenkavalier, 1911, Ariadne auf Naxos I, 1912 (Ariadne auf Naxos II, 1916), the Frau ohne Schatten, 1919, the Aegyptische Helena, 1928, and Arabella, 1933; two ballets - Josephslegende, 1914, and the Ruinen von Athen, 1924; one play with incidental music - the Bürger als Edelmann, 1918; a Kantate, 1914; and one film - the Rosenkavalier, 1926.

The very diversity and number of the body of works which this collaboration produced is in itself remarkable. Certainly this is one of the more significant facts abouth Strauss's and Hofmannsthal's co-operative efforts. Yet there is another distinguishing aspect: for possibly the first time in the history of German opera a significant poet consented to write libretti for a composer. (The first opera of this collaboration, Elektra, is excepted from this statement, because Hofmannsthal intended the text only for dramatic performance when he wrote it.) The Italian poet Metastasio, whose dramas and texts in Latin were so popular with the composers of the eighteenth century, is the only other poet in the history of German opera to have held a similar position for an extended period of time. It is questionable, however, whether Metastasio produced poetry that equals Hofmannsthal's in beauty of expression and depth of thought.

Willi Schuh emphasized the singularity of the Strauss-Hofmannsthal collaboration in his introduction to the third edition of their correspondence:

> Die Zusammenarbeit Richard Strauss' und Hugo von Hofmanns-
> thals - eines grossen Musikers und eines grossen Dichters - hat
> in der Geschichte des deutschen Musiktheaters nicht ihresglei-
> chen. (3)

The collaboration is thus viewed not only as a productive working relationship, but also as an extraordinary one in the history of the German theater.

One would expect when examining the collaboration from a logical point of view, that the two of them would have produced the very finest of works: one major

14

poet working with the most discussed German composer of the period 1890 - 1910
seems to promise significant works. Yet for many people, both literary and music
critics, the positive results did not occur or were exceeded in importance by negative factors. Among these critics is Strauss's biographer Norman Del Mar who
states:

> The span from Elektra [to Arabella] is incredibly wide and
> varied and, for all its temporary set-backs, marvelously fruit-
> ful. In the face of such productivity, with two undoubted and
> three near masterpieces to its credit, it seems almost petty to
> disparage the long relationship Strauss maintained with Hofmanns-
> thal. Nevertheless the suggestion cannot be avoided that in out-
> staying its original purpose the collaboration actually reached the
> point of doing harm to Strauss, who lost his initiative and with it
> his position of pre-eminence in the avant-garde of contemporary
> composition. (4)

At another point in his three-volume work Del Mar is very critical of Hofmannsthal:

> If we had not already had evidence of Hofmannsthal's complete
> self-absorption, to the point where he lost all sympathetic un-
> derstanding of his composer, it would have seemed hard to ex-
> plain his totally erroneous picture of how Strauss's mind worked. (5)

George R. Marek, another biographer of Strauss, censures Hofmannsthal severely:

> Hofmannsthal led Strauss partly up the garden path [after the
> success of the Rosenkavalier]. As the years passed, Hofmanns-
> thal became increasingly enamored of poetic conceits and became
> less interested in play and people, both vital to the operatic com-
> poser. To put it simply (perhaps too simply), he was no longer
> content to tell a story, tragic or charming; he needed to be allu-
> sive and revelatory. He began to operate with "symbols", those
> willing servants of the playwright which substitute for characters -
> but never substitute well. (6)

The music critics and biographers who have written about Strauss are, however, not the only ones to express displeasure with the Hofmannsthal-Strauss collaboration. From the literary critic and Hofmannsthal biographer Edgar Hederer
comes this comment:

> Das Wort des Dichters [Hofmannsthals] wiederum enthüllt oft
> mehr, als sich in der Musik begibt, öffnet sich nach innen, in-
> des der musikalische Vorgang und Ausdruck im rauschhaft Sinn-
> lichen bleibt. Allzu oft werden die zart bedeutenden Figuren der
> Dichtung von der breit strömenden Musik zugedeckt , und eine

verborgene Bedeutung geht verloren. Es kann geschehen, dass
die Musik, anstatt "Hieroglyphe eines Unaussprechlichen",
Berührung einer geheimen Sphäre und Verwandlung der Fabel
in ein nicht mehr Stoffliches zu sein, den geistigen und sittlichen
Sinn der Handlung vernachlässigt und den höheren Bezirk, dem
der Text zustrebt, nicht betritt. Ein Höheres, das sich befreien
will, bleibt gefangen im nur sinnlichen Element der Töne. (7)

Some critics have become so antagonistic toward the collaboration and its
alleged imperfections that they have even resorted to disparaging one or the other
of the pair:

How could Strauss and Hofmannsthal, with their contrasting natures, work together? How could the naturally cheerful, robust,
down-to-earth musician seek a close association with the pre-
cious, over-refined littérateur remote from reality, who described himself as a "poet, but no man of the theatre"? (8)

Und seltsamerweise gehörten seine Libretti für Richard Strauss
nach dem prachtvollen "Rosenkavalier" zu diesen [äthetischen
oder intellektuellen Experimenten], obwohl doch die sehr einfa-
che, durchaus nicht besonders verfeinerte oder intellektuell an-
spruchsvolle Natur des musikalischen Genies Richard Strauss ihm
bekannt sein musste. (9)

The bitterness on the part of Strauss's biographers seems to be rooted in the basic
assumption that the composer would have created better, or perhaps more popular
works, had Hofmannsthal not been his librettist. Conversely, the Hofmannsthal scholars assume that the poet would have produced either more lyric poetry or more purely dramatic works, had he not been associated with Strauss. Critics of Hofmannsthal writing in the early part of this century, such as members of the Stefan George
circle, felt that the writing of libretti was inferior work which should not be under-
taken by a serious poet.(10) Later critics more often express the opinion that the
subtleties of Hofmannsthal's creations are inundated by Strauss's sensual melodies
and brilliant orchestration. (11)

This latter opinion Hofmannsthal himself inadvertently encouraged by speaking critically of Strauss to close friends. Although the poet made these remarks in
private, they are public knowledge today and lend a semblance of authenticity to the
charge that Strauss's melodies overwhelm the texts. These quotations exemplify the
type of critical comments which the poet at times made:

Wenn ich einen raffinierteren künsterlischeren Komponisten
hätte. Alles was er sagt, was er sich wünscht, wonach er ten-
diert, degoutiert mich ziemlich stark. (12)

16

Strauss ist halt ein so fabelhaft unraffinierter Mensch. Hat eine
so fürchterliche Tendenz zum Trivialen, Kitschigen in sich. Was
er von mir verlangt an kleinen Aenderungen, Verbreiterungen etc.
geht immer nach dieser Richtung. . . . Eine merkwürdig ge-
mischte Natur, aber das ordinäre so gefährlich leicht aufsteigend
wie Grundwasser. (13)

Although it is apparent from the above quotations that the two artists were
not ideally suited to work with one another, the fact remains that they did endeavor
to cooperate with each other. Nor did they regard the collaboration lightly, as may
be deduced from their successful attempts to maintain their relationship. Even in
the face of Hofmannsthal's apparent personal dislike of Strauss, as evidenced by the
above letters, and also in the face of differences of artistic opinion, they both strove
to reach an accommodation with each other's desires. The following excerpt from a
letter of Hofmannsthal to Strauss reveals one of the problems which they faced and
were able to overcome:

Kessler sagte Sie würden noch zu mir kommen - leider sind Sie
nicht gekommen -, ich hätte Sie gerne noch gesehen, auch das
Folgende lieber gesagt als geschrieben. Kessler übergab mir,
als von Ihnen, einen Brief von G. Brecher, über den ich mich
etwas geärgert habe -, und zwar darum, weil Brecher eine, wenn
auch subalterne Figur Ihres Kreises ist. Für einen solchen Ihnen
nächst stehenden Schreiber - finde ich den Brief respektlos gegen
mich und darum nicht in Ordnung. Ich kann mich vollkommen darüber hinwegsetzen, wenn misswollende Journalisten gelegentlich
(wie es immer wieder vorkommt) an meinem Anteil einen Teil der
eigentlich Ihnen geltenden Rancune auslassen (Sie selbst haben, glaub
ich, das ganz richtige Wort vom Blitzableiter gebraucht), aber ich
würde es sehr übelnehmen, wenn ich denken müsste, dass in dem
Kreis der Leute, die Sie in der Hand haben, nicht verstanden oder
nicht gewürdigt wird, was meine Mitarbeit in drei stilistisch so ver-
schiedenen Fällen für Sie bedeutet, vor allem eben durch diese
stilistische Elemente. ''(Rosenkavalier'', ''Ariadne'', und auch
diesmal die Grundlage zu einer solchen Fresco-Symphonie [Rosen-
kavalier''legende].) (14)

In spite of the problems the two men encountered, neither was willing to allow the
collaboration to end or expressed any desire to end it. Strauss was well aware of the
contribution that Hofmannsthal was able to bring to him, voicing his appreciation at
one time to his librettist in this manner:

In einer Kritik aus Dresden las ich, dass das Wolf-Ferrari-Bat-
kasche Werk die richtige ''Wiedergeburt Molières'' (sic.!) aus
dem Geiste der Musik sei. Eben das, was mir mit ''Ariadne''
durch Ihr ''Ungeschick'' nicht gelungen ist. Der Mann hat von
Nietzsches ''Geburt der Tragödie aus dem Geiste der Musik''

einmal etwas läuten hören und lässt nun Molière durch Wolf-
Ferrari wiedergeboren werden.
    Lieber Freund, muss man nun all diesen Unsinn auf sich
sitzen lassen? Muss man nicht dagegen doch einmal in irgend-
einer Form seine Stimme erheben oder soll ich weiterhin ge-
duldig warten, bis die Leute von selbst dahinterkommen, ein-
zusehen, wie feinstilistisch gerade Ihre Arbeit in "Adriadne"
ist, wie aus Molière nur gerade das gerettet worden ist, was
in diesem Stück, wie in all seinen Stücken, unsterblich ist, wie
der Typus des Jourdain? Wie fein wir gerade im Lustspiel alles
aus Molière herausgezogen haben, was musikalisch ist, wie das
langsam zum eigentlichen Geist der Musik hinüberleitet und zu
Höhen hinaufführt, von denen auch der wiedergeborenste Molière
keine Ahnung haben konnte. (15)

Hofmannsthal, for his part, was also appreciative of Strauss's contribution to their
collaboration. The following lines were written by him to Strauss after the two of
them had met in Vienna in April of 1915, at which time Strauss played Acts I and II
of the Frau ohne Schatten:

Ihre Anregungen wirken alle nach, noch stärker das herrliche
Nachgefühl der gehörten Musik. Die Art, wie Sie den Kaiser in
der Musik geschaffen haben, gibt mir die bestimmteste Anwei-
sung, wie ich diese Figur in III zu behandeln habe. Er muss,
nachdem er aus der Versteinerung erwacht ist, seine Arie,
seine - völlig andere - "Gralserzählung" haben. Auch auf das
Verhältnis zu den Ungeborenen muss noch ein ganz anderes Licht
fallen . . . . (16)

Hofmannsthal and Strauss thus show a consideration and appreciation for each other
that is not often found in their respective biographers and scholars.

    Many of Hofmannsthal's and Strauss's biographers, such as Normal Del Mar,
George R. Marek, and Edgar Hederer, based their critical comments upon the hy-
pothesis that either Strauss or Hofmannsthal would have produced greater works had
he not collaborated with the other. Too many unknowable factors govern such an assumption for it to carry any significant weight. In contrast to this kind of procedure,
an inquiry based upon an analysis of the music, the libretto, and the visual effects -
including gesture, lighting, and stage sets - can produce valid results. It will even
be possible to focus upon the question of whether Strauss in his composition of the
libretto fulfilled Hofmannsthal's artistic intent.

    This kind of inquiry will, however, not produce an answer to the debate as to
the suitability of Hofmannsthal's texts for the composer Strauss. The results will be
more modest: they will be likely to show only where the two diverged or converged in
their understanding of each other's artistic goals. Provided a great amount of con-

vergence is found, the two must equally share the praise and the blame, for they fulfilled each other's artistic intentions well. If the degree of divergence is high, however, criticism of a type other than that customarily exhibited by their respective biographers is appropriate. Hofmannsthal may be criticized for not making his ideas clear to his collaborator and Strauss may be criticized for not sensing that the methods or goals which he was using were inappropriate for the text.

The opera the Frau ohne Schatten seems well suited for an inquiry of this nature for three reasons. First, critics are frequently at odds with each other in their assessments of this work. The following quotations demonstrate this lack of concord:

As his [Hofmannsthal's] imagination fashioned artificial blossoms he lost his way, amid countless verbal beauties, in the sphere of dark, personal subjectivity. He made things not easy but, on the contrary, very difficult for the spectator. . . . The music of the Frau ohne Schatten undoubtedly represents a new stage of creative development with regard to invention, technical accomplishment, dramatic force and spiritual significance. A work with such an abundance of broadly-flowing, rich-sounding music, which pours forth "like golden honey out of the dark honeycomb," [sic] signified a new summit in the sphere of dramatic music. . . . How plastic the tone symbols of this music are! What melodic and rhythmic power is contained in the remarkably characteristic motifs of Keikobad, the falcon, the Emperor and others! The composer here managed to create a certain amount of clarity in the half-darkness - a burst of light illumines the scene from time to time . . . . The music rises far above the literary aestheticism of the text. One has to keep a grip on the simple human symbols "in the realm of Keikobad." But can that be done?(17)

During the time that Hugo von Hofmannsthal was working on the libretto of Die Aegyptische Helena we used often to discuss problems of opera during our walks at Aussee, and Hofmannsthal was particularly interested in the question of how, as he put it, a librettist could best give the composer an opportunity for a fine musical passage. On one of these walks he suddenly asked me, "Why is the end of Rosenkavalier so effective while the end of Frau ohne Schatten is not? I thought for a moment, recalling the two dramatic situations.
In both operas the action is over by the time the final ensemble begins. In Rosenkavalier the trio of the Marschallin, Octavian, and Sophie comes first, then the duet of Octavian and Sophie, and the end is formed by the vignette-like mime of the little Blackamoor. In Frau ohne Schatten there is first the quartet of the two couples, the Emperor and Empress and the Dyer and his Wife, and then from above the final chorus of children's voices. Why is this ending not more effective, or at least

as effective, as the end of Rosenkavalier? As far as the text
is concerned it is undoubtedly more effective. What is wrong
with the music? Why is the poet's vision not fully realized?
  The answer I gave was this. "Both works use the orchestra symphonically. But in the Finale of Rosenkavalier Strauss
abandons this symphonic style and gives the voices, in both
trio and duet, formal melodies, important, new melodic ideas.
An unexpected new invention like this is always effective. We
need only think of the final duet in Aida. In Frau ohne Schatten,
on the other hand, Strauss combines themes from the opera
into an elaborate tissue, but the voices have no new material,
and, above all, nothing which can only be expressed in terms of
a vocal cantilena. This is the root of the failure."(18)

Diese Erzählung [the prose narrative of the Frau ohne Schatten],
zweifellos das ursprüngliche Produkt, ist eines der tiefsten Werke Hofmannsthals, ja der ganzen neueren deutschen Dichtung.
Hier gelang ihm alles, was er in den Bergwerken [the versions
of the Bergwerk zu Falun] immer wieder versucht hatte, ohne dass
dabei im ganzen mehr herausgekommen wäre als ein anmutig-
schwermütiges Märchen, mit Andeutungen eines schwer definier-
baren, offenbar nicht oder noch nicht ganz gelebten Tiefsinns.
"Die Frau ohne Schatten" ist das gelungene, zuende gestaltete
Gegenstück dazu. (19)

These diametrically opposed opinions suggest that a need exists for a detailed analysis of the opera which can provide an objective basis for assessments of it.

  Second, the plot of the Frau ohne Schatten exists in a prose narrative which
Hofmannsthal wrote both during and after the time when he was working on the libretto. Because the formal differences between narrative and drama require greater specificity and digression of the narrative, the prose story can become a valua-
ble tool for interpretation of the libretto. Among Hofmannsthal's and Strauss's common works only the Frau ohne Schatten exists in closely parallel forms. As a consequence, the libretto, the prose narrative, the score, and the correspondence between Hofmannsthal and Strauss comprise the primary source materials for the inquiry.

  Third, while Hofmannsthal and Strauss were working on this opera, they regarded it as their most significant work. Even after its completion and years of less
than enthusiastic reception by the general public, Strauss seemed to consider it his
finest work. (20) As for Hofmannsthal, within the poet's complete body of works, the
fairy-tale, both as narrative and as libretto, occupies a position of central importance.

INTRODUCTION

Genesis of the Frau ohne Schatten

Hofmannsthal's original inspiration for the Frau ohne Schatten seems to have occurred as early as 1911. During March of that year the poet complained to Strauss that the figures and actions of a new libretto (the later Frau ohne Schatten) were so attractive as to be disturbing to him as he was working on Ariadne auf Naxos (I). (21) Casual reference was made by both Hofmannsthal and Strauss during their collaboration on Ariadne (I), but Hofmannsthal only began to work seriously upon it in the summer and fall of 1912, at which time he wrote to Strauss:

> Ich schreibe Ihnen dies, weil ich weiss, dass es Ihnen Freude
> machen wird: dass mir seit einer Woche die ''Frau ohne Schat-
> ten'' mit Gewalt vor die Seele getreten ist und dass ich nun, erst
> nun diesen Stoff wirklich besitze, Glied für Glied, Bild für Bild,
> jeder Uebergang, jede Steigerung, alles im grossen Ganzen und
> zugleich im Einzelnsten, so dass ich mir wohl sagen kann: dies
> ist gerettet,- möge es uns beiden vergönnt sein, es auszuführen,
> so wie es jetzt vor mir schwebt. (22)

During the summer of 1913 Hofmannsthal wrote to Strauss that he had nearly completed the first two acts. (23) Curiously, however, Hofmannsthal did not press forward with the work on the new opera; his desire to have Strauss compose a ballet scenario which he and his friend Graf Harry Kessler had written appears to be responsible for the apparent procrastination. Kessler apparently feared that Strauss would quit working on the ballet, the Josephslegende, were he to receive any of the text of the Frau ohne Schatten. He, therefore, appealed to Hofmannsthal not to send the libretto to Strauss until the composition of the ballet was well on the way to completion. (24) Hofmannsthal accommodated his friend Kessler in this matter with the result that New Year's Day of 1914 arrived before Strauss received any of the libretto of the Frau ohne Schatten. In the spring and summer of 1914 Strauss worked on the composition of the first act; in mid-July of the same year Hofmannsthal sent Strauss the second act of the opera.

But at this point the assassination of the Archduke of Austria with the resultant outbreak of war in Europe interrupted their cooperative efforts: Hofmannsthal was recalled to military service. Although the Austrian government utilized him primarily for diplomatic missions so that he was not exposed to the dangers of frontline fighting, he was, nevertheless, occupied with matters other than the writing of the third act of the Frau ohne Schatten. Meanwhile, Strauss attempted to overcome a personal depression by immersing himself in the composition of Act I. (25)

During the months which followed Strauss continued to work on the opera, for he wrote to Hofmannsthal on the twenty-ninth of October that the second act was finished. Hofmannsthal, however, was prevented from any sustained efforts by his service in the Austrian army. As a result it was April, 1915, before he sent Strauss a short third act consisting of eighteen pages. (26) Strauss was, however, dissatisfied with the act, his many requests for additional verse lines indicating an apparent concern that it was too brief. (27) There is circumstantial evidence that this fear was caused because two of his close acquaintances confessed upon hearing the first two acts that they were totally incapable of comprehending the libretto; Strauss first requested verse lines for the third act which would recapitulate the preceding acts at the same time as he related the lack of comprehension of his friends. (28) The subsequent lengthening of Act III occurred at his behest (29) and at times against Hofmannsthal's wishes. (30) No immediate steps were, however, taken by the poet upon the composer's desire for more text; the two decided rather to discuss the act in a face-to-face meeting.

When Strauss was in Vienna later that same month, a thorough discussion of the text of the third act, which Hofmannsthal had previously sent to Strauss, appears to have taken place. Shortly after this meeting the composer received a revised version of the first scene of Act III, which he composed with his usual rapidity; Hofmannsthal received a note from him which was dated June 8, 1915, that the composition of the first scene was finished. Strauss had, however, because of an inability to contact Hofmannsthal, who during this spring was in Poland on diplomatic missions, been forced to write additional verses for speeches which he found to be too short. This breakdown in communication also caused Strauss to begin instrumentation of the two acts already finished, a task he customarily started only after he had completed the composition of a work. (31)

The second scene of Act III Hofmannsthal mailed to Strauss on July 7, but the third and final scenes of the text were not completed and sent to Strauss until the nineteenth of September. Moreover, Hofmannsthal found it necessary to send them by way of the Bavarian consulate since mail service had proved to be undependable. Other than a brief note from Strauss dated January 12, 1916, there is no mention of this opera in the correspondence until July 18, at which time Strauss requested more text for the third scene of Act III. This long interruption, from January until July, occurred because the collaborators chose this time to recast Ariadne auf Naxos. Only in August of 1916 was Strauss able to write to Hofmannsthal that he had completed sketching the third act. (32) The instrumentation he completed the next year in June. (33)

The genesis of the work offered here differs considerably from Hofmannsthal's personal recollection as it was published in Theater- und Musikwoche, Nr. 29, 1919. There he reported:

> 1913 schrieb ich dann den ersten und zweiten Akt und Strauss
> fing gleich zu komponieren an. Im Juli 1914, wenige Tage vor
> der Mobilisierung, hatte ich den dritten beendet. 1915 war die
> Komposition fertig, dann lag die Oper vier Jahre in Strauss'
> Schreibtisch. Wir konnten uns nicht entschliessen, sie während
> des Krieges spielen zu lassen. (34)

INTRODUCTION

The letters demonstrate that Hofmannsthal's memory was faulty about the dates.

From the first recorded inspiration on Hofmannsthal's part in March of 1911 until the completion of the instrumentation by Strauss in June of 1917, over six years passed. Nor, as has been suggested above, were these six years by any means what might be termed normal for the two artists. Externally, Hofmannsthal appears to have been the one who was the more disturbed by the events of World War I, for his recall to military service largely curtailed his poetic activity. Yet Strauss, although not called to actual military service, was not as untouched as appearances might suggest. Throughout the war he was greatly concerned that his only son would be called to active military duty. For some unknown reason, perhaps an undue influence upon the draft board, the son was not summoned until the summer of 1917. At this time the medical board which examined him declared him unfit for military service because he had, at twenty-one, "outgrown his strength." (35) In this way the catastrophe of World War I struck personally at Strauss, as well as at Hofmannsthal.

There can be no doubt that the amount of time required for the writing, composition, and orchestration of this work was lengthened by the war. No other of their common works required such a long period of time for its gestation. Nor can the effect be weighed solely in terms of a lengthened time span; undoubtedly a more concentrated effort, especially as far as the last act is concerned, would have proved helpful to the work.

Strauss and Hofmannsthal had agreed that this opera was not to be premiered during the war, but only after the war was over. This was apparently settled definitively at one of the times when Hofmannsthal and Strauss were together, perhaps in April of 1916 when Strauss played Acts I and II for Hofmannsthal. The correspondence reveals that the two of them treat the matter as a settled fact, with Hofmannsthal assuming this position as early as February 6, 1915:

> In einer Beziehung war ich, in bezug auf unser neues
> Werk, bisher immer guten Mutes: die Uebereinstimmung zwi-
> schen dem Ernst und der Wucht des Werkes mit dem rechten
> und bedeutenden Moment, wo wir damit hervortreten werden.
> Es wird nach diesem Kriege, zunächst in Deutschland, eine
> ganz bestimmte Atmosphäre fühlbar sein, mit ganz bestimm-
> ten Forderungen (auch Vorurteilen) gegenüber allen Dingen, vor
> allem auch den Künsten. In dieser Atmosphäre wird, abgese-
> hen von den sozusagen obligaten Anfeindungen, gerade die
> "Frau ohne Schatten", um des Themas wie um der Durch-
> führung willen, ausserordentlich gut und ehrenvoll bestehen
> können - wogegen eine künstlichere, spielerische Konzeption
> wie "Ariadne" mitsamt dem Molière gerade in diesem Mo-
> ment auf doppelten Widerstand gestossen wäre. (36)

INTRODUCTION

In addition to the suitability of the opera for the prevailing attitude of the post-war period, as stressed in the letter above, the difficulty of mounting such a large production for a premiere must also have contributed greatly to the decision to delay the first performance. The premiere took place accordingly in Vienna on the tenth of October, 1919.

During much of the time that Strauss and Hofmannsthal were collaborating on this opera, Hofmannsthal was also engaged in creating a prose narrative out of the same material. In a letter to Strauss dated July 12, 1914, he wrote:

> Das "Märchen" (Frau ohne Schatten) schreitet fort und soll,
> hoffe ich, unserem Werk, und vielleicht nicht nur im Ver-
> ständnis dieser Generation, sondern noch nachfolgenden zu-
> gute kommen. (37)

Hofmannsthal thus suggested that the prose piece could be validly used for understanding the libretto. The narrative was completed shortly after the premiere of the opera. Perhaps the initial performance inspired the poet to complete the prose version.

The following study of the opera springs from a desire to assess the opera objectively and to answer the question of whether or not Strauss in his composition and orchestration of the opera was successful in fulfilling Hofmannsthal's artistic intent; this intent will be disclosed through an analysis of the libretto and other available and relevant materials, including the prose narrative. The result, treating as it does both the text and the music, will provide a needed correction to the one-sided perspectives of the opera which were quoted in the first part of this chapter. In this respect one can emphasize with Karl-Joachim Krüger the need for an interdisciplinary approach to the joint works of Hofmannsthal and Strauss:

> Die Untersuchung ergibt, dass weder Hofmannsthal von Literatur-
> wissenschaft allein noch Strauss von der Musikwissenschaft allein
> begriffen werden können, sondern beide Disziplinen sich vereinen
> müssen, insonderheit, wenn man Hofmannsthals Operndichtungen,
> "deren Zurechnung eine der schwierigsten Aufgaben poesiegeschicht-
> licher Betrachtungen bleibt" (Masur), in das rechte Blickfeld be-
> kommen will. Das Hofmannsthal-Problem ist ein Beleg dafür, dass
> die grundsätzliche Vereinzelung der Disziplinen sehr leicht zu schie-
> fen Urteilen führen kann. So hofft die Untersuchung, auch ein metho-
> dologischer Beitrag zu sein. (38)

INTRODUCTION

Footnotes

(1) Although the two men exchanged letters in 1900 about a ballet scenario which Hofmannsthal proposed that Strauss should compose, the collaboration actually began with their work on Elektra; Strauss was then forty-one years old and Hofmannsthal was thirty-one.

(2) Richard Strauss - Hugo von Hofmannsthal: Briefwechsel, ed. Willi Schuh, 4th ed., Gesamtausgabe (Zurich: Atlantis Verlag, 1964), p. 17. Letters from this correspondence will subsequently be cited by author and date: Hofmannsthal to Strauss, 7. III. 1906. The Arabic numeral refers to the day; the Roman numeral to the month.

(3) "Vorbemerkungen zur Gesamtausgabe (Dritte Auflage 1964)," Strauss - Hofmannsthal: Briefwechsel, p. 10.

(4) Richard Strauss: A Critical Commentary on His Life and Works, 3 vols. (Philadelphia: Chilton Book Co., 1962-72), II: 437.

(5) Ibid., p. 127.

(6) Richard Strauss: The Life of a Non-Hero (New York: Simon and Schuster, 1967), p. 214.

(7) Hugo von Hofmannsthal (Frankfurt a.M.: S. Fischer Verlag, 1960), pp. 211-12.

(8) Ernst Krause, Richard Strauss: The Man and His Work, trans. John Coombs (London: Collet's, 1964), p. 390. (German edition. Leipzig: VEB Breitkopf and Härtel, 1955.)

(9) Willy Haas, Hugo von Hofmannsthal, Köpfe des zwanzigsten Jahrhunderts, vol. 34 (Berlin: Colloquium Verlag Otto H. Hess, 1964), p. 48.

(10) Friedrich Gundolf, "Das Bild Georges," Jahrbuch für die geistige Bewegung, I (1910), excerpts reprinted in Hofmannsthal im Urteil seiner Kritiker: Dokumente zur Wirkungsgeschichte Hugo von Hofmannsthals in Deutschland, ed. Gotthart Wunberg (Frankfurt: Athenäum, 1972), p. 234.

(11) Hederer, pp. 211-212.

(12) Hugo von Hofmannsthal - Harry Graf Kessler: Briefwechsel 1898-1929, ed. Hilde Burger (Frankfurt a.M.: Insel Verlag, 1968), p. 244, 12. VI. 1909.

(13) Ibid., pp. 242-43, Hofmannsthal an Kessler, 12. VI. 1909.

INTRODUCTION

(14) Briefwechsel, Hofmannsthal to Strauss, 20.(?) V. 1914. Kessler is Graf Harry Kessler, a friend of Hofmannsthal.

(15) Ibid., Strauss to Hofmannsthal, 15. XII. 1913.

(16) Ibid., Hofmannsthal to Strauss, 14. V. 1915.

(17) Krause, Strauss, pp. 398, 401-03, passim. The quotation is a translation of the line "Wie schwerer Honig aus den hohlen Waben" from Hofmannsthal's poem "Ballade des äusseren Lebens" (1895).

(18) Egon Wellesz, "Three Lectures on Opera: (a) The Problem of Form," Essays on Opera, trans. Patricia Kean (London: Dennis Dobson Ltd., 1950), pp. 104-05.

(19) Haas, Hofmannsthal, p. 49.

(20) Richard Strauss, "Erinnerungen an die ersten Aufführungen meiner Opern (1942)," Betrachtungen und Erinnerungen, ed. Willi Schuh (Zurich: Atlantis Verlag, 1949), pp. 201-02.

(21) Briefwechsel, Hofmannsthal to Strauss, 20. III. 1911.

(22) Ibid., Hofmannsthal to Strauss, 8. IX. 1912.

(23) Ibid., Hofmannsthal to Strauss, 3. VI. 1913.

(24) Hofmannsthal - Kessler: Briefwechsel, Kessler to Hofmannsthal, 4. VI. 1913, p. 362.

(25) Briefwechsel, Strauss to Hofmannsthal's wife, Gerty von Hofmannsthal, 22. VIII. 1914.

(26) Ibid., Hofmannsthal to Strauss, 26. III. 1915.

(27) Ibid., Strauss to Hofmannsthal, 15. IV. 1915.

(28) Ibid., Strauss to Hofmannsthal, 5. IV. 1915.

(29) Ibid., Strauss to Hofmannsthal, 15. IV. 1915.

(30) Ibid., Hofmannsthal to Strauss, 24. VII. 1916.

(31) Ibid., Strauss to Hofmannsthal, 8. VI. 1915.

(32) Ibid., Strauss to Hofmannsthal, ca. 16. VIII. 1916.

(33)   Ibid., Strauss to Hofmannsthal, 28. VI. 1917.

(34)   Quoted from Franz Grasberger, Richard Strauss und die Wiener Oper (Tutzing: H. Schneider, 1969), pp. 183-84.

(35)   Del Mar, Strauss, II: 156.

(36)   Briefwechsel, Hofmannsthal to Strauss, 6. II. 1915.

(37)   Briefwechsel.

(38)   Hugo von Hofmannsthal und Richard Strauss: Versuch einer Deutung des künstlerischen Weges Hugo von Hofmannsthals, Neue Deutsche Forschungen: Abteilung Neuere Deutsche Literaturgeschichte, vol. 3 (Berlin: Junker und Dünnhaupt, 1935), p. 273. Masur is not identified in the book.

CHAPTER II

OPERA, HUGO VON HOFMANNSTHAL, AND RICHARD STRAUSS

A discussion of any literary or musical work must proceed under certain assumptions concerning the nature of the work being analyzed. The genre of opera contains such diverse works that it seems imperative to state these assumptions when an opera is to be the subject of inquiry. This chapter attempts, therefore, to define some of the aesthetic ideas upon which this study is based. An additional goal will be to discuss the factors which seem to have led Hofmannsthal to write libretti and Strauss to compose operas.

Opera as an Art-Form

Susanne K. Langer, one of the most eminent aetheticians living today, makes these statements about music in her book Feeling and Form: "the function of music is not stimulation of feeling, but expression of it . . ." (1); "music makes time audible, and its form and continuity sensible."(2) From her point of view, therefore, music expresses experiential time, or time as it is felt, not as the clock measures it. Langer elaborates her theory of music in this manner:

> The tonal structures we call "music" bear a close logical simi-
> larity to the forms of human feeling - forms of growth and of
> attenuation, flowing and stowing, conflict and resolution, speed,
> arrest, terrific excitement, calm, or subtle activation and dreamy
> lapses - not joy and sorrow perhaps, but the poignancy of either
> and both - the greatness and brevity and eternal passing of every-
> thing vitally felt. Such is the pattern, or logical form, of sen-
> tience; and the pattern of music is that same form worked out in
> pure, measured sound and silence. Music is a tonal analogue of
> emotive life. (3)

Music, therefore, expresses feelings by presenting them to us in their logical contours. The expression of emotions which thus occurs presents time as it is experienced. Although this experienced or felt time requires time as it is measured by the clock in which to develop and recede, the ultimate effect is one of suspension of clock time; the figures and shapes of the music establish their own time. The percipient will recognize this occurrence as a quality or as a characteristic; it is in reality its essence. Opera, because it is one particular type of music, also evidences this characteristic.

Opera is, however, more than music; it is also drama. And drama, like music, has a special relationship to time. The relationship is in this case not one of the creation of a time independent of clock time, such as occurs by means of the configurations of the music, though, but a relationship wherein the tendency of time as experienced is to leap beyond the present to the future. Langer states that the

28

"basic abstraction [of drama] is the act, which springs from the past, but is directed toward the future, and is always great with things to come. "(4)

A logical antithesis is in evidence here. The shapes and figures of music
establish an independent realm of time wherein the emphasis falls on the Now; in
contrast to this emphasis on the Now which occurs in music, drama is concerned
with the Future, or with the consequences of acts performed in the Now.

Opera, as a form in which music and drama are combined into a whole, is
threatened by two failings, either of which will diminish the effectiveness of the
form. On the one side, too great a time span of lyrical expression, i.e., too much
emphasis on the musical aspects of opera wherein the Now predominates, will dull
the dramatic action to the point of boredom. On the other side, too great an emphasis
upon action, with its predominant concern being the Future, will result in a loss of
musical interest. The librettist and the composer must eliminate excesses on either
side if their work is to be viable.

Because music introduces such a great retarding quality into dramatic action, i.e., emphasis on the Now at the expense of emphasis on the Future, it would
appear that some types of texts may be better suited than others for composition into operas. Texts taken from the Realistic movement in literature would appear to be
generally difficult to assimilate into a libretto, for it is doubtful that such a libretto -
for example, one based upon Gerhart Hauptmann's Die Weber - would make suffi-
cient allowance for the emphasis upon the Now of its musical setting. One writer on
opera even demands the opposite of naturalism for libretti:

> The vital nerve center of the musical-dramatic work is embodiment,
> representation of the unreal, comprehensible portrayal of higher
> and especially inner experience. (5)

A libretto which fulfills this description would appear to be far more likely to be
successful in a musical setting than one which does not; the portrayal of "inner experience" which is here viewed as necessary for an opera libretto would appear to
provide the composer with a subject which could be easily assimilated into music,
music seen as a "tonal analogue of emotive life. "(6)

Easy intelligibility is also a desirable quality for a libretto, for the difficulty
of understanding words which are sung cannot be overestimated. One way to accomplish this without descending to the level of the banal would be to employ archetypal
figures in situations originated by the librettist. A desire to fulfill the need for comprehensibility without resorting to the commonplace has possibly been one of the mo-
tivating factors behind the frequent choice of myth or fairy-tale as the framework for
an opera libretto.

When archetypal figures derived from fairy-tale, legend, or myth are set in
contexts new to the audience, the librettist offers the listeners a vision or idea about

29

life which may add to their knowledge about and experience of life. Philip Wheelwright emphasized this quality in his book Metaphor and Reality:

> To speak forth honestly is to report the world as it is beheld
> (however precariously) in one's own perspective. Things have
> contexts, but only a person has perspectives. The essential
> excuse for writing, then, is to unveil as best one can some
> perspective that has not already become ordered into a public
> map. (7)

Archetypal figures in original situations, therefore, would appear to be well-suited
for opera texts, for Wheelwright's demand for an original perspective would be fulfilled while at the same time comprehensibility would be aided. Unusual and yet not
unusual, new and yet not new, would appear to be a useful criterion here.

Not only must an opera reconcile the antithetical qualities of drama and music with regard to time if it is to be successful, but the innumerable difficulties inherent in any dramatic production or musical performance must also be overcome.
Appropriate interpretation and accurate performance of pitch, rhythm, and the many
other factors which constitute a successful reading of a large-scale musical work
are essential from a musical point of view; suitable gestures and facial expressions
plus apt costuming, staging, lighting, and sets are necessary from the dramatic. As
for the performance itself, there is a need for a balance between the vocal line, often enough sung from the side or rear of a stage, and the orchestra. Moreover, the
dramatic aspect of an opera will suffer greatly if the plot cannot be followed, either
because of poor diction on the part of the singers or because of the conductor's mis-
judgment about balance between the singers and the orchestra. The very great number of factors involved make the writing, composition, and production of a successful opera probably the most difficult of all artistic endeavors.

Opera is, in summary, a hybrid form combining both music and drama – two
art-forms which bear a logical antithesis to each other: music establishes an independent realm of time wherein the emphasis falls on the Now, while drama is concerned with the Future, or with the consequences of acts performed in the Now. The
reconciling of these antithetical natures is the supreme task which a composer and
a librettist are called upon to perform. Perhaps this difficulty can be surmounted
with a carefully considered choice for the subject of the libretto, eliminating those
aspects of drama, such as realism, which would appear to be problematical as far
as assimilation into the music is concerned. Comprehensibility of the text, perhaps
through the use of archetypal figures in original situations, may also aid the librettist and the composer as they seek to reconcile the antithetical natures of music and
drama, for opera as a form is viable only when the elements of music and drama
combine to form a whole.

OPERA, HUGO VON HOFMANNSTHAL, AND RICHARD STRAUSS

Hofmannsthal and Opera

Although ideas and commentary concerning opera are not lacking in Hofmannsthal's collected works, he did not theorize about it. In fact, he felt in general a deep aversion to abstractions. This distrust he expressed in later life in this manner:

> Das Leben ist ein Kampf zwischen der puren Vitalität und den Formen. Das meinte Goethe, als er sagte, dass den Formen, allen, auch den höchsten, etwas Erstarrendes, Todbringendes innewohne. Wir sind immer in Gefahr, das Leben an die Institutionen zu verlieren, an die Abstraktionen, an die Worte (auch sie sind Formen). (8)

As a consequence, anyone wishing to know Hofmannsthal's ideas on a subject must compile relevant comments from various sources. Opera constitutes no exception to this generalization.

One comment about opera which Hofmannsthal made in 1919, the year of the premiere of the Frau ohne Schatten, was quoted from Goethe's Tag- und Jahreshefte, 1789:

> - "Die reine Opernform, welche vielleicht die günstigste aller dramatischen bleibt . . . "

> (A 192.)

That Hofmannsthal regarded opera not only favorably but also highly is evident from this comment, as well as from the more salient fact that he engaged in writing opera libretti from 1906, when he revised Elektra for Strauss, until his death in 1929, at which time he had just finished the libretto of Arabella. As far as theories are concerned, however, neither this quotation nor the more tangible libretti provides a great deal of information.

Hofmannsthal employed another quotation from Goethe in an introduction which he wrote for a volume of Goethe's Singspiele and operas: "Musik füllt den Augenblick am entschiedensten." (P IV 174.) In choosing this particular quotation Hofmannsthal apparently was saying that music emphasizes the quality of eternal significance which, were the rapidly passing moment bare and alone, might not be noticed. A major theme in the poet's body of works has been struck in this allusion to the swift passage of time. Some of the very earliest of Hofmannsthal's works, for example the verse play Gestern (1891), exemplify this interest. In this play the hero Andrea reverses his initial commitment to the sensual pleasures of each moment and says: "Was einmal war, das lebt auch ewig fort." (GLD 179.) In stressing the importance which music gives to the single moment ("Musik füllt den Augenblick am entschiedensten") Hofmannsthal indicated an intuitive awareness of the special relationship of music to time, of the apparent suspension of time as measured by the

31

clock and of the establishment of an experiential, or emotive, span of time.

That Hofmannsthal expended so much effort in attempting to come to terms with time and its swift passage may perhaps be ascribed to the Viennese philosophical atmosphere of the 1890's. William H. Rey in his article "Die Drohung der Zeit in Hofmannsthals Frühwerk" states:

> Bestimmend für Hofmannsthals Anfang war jedoch die Tatsache,
> dass er sich im Augenblick seines geistigen Erwachens dem Welt-
> bild und der Lebensauffassung des Wiener Impressionismus gegen-
> übersah. . . . Er sah sich einer Welt ohne Substanz, ohne tieferen
> Sinn, ohne vorgegebene Ordnung gegenüber. Diese Welt hatte die
> Verbindung mit dem Absoluten verloren und unterstand nur noch
> dem Diktat der verrinnenden Zeit. . . . Nur der Moment habe
> Gültigkeit, die Dauer sei eine Illusion. (9)

Such an attitude toward life seems to beg for a re-definition of the relationship of life to time.

Perhaps it is not an exaggeration to state that exposure to this attitude toward life as it was specifically formulated in the philosophy of Ernst Mach was instrumental in forcing Hofmannsthal to become a poet. The young man apparently became acquainted with the Machian philosophy, which stresses the lack of continuity of substances, personalities, and relationships, (10) at the University of Vienna in the early 1890's. This experience seems to have driven him to search for order and relationship, which is one of his definitions of the poetic task:

> Die dichterische Aufgabe ist Reinigung, Gliederung, Artikulation
> des Lebensstoffes. Im Leben herrscht das grässlich Widersinnige,
> ein furchtbares Wüten der Materie - als Erblichkeit, innerer
> Zwang, Dummheit, Bosheit, innerlichste Niedertracht -, im Gei-
> stigen eine Zerfahrenheit, Inkonsistenz bis ins Unglaubliche -
> das ist der Augiasstall, der immer wieder gereinigt und in einen
> Tempel verwandelt werden will.
>
> (A 62.)

There is a striking similarity between this definition of the task of art and the one offered by Langer:

> Every good work of art has, I think, something that may be said
> to come from the world, and that bespeaks the artist's own feel-
> ing about life. This accords with the intellectual and, indeed,
> the biological importance of art: we are driven to the symboli-
> zation and articulation of feeling when we must understand it to
> keep ourselves oriented in society and nature. (11)

OPERA, HUGO VON HOFMANNSTHAL, AND RICHARD STRAUSS

The relationship between the transitory nature of time and indistinctness in the material and spiritual world appears at first to be remote; a relationship does, however, exist. The fleeting moment admits of no reflection on the past, nor on the future, but allows only kaleidoscopic change - a chaotic shifting of colors, images, and sounds, none of which has any relationship to anything else. Articulation and separation ("Gliederung, Artikulation"), as completed processes, re-establish qualities and shapes so that they may once more exist in relationship to each other. When the poet's work is viewed in this light, the poet himself becomes the architect of material and intellectual relationships. In this sense one is tempted to say of Hofmannsthal as he said of his young friend Carl J. Burckhardt:

Wesen dieser Art ist keine Bahn vorgezeichnet - und keine der vorgezeichneten Bahnen tut ihnen genug. Sie müssen das scheinbar Fern-Abliegende auf eine neue Weise aneinanderknüpfen, aus einer unerwarteten Combination von Elementen bauen sie sich ihre Welt, sie meinen damit nur für sich selber die atembare Luft herzustellen und schaffen neue Typen der geistigen Existenz. (12)

Hofmannsthal's intuitive feeling for music must also have assured him that within the major-minor tonal system with which he was familiar, relationship was the unspoken by-word. For although the tonal system was rapidly disintegrating or had even been abandoned in the avant-garde music of his time, the new music - such as Strauss's operas - with which he was acquainted still functioned within this system. It is only in the twelve-tone system of composition or other non-tertian harmonic systems, wherein each note stands on the same footing as every other note, that the paradoxical situation of non-relationship occurs. The fact that in the major-minor tonal system a note has significance in its functional relationship within the total work appears not to have been overlooked by Hofmannsthal.

The poet, perhaps because of the emphasis on the transitory aspects of life which dominated Viennese philosophical thought during the final decade of the nineteenth century, was eager to give things a shape so that relationships might exist. The solution to his problem would only superficially appear to be poetic creation: "Die dichterische Aufgabe ist Reinigung, Gliederung, Artikulation des Lebensstoffes." (A 62.) Life did not present itself that simply either to the young or to the mature Hofmannsthal. He faced an agonizing doubt in the efficacy of words, even as early as 1891, when these lines - the last stanza of a much longer poem - were written:

Der Schatten eines Toten . . .

Das ist vielleicht das Letzte was uns bleibt,
Wenn der Gedanke ungedacht schon lügt:
Dass auf ein zitternd Herz das andere lauscht
Und leisen Drucks zur Hand die Hand sich fügt . . .
(GLD 493.)

If "the thought – not yet thought – lies," "the problem is distinctly one of the process of petrification which is inherent in language itself. Owen Barfield in his significant book Poetic Diction: A Study in Meaning describes this process for the world "spiritus":

> . . . such a purely material content as "wind," on the one hand, and on the other, such a purely abstract content as "the principle of life within man or animal" are both late arrivals in human consciousness. Their abstractness and their simplicity are alike evidence of long ages of intellectual evolution. So far from the psychic meaning of "spiritus" having arisen because someone had the abstract idea "principle of life . . ." and wanted a word for it, the abstract idea "principle of life" is itself a product of the old concrete meaning "spiritus," which contained within itself the germs of both later significations. We must, therefore, imagine a time when "spiritus" or πνεῦμα, or older words from which these had descended, meant neither breath, nor wind, nor spirit, nor yet all three of these things, but when they simply had their own old peculiar meaning, which has since, in the course of the evolution of consciousness, crystallized into the three meanings specified – and no doubt into others also, for which separate words had already been found by Greek and Roman times. (13)

Hofmannsthal, in rejecting language and thought even before it has been utilized, obviously is rejecting the basic process by which language operates. He faces here the poet's dilemma of being forced to choose beween static terms whose meanings are by habit known to all speakers of a language and which, therefore, can express nothing new and freshly coined terms which are capable of expressing his new ideas but whose meanings may only be dimly perceived by his readers or audiences.

Although Hofmannsthal obviously possessed a highly poetic imagination, his skepticism that language was a fit medium for the expression of his ideas led him to turn away from the creation of lyric poetry and to search for other media of expression. The theater was early an interest, but his search for adequate means of expression led him beyond the traditional dramatic forms to the writing of opera libretti and of scenarios for both the ballet and the motion picture. He stressed repeatedly the importance of gesture and of other non-verbal modes of expression:

> Die Leute sind es nämlich müde, reden zu hören. Sie haben einen tiefen Ekel vor den Worten: Denn die Worte haben sich vor die Dinge gestellt. Das Hörensagen hat die Welt verschluckt.
> So ist eine verzweifelte Liebe zu allen Künsten erwacht, die schweigend ausgeübt werden: die Musik, das Tanzen und alle Künste der Akrobaten und Gaukler.
> (P I. 228.)

OPERA, HUGO VON HOFMANNSTHAL, AND RICHARD STRAUSS

One other aspect of Hofmannsthal's outlook on life which seems to have been instrumental in leading him to opera was his concern for the isolated individual - the individual who is unable to bridge the gulf between himself and others. Many of his early writings deal with this type of character. Der Tor und der Tod and Das Märchen der 672. Nacht are two particularly apt portrayals of this concern. Both works depict individuals for whom life is singularly devoid of emotional depth, primarily because neither has established satisfactory relationships with other people; they have instead devoted their efforts to the acquiring of beautiful objects of art. Hofmannsthal was not content, however, with a mere portrayal of the alienated person. He rejected this kind of isolated life by passing a negative judgment upon those who lived in this manner and also by holding these people accountable and responsible for their unhappy lives.

In contrast to many of Hofmannsthal's early works, which frequently portray and condemn the individual in his estrangement from a community, many of the poet's middle and late works depict the isolated individual as he attempts to bridge the gap between himself and others. The opera the Frau ohne Schatten is representative of this latter type. Even this artistic development - the movement from a negatively tinged condemnation of the isolated individual to the more positive depiction of the integration of the once isolated person into a community - seems not to have been wholly satisfactory to the poet. He seemed eager that his works should provide more than an example of how an individual might overcome his isolation. He also desired that his creative efforts should help to create a community, a community which he sensed was lacking in Austria and Germany at that time. He described this deficiency in "Der dritte Brief eines Zurückgekehrten":

> Sie [die Deutschen und die Oesterreicher] haben ein Oben und Un-
> ten, ein Besser und Schlechter, ein Gröber und Feiner, ein Rechts
> und Links, ein Füreinander und Gegeneinander, und bürgerliche
> Verhältnisse und adelige Verhältnisse und Universitätskreise und
> Finanzkreise: aber was in dem allen fehlt, ist eine wahre Dich-
> tigkeit der Verhältnisse: es hakt nichts ins andere ein - es ist
> irgend etwas nicht drin, wofür ich Dir den Kunstausdruck nicht
> zu finden weiss, was aber doch im englischen Wesen drin ist,
> so grandios und vielfältig es ist, und im Maoriwesen drin ist,
> so kindisch und kunstlos dieses ist: das Gemeinschaftsbildende,
> all das Ursprüngliche davon, das was im Herzen sitzt.
> (P II 292-93.)

That Hofmannsthal felt the theater was an instrument for forging ties between people may be seen from this quotation:

> Aber der Dramatiker hätte sein Spiel schon verloren, wenn es
> ihm nicht gelänge, die Zuschauer ebenso wie die Schauspieler
> zu seinem mittätigen Werkzeug zu machen; nicht umsonst sind
> die Zuschauer eines Schauspieles Nachkommen des ursprüng-

35

lichsten Chores, einer tanzenden und singenden Schar, die den
Protagonisten, den geopferten Heros, umgab, mit ihm litt und
jubelte; ja die Zuschauer sind niemals etwas anderes als dieser
erweiterte Chor, also Mitspieler und Halluzinierte.

(A 328-29.)

This chorus is obviously none other than the Dionysian chorus of Attic tragedy as
characterized by Friedrich Nietzsche:

Singend und tanzend äussert sich der Mensch als Mitglied einer höheren Gemeinsamkeit: er hat das Gehen und das Sprechen verlernt und ist auf dem Wege, tanzend in die Lüfte em-
porzufliegen. (14)

The theater was thus viewed by Hofmannsthal as an agent which was capable of molding the many isolated individuals of the audience into a community.

There were, therefore, three primary factors which influenced Hofmannsthal to write opera libretti. These were 1) a desire to give significance to the Present, that is, to the moment being lived now, 2) a despair over the efficacy of words,
and 3) a desire to create a community which would overcome individual isolation.

Strauss and Opera

Like Hofmannsthal, Strauss was not given to theorizing about his work, but in
comparison to the poet Strauss's theoretical comments on opera are so few as to be
almost non-existent. In one of these comments he took exception to both of the views
then in vogue about music:

Unsere Musikgelehrten - ich nenne die beiden Hauptnamen:
Friedrich von Hausegger ("Musik als Ausdruck") und
Eduard Hanslick ("Musik als tönend bewegte Form") - haben
Formulierungen gegeben, die seither als feindliche Gegensätze
gelten. Dies ist falsch. Es sind die beiden Formen musikali-
schen Gestaltens, die sich gegenseitig ergänzen. (15)

These comments approximate closely some of the primary ideas developed by Langer in her systematic theory of aesthetics. Perhaps the underlying factor in the similarity of their ideas lies in the attitudes toward music which existed in the Vienna
of the 1920's. Not only was Strauss living in the city during this time while he directed the Vienna State Opera, but Langer was a student there during these years.

Most of what Strauss wrote on opera avoids aesthetic discussions in order to
focus on technical problems. Some topics which he considered were: the need to organize one good state opera company as a replacement for many indifferent city opera

companies; the need to synchronize operatic singing and the gestures on stage with the ebb and surge of the music in the orchestra; the need to compose in a manner which would allow comprehension of the text. (16) These subjects reflect Strauss's primary relationship to opera as a practitioner of the art and not as a philosopher. In this respect Hofmannsthal and Strauss were similar in their attitudes.

Also like Hofmannsthal, Strauss began his career in a field which was somewhat removed from opera; he initially composed and conducted instrumental music. The turning of Strauss to the composition of opera, however, may in no way be regarded as unusual as the poet's rejection of lyric poetry for the sake of stage plays and opera libretti. Opera, although differing in many respects from instrumental music, has long been a traditional genre in which composers have exercised their creativity. Moreover, very few composers have resisted the temptation to write at least one work in this form. Strauss began his career, however, as a composer in what might be termed the classical forms, such as sonata allegro form, rather than in the avant-garde forms of his time – the tone-poem and the music-drama. The forms of these avant-garde works were determined by exterior ideas, such as might be presented by poems or prose descriptions, rather, than by purely musical considerations. Strauss's early indifference to, or neglect of, this kind of composition placed him among the composers of traditional forms, with men such as Brahms for companions. In the music controversy of that day he thus ranged himself among the conservatives against Richard Wagner and Franz Liszt.

Only when Strauss discarded classical forms for the sake of the tone-poem did his individual genius manifest itself. Because his early musical education, which was overseen by his musician father, was conducted strictly within the confines of the classical tradition, this development took place only after he had left home and was able to make a thorough study of the scores and writings of Liszt and Wagner. Strauss himself gave credit to Alexander Ritter, a violinist in the Meiningen orchestra which Strauss conducted during the 1885–86 season, for his introduction to these new musical forms:

> Durch die Erziehung hafteten mir noch immer manche Vorurteile gegen das Wagnersche und besonders das Lisztsche Kunstwerk an, ich kannte kaum Richard Wagners Schriften. Mit ihnen und Schopenhauer machte mich Ritter in erklärender Ausdauer bekannt und vertraut, bewies mir, dass der Weg von dem "Ausdrucksmusiker" Beethoven . . . über Liszt führe, der mit Wagner richtig erkannt hatte, dass mit Beethoven die Sonatenform bis aufs Aeusserste erweitert worden . . . .
> Neue Gedanken müssen sich neue Formen suchen – dieses Lisztsche Grundprinzip seiner sinfonischen Werke, in denen tatsächlich die poetische Idee auch zugleich das formbildende Element war, wurde mir von da ab der Leitfaden für meine eigenen sinfonischen Arbeiten. (17)

Strauss composed his first work according to a literary program, Aus Italien, that same year, 1886. His absolute commitment to this kind of music is demonstrated most forcibly by the kinds of works he wrote after this date: orchestral tone-poems, operas, and songs form the greater part of the opus numbers from this year forward. Norman Del Mar in discussing this change in Strauss's style states:

> Strauss only found himself as a composer when his imagination
> was stimulated by literary or other external influences, and it
> is arguable that had he not, through the encouragement of some
> Alexander Ritter, found emancipation away from the classical
> forms of Absolute Music in which he had grown up, he might
> never have blossomed into an outstanding genius at all. He him-
> self later acknowledged this: "I have long recognized" he wrote,
> "that when composing I am unable to set anything down without a
> programme to guide me". (18)

The radical influence which this new music had upon Strauss's compositional style can hardly be overestimated. In the space of a few short years Strauss the symphonist and writer of chamber music became Strauss the composer of tone-poems and operas.

Footnotes

(1) Feeling and Form: A Theory of Art Developed from "Philosophy in a New Key" (New York: Charles Scribner's Sons, 1953), p. 28.

(2) Ibid., p. 110. Ms. Langer's italics.

(3) Ibid., p. 27.

(4) Ibid., p. 306.

(5) Max Kraussold, "Musik und Mythus in ihrem Verhältnis," Die Musik 18 (1925-26): 178-87, cited from a reprint in translation in Reflections on Art: A Source Book of Writings by Artists, Critics, and Philosophers, ed. Susanne K. Langer (Baltimore: Johns Hopkins Press, 1958), p. 328.

(6) Langer, Feeling and Form, p. 27.

(7) (Bloomington, Indiana: Indiana University Press, 1962), pp. 15-16.

(8)   Hugo von Hofmannsthal, Prosa IV, Gesammelte Werke in Einzelausgaben,
      ed. Herbert Steiner (Frankfurt: Fischer Verlag, 1955), p. 519. All quotations
      of Hofmannsthal will be taken from this edition of his collected works. Subse-
      quent references to any volume will be given in the body of the text according
      to the abbreviations given below. For example: P IV 519.
          Aufzeichnungen (Frankfurt: Fischer Verlag, 1959): A.
          Dramen I (Frankfurt: Fischer Verlag, 1953): D I.
          Dramen II (Frankfurt: Fischer Verlag, 1954): D II.
          Dramen III (Frankfurt: Fischer Verlag, 1957): D III.
          Dramen IV (Frankfurt: Fischer Verlag, 1958): D IV.
          Erzählungen, Die (Stockholm: Bermann-Fischer Verlag, 1946): E.
          Gedichte und lyrische Dramen (Stockholm: Bermann-Fischer Verlag,
              1946): GLD
          Lustspiele I (Stockholm: Bermann-Fischer Verlag, 1947): L I.
          Lustspiele II (Stockholm: Bermann-Fischer Verlag, 1948): L II.
          Lustspiele III (Frankfurt: Fischer Verlag, 1956): L III.
          Lustspiele IV (Frankfurt: Fischer Verlag, 1956): L IV.
          Prosa I (Frankfurt: Fischer Verlag, 1950): P I.
          Prosa II (Frankfurt: Fischer Verlag, 1951): P II.
          Prosa III (Frankfurt: Fischer Verlag, 1952): P III.
          Prosa IV (Frankfurt: Fischer Verlag, 1955): P IV.

(9)   Reprinted in Hugo von Hofmannsthal, ed. Sibylle Bauer, Wege der Forschung,
      vol. 183 (Darmstadt: Wissenschaftliche Buchgesellschaft, 1968), pp. 171-72,
      passim.

(10) Ernst Mach, The Analysis of Sensations and the Relation of the Physical to the
      Psychical, trans. from the 1st ed. by C. M. Williams, rev. and trans. from
      the 5th ed. by Sydney Waterlow, with a New Introduction by Thomas A. Szasz
      (New York: Dover Publications, Inc., 1959), pp. 2-3.

(11) Feeling and Form, p. 253. Ms. Langer's italics.

(12) Hugo von Hofmannsthal - Carl J. Burckhardt: Briefwechsel, ed. Carl J. Burck-
      hardt (Frankfurt: Fischer Verlag, 1956), p. 42. Hofmannsthal to Burckhardt's
      mother, 26. VII. 1920.

(13) With an Introduction by Howard Nemerov (London: Faber and Gwyer Ltd.,
      1928; reprinted in New York: McGraw Hill Book Co., 1964), pp. 80-81.

(14) Die Geburt der Tragödie oder Griechentum und Pessimismus; Werke in drei
      Bänden, ed. Karl Schlechta (Munich: Carl Hanser Verlag, 1966), I:25.

(15) Richard Strauss, "Vom melodischen Einfall," Betrachtungen und Erinnerun-
      gen, ed. Willi Schuh (Zurich: Atlantis Verlag, 1949), pp. 138-39.

(16) Betrachungen, passim.

(17) "Aus meinen Jugend- und Lehrjahren," Betrachtungen, p. 168.

(18) Richard Strauss: A Critical Commentary on His Life and Works, 3 vols. (Philadelphia: Chilton Book Co., 1962-1972), II: 272.

CHAPTER III

THE TEXT OF THE FRAU OHNE SCHATTEN

A valid analysis of the opera the Frau ohne Schatten must proceed by means of a study of its two primary elements, music and drama. The drama of this opera, which consists of actions or decisions having irrevocable consequences, (1) is expressed most consistently in the words of the text, for language mediates between the different figures of the opera. That aspect of the Frau ohne Schatten which expresses this mediation, primarily the text, is discussed in this chapter; the analysis of the music and its relationship to the drama of the opera is reserved for the succeeding chapter.

Symbols in the Text of the Frau ohne Schatten

Definition of Symbols

Mankind has often been defined by means of its particular ability to use language. Luther's translation of the Bible (Biblia Germanica, 1545) contains a preface to the Psalms in which he praises man's capacity for speech, calling it the one characteristic of man which most specifically separates him from the animals:

> "Das edlest werck am Menschen
> ist / das er reden kann."

ES ist ja ein stummer Mensch gegen einem redenden /
schier als ein halb todter Mensch zu achten. Und kein
krefftiger noch edler werck am Menschen ist / denn reden /
Sintemal der Mensch durchs reden von andern Thieren am
meisten gescheiden wird / mehr denn durch die gestalt
oder ander werck. Weil auch wol ein holtz kan eines
Menschen gestalt durch Schnitzer kunst haben. Und ein
Thier so wol sehen / hören / riechen / singen / gehen /
stehen / essen / trincken / fasten / dürsten / Hunger /
frost und hart lager leiden kan / als ein Mensch. (2)

Although twentieth century man is unlikely to look upon his ability to speak as evidence of his superiority over the other creatures of the earth, his ability to use language is still regarded by many as his distinguishing feature: "Man is, perhaps uniquely, the symbolizing animal; he not only performs, he also means and intends and seeks to know."(3) Suzanne K. Langer expresses a similar idea about man's distinguishing feature:

THE TEXT OF THE FRAU OHNE SCHATTEN

> Not higher sensitivity, not longer memory or even quicker
> association sets man so far above other animals that he can
> regard them as denizens of a lower world: no, it is the
> power of using symbols - the power of speech - that makes
> him lord of the earth. (4)

As may be deduced from the preceding two quotations, man's view of himself and
the world is changing from a two-sided conception wherein man and his subjective
emotions are posited as confronting an external, objective world to a conception
wherein language mediates between subjective man and the objective world. Wheelwright expresses this idea as follows:

> . . . the traditional Cartesian dualism of mind vs. matter,
> or in its later forms subjective vs. objective, which has tend-
> ed to give shape and direction to much of the philosophical
> thought since the seventeenth century, has begun to yield in
> many quarters to a threefold thought-structure, in which sub-
> ject, object, and linguistic medium play irreducible and
> intercausative roles in the formation of what, for want of a
> better name, we may call reality. (5)

Langer also rejects the subject-object dichotomy, but she places far greater emphasis on the symbolic transformation of sense data than Wheelwright does. Her conception of symbolism is correspondingly broader, embracing as it does nearly all
of the activities in which man engages:

> The fact that the human brain is constantly carrying on
> a process of symbolic transformation of the experiental data
> that come to it causes it to be a veritable fountain of more or
> less spontaneous ideas. As all registered experience tends
> to terminate in action, it is only natural that a typically human
> function should require a typically human form of overt activity;
> and that is just what we find in the sheer expression of ideas.
> This is the activity of which beasts appear to have no need. And
> it accounts for just those traits in man which he does not hold in
> common with the other animals - ritual, art, laughter, weeping,
> speech, superstition, and scientific genius.
> Only a part - howbeit a very important part - of our
> behavior is practical. Only some of our expressions are signs,
> indicative or mnemonic, and belong to the heightened animal
> wisdom called common sense; and only a small and relatively
> unimportant part are immediate signs of feeling. The remain-
> der serve simply to express, i.e. to act upon, without practi-
> cal purpose, without any view to satisfying other needs than
> the need of completing in overt action the brain's symbolic
> process. (6)

42

THE TEXT OF THE <u>FRAU OHNE SCHATTEN</u>

The following discussion of man's symbolic activities is restricted to language. When conceived in this sense, speech is a symbol or a sign, the difference between the two depending upon the type of relationship of the word to the thing to which reference is made, or the referrent. If a relationship exists wherein the word signals the presence of the object which it denotes – in much the same way that a ringing doorbell signals that someone is at the door, the word is functioning as a sign. This occurs every time the arrival of the president is announced with the words "the President of the United States," to which signal those gathered respond by standing in respect. If, on the other hand, the word is used by a speaker to recall a <u>conception</u> of an object to his or someone else's attention, the word is functioning as a symbol: "In talking <u>about</u> things we have conceptions of them, not the things themselves; and it is the conceptions, not the things, that symbols directly 'mean'."(7) A child who requests a drink without pointing to a faucet or a cup is utilizing words to express his conception of his need. This symbolizing function of words is radically different from the signalling function of words. The symbolizing function rests upon a four-sided relationship which includes 1) the speaker or subject, 2) the thing spoken of or object, 3) the word, and 4) the subject's conception of the object; the signalling function rests upon only three – subject, object, and word.

Symbols, as defined in this manner demonstrate a wide variation in the exactitude with which they convey the speaker's conception to the listener. A closed relationship may occur, closed in the sense that the conception is completely defined. This use of symbols occurs in scientific and philosophic writings where the author seeks by definition of his terms to convey his conceptions as precisely and as completely as possible. Somewhat surprisingly, the common transactions of everyday life are also expressed in this type of language, the speaker's conceptions being readily apparent to the listener, as in a child's request for a glass of water. In occurrences like this of ordinary life, however, and in distinction to the closed language by stipulation of science and philosophy, habit and stereotype are the forces which produce complete definition of conception. Transparency of this type is typical of closed symbolic language.

In contrast both to the stipulated conceptions of philosophy and science and also to the stereotyped conceptions employed in casual conversations, artistic writings, from lyric poetry to imaginative essay, often exhibit pluriconceptions, paradoxes, and deliberate ambiguities. A poet may establish, for example, a relationship between the life-giving liquid which one individual offers to another and the communion chalice of the Christian heritage. The beverage and the cup thus take on a range of meaning which may run the gamut from the popular Christian belief in a "hereafter" to a more general ideal of service to others. If the poet wishes to speak more exactly to his audience, he will employ additional words and phrases which will clarify the conception which he intends to convey. He may even shift the emphasis of the poem to the <u>lack of communion</u> for which the two are destined; he does not achieve this end, however, by defining the words which he uses, as do the scientist and the philosopher.

43

Owen Barfield, in an early study of meaning, contrasted the different kinds of meanings which are exhibited by philosophy and poetry:

> Words whose meanings are relatively fixed and established, words which can be defined - words, that is, which are used with precisely the same connotation by different speakers - are <u>results</u>, they are <u>things become.</u> The arrangement and rearrangement of such univocal terms in a series of propositions is the function of <u>logic</u>, whose object is elucidation and elimination of error. The poetic has nothing to do with this. It can only manifest itself as <u>fresh meaning</u>; it operates essentially <u>within</u> the individual term, which it creates and recreates by the magic of new combinations. (8)

In an attempt to impart new knowledge, or to convey "fresh meaning," therefore, the artist utilizes symbols in new and often striking ways, thereby creating and disclosing "certain hitherto unknown, unguessed aspects of What Is." (9) Any structure of stipulated meanings the poet will necessarily reject, unless his purpose is either to repeat what someone else has said or to write philosophy, for these are the required correlatives to the employment of a language composed of defined symbols. Assuming both that the poet or writer has a personal perspective and also that he desires to communicate this perspective to others, one cannot avoid the conclusion that he will employ language in an original manner, for symbols of this type are language's method of negotiating new insights. (10)

If artistic symbols, as contrasted to the stipulated symbols of science and philosophy, are to be successful in their task of revealing previously unknown or unperceived aspects of reality, they will exhibit the tendency of working toward the unknown from the known. This occurs in what is variously termed as metaphor, image, simile, and symbol. All of these words refer to a process of elucidating something which is difficult to comprehend by means of likening it to something more familiar. In the expression "God the Father," for example, the word "God" is illuminated by the word "Father." The words which are used to refer to this process may be distinguished from one another: "image" stresses the concrete aspect of a comparison; "simile" stresses a particular grammatical structure (use of the word "like"); "metaphor" is commonly used to suggest the comparison or juxtaposition of differing things or conceptions; "symbol," used in this specialized sense and in distinction to its reference to linguistic medium, suggests repeated use of a linguistic expression and its conception with a subsequent broad understanding among a widespread populace. These distinctions are not as significant, however, as their basic similarity of function, which is to reveal some aspect of "the infinitude of What Is - the infinitude of actual and potential experience . . . . "(11)

A pragmatist and supposed realist may object to the assertion that poetry is basically a revelation of reality, preferring in his own mind to find reality in the measurable differences of atomic weights and light-years, in "facts." The answer to this objection lies in a reiteration of the basic thesis that for people the fullest

reality consists of a three-fold inter-related and inter-causative structure of subject, object, and linguistic medium (including both words and conceptions), and not
in a measuring of the similarities and differences of objects or things which stand
in opposition to the subject. This is not to say that facts do not exist, for obviously
one can, for example, measure distances and record one's findings for others to
read and use. Nor are procedures of this kind unimportant to man, as demonstrated
by the tremendous capabilities given man by science and technology. This view of
reality, with its systematic refusal to admit both the subjective element of man and
also the symbolistic character of the medium in which it records its findings, tends
to be so simplistic, however, as to be inadequate.

A story about the relationship between a woman and a man is not greatly en-
hanced with a recital of basic facts, such as their respective heights, weights, and
rates of respirations. Yet a revelation of such a relationship, at least in its emotional aspects, may be as meaningful, hence, real, to a person as a knowledge of
the rate of speed at which the universe is expanding. Viewed from this vantage-
point, modern science and technology reveal their roots in the subject-object dichotomy which up to this century has been characteristic of modern thought patterns.
Contemporary man seems to be faced with the need to revise this simplistic conception of reality in order to give greater consideration to his subjective elements and
to his linguistic medium. Poetry, where reality in a more holistic sense is disclosed, can lead man in this direction.

This definition of artistic symbols - words and word structures which,
especially in original combinations, offer a fresh perspective on reality - makes of
the poet a visionary or prophet, one who sees possible modes of life beyond those
presently in existence. Unlike the visionary, who may be given to living his visions
in a dream-like state, or the prophet, who is doomed to fail in his attempts to mold
a misunderstanding and intractable society after his vision, however, the poet creates a symbolic reality, a structure of conceptions in words:

> Art, then, takes up experience and boldly wrenches it into new
> shapes; it does not so much hold the mirror up to nature as it
> confronts nature with a new, fresh, and unique version of it-
> self. (12)

This confrontation between traditional views of nature and the artist's "new, fresh,
and unique version" of it may be instrumental in creating a new sense of reality for
others, for the conceptions which people hold of nature are basic to their determina-
tion of what constitutes reality.

The artistic symbols which a poet or writer uses may be private and con-
fined to one particular work or they may be more generally used. Wheelwright differentiated types of symbols in this manner:

A symbol may complete its work as the presiding image of
a particular poem; it may be repeated and developed by a
certain poet as having special importance and significance
for him personally; it may develop literary life ("ancestral
vitality") by being passed from poet to poet, being mingled
and stirred to new life in fresh poetic contacts; it may have
significance for an entire cultural group or an entire body
of religious believers; and finally it may be archetypal, in
the sense of tending to have a fairly similar significance
for all or a large portion of mankind, independently of
borrowings and historical influences. (13)

Hofmannsthal's Use of Artistic Symbols in
the <u>Frau ohne Schatten</u>

Hugo von Hofmannsthal used artistic symbols which range from the personal to the archetypal as he strove to make his vision clear to his readers and listeners in the <u>Frau ohne Schatten</u>. In keeping with the poet's belief that even situations
are symbolical in nature (A 14) and expressive of life's secrets, (14) certain gestures
and even manners of speaking attain a symbolical significance. The vision which he
wished to convey by means of his poetry, including the gestures and the manners of
speaking of the opera's principal figures, is concerned with both the most problematical and also the most varied aspect of human life: relationships among people. Because this vision deals with a tremendous range of possibilities, Hofmannsthal used
many symbols. These will be grouped and discussed in the succeeding sections of
this chapter according to the character which the various symbols most illuminate;
they will be extracted from both the prose narrative and the libretto, a procedure
which allows each version to enlarge upon and qualify the meaning of the other. Preceding the discussion of the symbols is a synopsis of the libretto, which provides
the context in which the symbols belong. The decision to discuss the symbols apart
from the analysis of the opera as a whole, which is given in Chapter IV, stems from
the nature of symbols themselves. The new knowledge they give, "the bright center
of particularity that is singled out for attention," is often surrounded by an aura of
secondary import, "the dim tail-of-the-eye impression of qualities and meanings
and perspectives that was left out."(15) The secondary import, when exhaustively
studied, may be observed to modify "the bright center of particularity" of the primary knowledge. The resultant meaning-complexes are too lengthy for discussion
within the space restrictions imposed by a table, which is the format of the analysis
in Chapter IV.

Synopsis of the Libretto the <u>Frau ohne Schatten</u>

The Emperor of the South Sea Islands, while hunting one day, was on the
verge of hurling his spear at a beautiful, white gazelle. At the last instant before he
threw his weapon, the animal turned into a lovely fairy. The Emperor, enchanted by

46

her beauty, made her his Empress. Since their marriage the two of them have spent every night together expressing their infatuation for each other. (This hunting incident, which precedes the opening scene of the opera by one year, is recounted by both the Empress and the Emperor during Act I scene i.)

The opening of the curtain upon the first scene of the opera reveals a figure, the Empress' Nurse, crouched in the dark upon the roof of a palace. A messenger from the Empress-fairy's father, Keikobad, arrives and inquires of the Nurse whether the Empress throws a shadow yet. The Nurse answers, "None!" as she has to the eleven previous messengers of the eleven preceding months. The twelfth Messenger, upon receiving this news, announces that only three days remain to the Emperor and the Empress. If at the end of this period the Empress does not throw a shadow, she will have to return to her father and the Emperor will turn to stone. The Nurse greets this news joyously, for she is eager to be free of mankind and return to the fairy kingdom. She resolves not to tell the Empress of this threat to her husband and lover, just as she has kept the appearance of the eleven previous messengers secret.

The Messenger disappears as the Emperor comes from the room situated on the roof of the palace to inform the Nurse that he is going to hunt today as is his custom. He may, moreover, be absent for as long as three days, because he intends to search for his missing Red Falcon; he bids the Nurse to protect the Empress. As she assents she thinks gleefully that the Emperor's three-day absence will assure that he turns to stone.

After his departure the Nurse takes a lamp and enters the roof-top chamber in order to determine whether the Empress still is free of a shadow. Triumphantly, she ascertains that this is indeed the case, but in the process she awakens her mistress. The Empress reacts to being awakened by rebuking the Nurse, for she would much rather sleep and dream than face the boredom of being alone all day in the castle. (The Emperor is responsible for this solitary existence, for he, fearing detriment to her fairy aspects, forbids her to associate with human beings.) The Empress desires to dream, for then she can once again transform herself into the creatures of the air, land, and sea, just as she had actually done before she lost her magic Talisman during the initial euphoric encounter with the Emperor. Were she to recover the Talisman, she states, she would reappear every day as a new prey to the hunting Emperor.

As the Empress and the Nurse reflect on the disappearance of the Talisman, the Emperor's Red Falcon returns to the palace after an absence of a year. The bird had flown away from the couple after the Emperor had in anger thrown a dagger at it and wounded it. The Red Falcon informs the Empress of the curse which is likely to overtake the Emperor because she throws no shadow.

The Empress resolves to obtain a shadow and save her beloved husband from turning to stone. Initially, the Nurse refuses to help, but the strong will of the

47

THE TEXT OF THE <u>FRAU OHNE SCHATTEN</u>

Empress soon forces her to consent. As a new day dawns, the two of them fly down
to a city in search of a shadow.

The second scene of Act I presents a dyer's hovel where three misshapen
young men are fighting. A young woman angrily throws a bucket of water over them,
with the result that they cease fighting with each other in order to heap abuse upon
her. The argument continues until Barak, the woman's husband enters; the Wife
gives him this ultimatum:

> Aus dem Haus mir mit diesen!
> Du, schaff sie mir fort!
> Oder es ist meines Bleibens nicht länger bei dir!
> (D III 164.)

Barak sends his three brothers outside to work with the dye vats and attempts to placate the Wife's anger by pointing out their dependence upon him. As he
leaves to go to market, however, the frustration and dissatisfaction of the Wife,
rather than having been ameliorated by his words, have increased.

At this point the Nurse and the Empress enter, disguised as poor country
people. The Nurse ingratiates herself with the Wife and eventually suggests that
riches and slaves for an eternity would be a fair exchange for the Wife's shadow. In
astonishment the woman watches and listens as a pavilion suitable for a princess
appears before her eyes and slaves call out longingly for their mistress. As the
Wife begins to speak, the vision fades, whetting her appetite for the leisure and
riches which she believes to be within her grasp. The Nurse, aware that she nearly
has the Wife's consent in advance, broaches the terms of a pact: she (the Nurse) and
"her daughter" (the Empress) will serve the Wife for three days, during which time
Barak the Dyer is not to come near her. After the three days have passed, the Wife
will formally deny her prospective children entrance into the world. She will then
lose her shadow and begin to experience eternal joy, beauty, and wealth. The Wife,
acknowledging that she has no desire to become a mother, agrees.

With a pact concluded, the Nurse magically separates the marriage bed into two parts and prepares a supper for Barak of fried fish. The Nurse and Empress
disappear, leaving the Wife to listen anxiously to a mournful sound which appears to
emanate from the fire: "Mutter, Mutter, lass uns nach Hause! / Die Tür ist verrie-
gelt, wir finden nicht ein . . . ." (D III 178.) As the fire dies down, the voices
cease, but the Wife is still frightened. While she fearfully wipes away beads of per-
spiration, Barak enters. Upon his return the Wife disappears behind the curtain
that shields her half of the bed. Barak, giving up hope of speaking with her, settles
down to sleep for the night while outside the night watchmen sing their praise of
married love. This hymn concludes Act I.

Act II scene i opens with Barak again readying himself to go to market. The
Empress, disguised as a serving maid, helps him. As soon as he has left, the Nurse

48

conjures forth the apparition of a youth who had at one time attracted the attention
of the Wife. She, drawn toward him and yet repulsed by him, is prevented from making any decision when the Empress announces the return of Barak. The Three Brothers and a crowd of Beggar Children accompany him as he enters, carrying a huge
platter piled high with delicacies. Meanwhile, the Nurse has effected the disappearance of the Youth as quickly as she had his appearance. The delight of the Brothers
and the Beggar Children in the food provided by Barak gives the hovel an atmosphere
of celebration in which the Wife refuses to take part. Barak does not sense her unhappiness, so intent is he upon praising the fine things which he has bought. Frus-
trated at his insensitivity to her needs, the Wife lashes out at him verbally and then
bursts into tears. Barak's reaction is one of resignation and forgiveness. The scene
closes as Barak offers food to the Children and the Three Brothers; they in turn
praise his goodness and generosity. Simultaneously the Wife expresses dissatisfaction with her life. This concludes the portrayal of the events of the first day of the
pact; concurrently, the first of the three days left to the Emperor has passed.

Act II scene ii is set in the forest outside the Falconer House, where the
Empress had claimed in a note to the Emperor that she would be spending the three
days of his absence. The Emperor arrives, led by the Red Falcon, and hides among
the trees to observe the house. Upon discovering it to be empty, a sense of impending doom overcomes him. As the Empress and the Nurse fly past him to the lodge,
the Emperor realizes that the Empress has deceived him, for it is obvious to him
that she has been associating with people rather than spending the day in solitude.
His immediate reaction is one of sorrow at her deceit, but this emotion quickly
gives way to anger, and he determines to kill her. He is, however, unable to decide
which of his weapons is suitable to execute his death sentence. His indecision leads
him to the realization that he cannot kill her. He leaves without even attempting to
talk to her, telling the Falcon to lead him to a distant rocky cliff where no one will
be able to hear him mourn.

The third scene of Act II is again set in the Dyer's hut and portrays the second day of the pact. As before, Barak is at work, preparing to go to market. He
requests a drink from the Wife, but she refuses to serve him, sending the Empress
in her stead. The drink, prepared with a sleeping potion by the Nurse, causes Barak to fall asleep. When the Wife discovers what has occurred, her concern for Barak is so great that she calls gently to him; she does not, however, awaken him at
this time.

The Nurse, eager to take advantage of the opportunity which Barak's sleep
provides, once more conjures forth the apparition of the Youth. But the Wife does
not willingly follow the Nurse's lead. Rather than be drawn into the erotic situation
which the Nurse has prepared for her, she demands her wraps so that she may take
a walk. As the Youth falls over, seemingly unconscious at her rejection, she pauses.
The Youth utilizes this opportunity to grasp her hand; meanwhile, the Nurse pushes
the Empress out the door and follows. Almost prey to the trap set by the Nurse, the
Wife suddenly remembers Barak. She rushes to awaken him, and cries out to him

49

to protect his home from robbers and to take care of her. The Empress helps her to awaken him, while the Nurse magically causes the Youth to disappear.

Barak, only partly conscious, grabs his hammer and calls for the Brothers to help him rid their home of thieves. But the Wife now denies the existence of any intruders and criticizes Barak for his stupid behavior. The Dyer is moved that she is concerned about him, but immediately forgets this tenderness when he discovers a broken mortar. He fears that the damaged work utensil and the inexplicable day-time nap presage a growing incapacity on his part to care for those entrusted to him. Angry that Barak does not acknowledge more fittingly the tenderness which she has exhibited toward him, the Wife calls him an ass and leaves for a walk, taking the Nurse with her. Barak, confused and sad, remains behind. As he sits, presumably alone in the hut, he becomes aware that someone is with him and asks who might be there. The Empress replies, as she picks up his tools: "Ich, mein Gebieter, deine Dienerin!" (D III 201.)

The fourth scene of Act II focuses on the relationship between the Empress and the Emperor and upon the Emperor's seemingly relentless movement toward his stony fate. In this scene, however, the Emperor's approaching doom is seen through the eyes of the Empress; by contrast, Act II scene ii presents events from the point of view of the Emperor.

It is night and the Empress sleeps in the Falconer House with the Nurse at her feet. Her sleep is troubled by dreams of Barak and she murmurs in her sleep:

> Sieh – Amme – sieh
> des Mannes Aug, wie es sich quält!
> Vor solchen Blicken liegen Cherubim
> auf ihrem Angesicht!
> (D III 201.)

The dream then shifts to a vision, enacted on the stage, of the Emperor entering a rocky, grave-like cavern. The Empress, fully aware of her responsibility both for the turning of the Emperor to stone and for Barak's suffering, awakens with a start.

Act II scene v portrays the activities in the Dyer's hut on the third day – the final day both for the pact and also for the Emperor. Barak and the Brothers display awareness of the intrusion of a dark power into their world. The Nurse also comments upon the apparent interference of superior powers, while at the same time she asserts that the terms of the pact are inviolate.

In an ensemble wherein Barak, the Nurse, and the Three Brothers express their reaction to these unnatural events, the Empress rues her interference in the lives of Barak and the Wife. The Wife simultaneously determines that she can no longer stand to live in the Dyer's hut. She tells Barak that she has been receiving a friend in his absence and that she is determined to live in the glory that will be hers

50

when she has renounced her shadow and with it her children. The Nurse immediately prompts her to speak a formal renunciation. Barak, galvanized to action by the
Wife's words, calls to the Brothers to light a fire so that he can see her face. When
the light reveals the Wife to be without a shadow, Barak breaks into a rage; he will
drown the "whore." As the Brothers attempt to prevent him from doing any violence,
the Nurse conjures a sword into Barak's hand. Simultaneously, the Empress refuses
to grasp the shadow, for in her opinion blood is upon it. The Wife sees Barak standing before her as her judge and attempts to tell him that she really has not done
those deeds of which she spoke. Awed by the power he has assumed in this role, she
surrenders herself to him for his judgment. At this instant, in the midst of an earth-
quake and a flood, both Barak and the Wife disappear from sight. Complete darkness
ends the scene and the act.

The curtain of Act III rises to reveal Barak and the Wife imprisoned in separate rocky caverns. Neither hears the other call, yet each longs to be helpful to
the other. The mighty anger of Barak, precipitated by the frivolous words of the
Wife, has led each to a true insight into the other's deepest being. Although each believes himself now lost to the other, the superior powers which interceded at the
end of the second act and transported them to this prison intervene once again to release them from their cells. Nevertheless, they do not meet at this time. Throughout the remainder of the act they search for one another, periodically calling out
each other's names.

The second scene of Act III shows a great rocky cavern with a temple-like
entrance. The Empress, arriving with the Nurse in a boat, realizes that they have
come to her father's palace. Hearing the call of horns in the distance, she perceives
that she is to be judged and begins to climb the steps leading to the gate. She will not
listen to the Nurse's warning of the punishment which awaits her there for associating with men. Instead, her thoughts turn to the petrified Emperor and to the fact
that she is responsible for the fate which has befallen him.

The Empress, observing the Nurse's fear, questions her closely about
where the gate leads. Learning that one enters there to the "Water of Life," the
Empress responds with sudden comprehension: "to the Threshold of Death!" She
envisions the petrified Emperor here, but feels that she can restore him to life by
sprinkling him with the magical Water of Life. She asks the Nurse if the Water of
Life is the blood of her own veins which she must let flow. In answer, the Nurse informs her that there actually is a spring in the interior of the mountain, but that to
a being from the spirit world this spring-water is deadly. Still the Empress climbs
the steps to the gate while the Nurse anxiously attempts to dissuade her. The Empress, confidently radiant in the appropriateness of her decision, informs the Nurse
that she goes to receive judgment upon the acts which she has committed among men.
She perceives, she says, the greatness of men in their suffering; it is her intention
from this point on to live among them. Moreover, she no longer needs or desires
the Nurse to be her helper and companion.

THE TEXT OF THE <u>FRAU OHNE SCHATTEN</u>

After the Empress enters the gate which leads into the mountain, the Nurse curses mankind for having ruined her child's "crystal soul." As she curses, Barak and the Wife enter separately, each in search of the other. The Nurse sends them off in opposite directions and then gathers up enough courage to attempt to follow and help the Empress. As she approaches the gate, however, the Messenger appears and prevents her entrance. Following a long argument the Nurse tries to push past him, but he shoves her down the steps and into the boat, commanding it to carry her back into the midst of mankind; she is to dwell among those she hates.

Act III scene iii takes place in a temple-like room in the interior of the mountain. The Empress enters as ministering spirits, who light the way, advise her:

> Erster: Hab Ehrfucht!
> Zweiter: Mut!
> Dritter: Erfülle dein Geschick!
> (D III 231.)

The Empress, alone now, speaks to a curtained niche in the wall, assuming Keikobad's presence there. She claims a place among men for herself, even though she has been unable to barter or buy a shadow. A fountain of golden water springing from the floor is the only answer she receives. As the Empress, denying any need for water to refresh herself, retreats from the fountain, a voice instructs her to drink of the water so that the shadow of the Wife might become her shadow. The Empress, exhibiting a newly-acquired freedom from exterior influences, acknowledges her indebtedness to Barak, and the water slowly sinks. When she declares that she will not drink, the fountain subsides completely.

Upon the disappearance of the fountain the Empress demands that Keikobad show himself and pass judgment upon her. The curtained niche gradually becomes lighted, exposing not Keikobad, but the stony form of the Emperor. Horrified, the Empress requests to die with him, for she recognizes that it is her fault that he has been punished in this way. When the stony glance of the Emperor observes her lack of a shadow, she cries out that she cannot help.

Again a stream of golden water springs from the floor and again a voice, promising the rejuvenation of the Emperor with this act, instructs her to drink. In desperation the Empress implores Keikobad not to tempt her. As if to strengthen her resolve, the voices of Barak and the Wife call out in the distance. The Empress, torn by inner conflict, cries out: "Ich - will - nicht!" (D III 237.) The fountain subsides and the room momentarily darkens.

A bright light from above reveals a dark shadow extending from the Empress. The Emperor rises, telling her that as he lay dying he was informed that he might rise from the depths of his own grave when the crystal heart of the Empress broke with a cry. As he sings, the light increases in intensity, and silvery voices call to them from a distance: the Unborn Children are greeting their parents.

The final scene opens with the Wife continuing her search for Barak: she would prefer to die by his sword rather than live without his love. From the opposite side of a deep abyss Barak calls to her to remain in one place in order that he might find her. As they behold one another, the Wife's dark shadow, now restored to her, extends across the abyss from her to him. In delight they call to each other while a golden bridge replaces the shadow and magically enables their reunion.

In a final outburst of joy Barak, the Emperor, the Empress, and the Wife, all praise the outcome of their trials. The opera ends with the voices of the Unborn Children sounding from the orchestra:

> Vater, dir drohet nichts,
> siehe, es schwindet schon,
> Mutter, das Aengstliche,
> das euch beirrte.
>
> Wäre denn je ein Fest,
> wären nicht insgeheim
> wir die Geladenen,
> wir auch die Wirte!
> (D III 242.)

In summary, Act I presents the curse of petrification which threatens the Emperor at the end of three days should the Empress be unable to obtain a shadow. The Empress and the Nurse appear to be close to this goal when the Wife agrees to their terms of barter for the shadow. Act II presents the events of the succeeding three days and two nights, which constitute both the deadline for the Emperor and also the duration of the pact. During this time the Empress begins to rue her decision to interfere in the lives of others in order to obtain a shadow. The steady progression of the Emperor toward his stony fate is also presented in this act. Act III presents the Empress at the juncture of an ultimate decision: she can save the Emperor from a fate for which she shares the responsibility only by destroying Barak's happiness or she can deny help to the Emperor, abandoning him to his stony fate, in an attempt to help Barak. Only the interference of a higher power can help her out of this tragic dilemma. When she outwardly reveals the torment of her soul over this decision and cries out in anguish, the higher powers restore the Emperor to her without the destruction of Barak's life. Barak and the Wife are reunited while the Nurse is banished from the spirit world.

THE TEXT TO THE FRAU OHNE SCHATTEN

Symbols Pertaining to the Empress

Schatten, Licht

Light, brightness, and the lack of a shadow are the characteristics which Hofmannsthal most frequently ascribed to the Empress. According to the prose narrative, she has a body of rock crystal (Bergkristall); in the libretto the Nurse states that ''light travels through the Empress' body as though she were made of glass'':

> Durch ihren Leib
> wandelt das Licht,
> als wäre sie gläsern.
> (D III 150.)

When the Messenger inquires whether she throws a shadow, the answer is ''Keinen! Keinen!'' (D III 150.) These complementary symbols - transparency and the lack of a shadow - distinguish the physical appearance of the Empress from that of any other being. In this manner Hofmannsthal implies that the Empress is unique. Whether one interprets these qualities _ transparency and the lack of a shadow - as symbolical of the supra-human within a human being or as literally descriptive of the physical characteristics of a fairy, these physical traits signify a rarity that bespeaks superiority. In contrast to the mangled uniqueness of the Three Brothers, the singularity of her being is radiance and beauty.

These physical features are also a means of symbolizing the Empress' descent from Keikobad, the king of spirits, for Hofmannsthal often associated light and spirituality:

> Zu ihrem Animalischen haben diese Geschöpfe [ein paar Ziegen] etwas Göttliches hinzu, aus der Luft: dieses Licht is die unauf-hörliche Hochzeit des Geistes mit der Welt.
> (P IV 155.)

The relationship between light and spirituality is made explicit in the Empress' recollections of her father: '' . . . er trug keine Krone, aber die Stirne selber glänzte wie ein Diadem. '' (E 358.) Hofmannsthal described here a nobility of spirit, rather than a nobility of riches and power, and symbolized this spiritual nobility by juxtaposing light, forehead, and diadem. In doing this he appropriated the typically Middle Eastern association of light with a spiritual deity.

In addition to light, Hofmannsthal associated with Keikobad one other quality, which is signified by the location of his palace in a rocky cliff:

> . . . hinter ihnen [den Bäumen] stiegen die schwarzen glänzen-den Felsen empor, aus deren finsterer mächtiger Masse der ganze Bereich von Keikobads verborgener Residenz aufgebaut war.
> (E 349.)

THE TEXT TO THE FRAU OHNE SCHATTEN

Unlike plants and animals, rocks do not grow; they are static. Nor does light, the other primary quality associated with Keikobad, admit of growth and development; it is either present or it is absent. In short, both rocks and light are expressions of absolutes. As Keikobad's daughter, the Empress has inherited this quality of absoluteness or perfection; her body of rock symbolizes that she has never experienced growth.

Keikobad's imposing and immovable place of residence also signifies the security of his personality; rather than blowing hither and yon with the opinions and whims of others, he firmly and steadfastly maintains the course of his own being. The cliff residence thus assumes a symbolism akin to that held by Sigismund's tower in the Turm. As the Empress develops and comes to resemble her father, she discovers a similar strength within herself:

> Sie sah mit einem Blick, als schwebe sie ausserhalb, sich sel-
> ber dastehen, zu ihren Füssen den Schatten des fremden Weibes,
> der ihr verfallen war, drüben die Statue. Das furchtbare Gefühl
> der Wirklichkeit hielt alles zusammen mit eisernen Banden. Die
> Kälte wehte zu ihr herüber bis ins Innerste und lähmte sie. Sie
> konnte keinen Schritt tun, nicht vor- noch rückwärts. Sie konnte
> nichts als dies: trinken und den Schatten gewinnen oder die Schale
> ausgiessen. Sie meinte vernichtet zu werden und drängte sich
> ganz in sich zusammen; aus ihrer eigenen diamantenen Tiefe stie-
> gen Worte in ihr auf, deutlich, so als würden sie gesungen in grosser
> Ferne; sie hatte sie nur nachzusprechen. Sie sprach sie nach,
> ohne Zögern. ''Dir Barak bin ich mich schuldig!'' sprach sie,
> streckte den Arm mit der Schale gerade vor sich hin und goss die
> Schale aus vor die Füsse der verhüllten Gestalt.
>
> (E 368-69.)

Keikobad's imposing strength, intimated by the impregnability of his place of residence, pre-figures the spiritual power which the Empress here exhibits.

The Empress has not only been denied by the Emperor the opportunity for growth, in the sense of expanding her understanding of the world, she has never shared in the dark aspects of human life, such as suffering, guilt, and ultimately death. Here lies the reason for the complementary symbol to her radiance, for the lack of the shadow. The relationship between the shadow and the dark aspects of life is made explicit in this speech of the Empress from the prose narrative:

> Es ist das Schattenwerfen mit dem sie der Erde ihr Dasein
> heimzahlen. Ich wusste nicht, dass ihnen dieses dunkle Ding
> so viel gilt.
>
> (E 262.)

55

The Empress here considers the shadow to be the price of being, the price of life on earth. On this subject Hofmannsthal made other, perhaps more revealing comments. In criticizing a book of short stories by Peter Altenberg in the 1890's he stated:

> Es [das Buch(16)] ist verliebt in das Leben, allzu verliebt . . . .
> Es gibt eine zurückhaltendere Art, dem Leben zu huldigen,
> eine grössere, herbere Art, ihm zu sagen, dass es grenzen-
> los wundervoll, unerschöpflich und erhaben ist und wert, mit
> dem Tod bezahlt zu werden.
>
> (P I 270.)

> Sie [Künstler und Kinder] sind die einzigen die das Leben als
> Ganzes zu fassen vermögen. Sie sind die einzigen, die über den
> Tod, den Preis des Lebens etwas sagen dürfen.
>
> (P I 276.)

The ultimate price of life is death; the temporary price of life is the shadow, or physical and emotional pain, suffering, transgressions against others, and consciousness of death. Until the Empress experiences these aspects of life, she will not be a human being. Until she is fully human, moreover, she will be unable to throw a shadow. The Empress is given the awe-inspiring task of integrating sorrow, suffering, transgressions against others, and death into her life. When this is accomplished, she will be able to throw a shadow.

Kinder

As a further symbol of her humanity, the Empress will also be able to bear children. The change from sterility to fruitfulness, a polarity frequently treated by Hofmannsthal - as in, for example, the opening lines of <u>Der Tor und der Tod</u>, symbolizes that an individual has completed the path which leads from egocentric isolation to life within a community. The Empress travels this path, rejecting the isolation of the palace and the sterility of life within its well-regulated halls for the encounter with the ugly, and yet fruitful, aspects of life within Barak's hut. In his notebook ''Ad me ipsum'' Hofmannsthal clearly stated this relationship between the child and society:

> Der Weg zum Sozialen als Weg zum höheren Selbst:
> der nicht-mystische Weg.
>   a) durch die Tat
>   b) durch das Werk
>   c) durch das Kind
>
> (A 217.)

The tie between humanity and child-bearing is made explicit in the case of the Wife. The terms of the pact require that she deny life to her children; this denial will be equivalent to the loss of her shadow or the loss of her humanity. The Nurse states:

> "Dann nimmst du sieben solcher Fischlein, wirfst sie mit
> der linken Hand über die rechte Schulter ins Wasser und
> sagst dreimal: 'Weichet von mir, ihr Verfluchten, und
> wohnet bei meinem Schatten.' "
>
> (E 278.)

Seen in this light and applied to the case of the Empress, the Unborn Children, who sing at times throughout the opera and who close the final scene, are as much a symbol of full humanity as is the shadow.

Perhaps a greater understanding of the role of the Unborn Children can be attained through a reading of this interpretation by Edgar Hederer:

> Das Kind ist Zeichen eines Siegs des sich verschenkenden
> Herzens, Lohn für Unterwerfung unter das irdische Ge-
> setz. (17)

Hederer emphasizes that aspect of bearing children which constitutes a voluntary restriction upon oneself. Children are the reward for those who learn loyalty to another individual, even to the point of self-denial.

Gazelle, Vogel, Fisch

Hofmannsthal associated several animals with the Empress in an attempt to suggest the sense of unity between the self and the world which the Empress experienced before her marriage to the Emperor. He wrote that the Empress was able to transform herself at will into a bird or a gazelle, according to the libretto, and into a fish, an otter, a snake, or a kite, according to the prose narrative. These are representatives of many animal species - of those which fly and are at home in the air, of those which swim and live in the water, of those which run or crawl on the land, of those which are almost equally at home in the water and on the land. With the Empress' quality of lightness and brightness representing fire, she thus partakes of all four elements of the earth: air, earth, water, and fire. There is, therefore, no limitation upon the world of the Empress; she is at home everywhere.

A second quality of animals which impressed Hofmannsthal was the sense of immediacy with which animals experience the world. It is the absence of this particular quality which is bemoaned by the Fool in Hofmannsthal's early verse play Der Tor und der Tod:

THE TEXT OF THE FRAU OHNE SCHATTEN

Was weiss denn ich vom Menschenleben?
Bin freilich scheinbar drin gestanden,
Aber ich hab es höchstens verstanden,
Konnte mich nie darein verweben.
Hab mich niemals daran verloren.
. . . .
Wenn ich von guten Gaben der Natur
Je eine Regung, einen Hauch erfuhr,
So nannte ihn mein überwacher Sinn
Unfähig des Vergessens, grell beim Namen.
Und wie dann tausende Vergleiche kamen,
War das Vertrauen, war das Glück dahin.

                                 (GLD 201-202.)

Hofmannsthal here placed a high value upon the ability to experience life without analysis; in contrast to man, this manner of experiencing life is paramount in animals. The Empress, when she was capable of experiencing life as an animal, was, therefore, not only everywhere at home in the world, but her life was characterized by a sense of immediacy and a lack of reflection.

When the Empress was captured by the Emperor, she was in the shape of a gazelle. Erwin Kobel attributes the following qualities to this family of animals:

> Anmut und Scheu, ein Heraustreten und Dastehen, ein Sich-
> entziehen und Verbergen, etwas Leichtes und Ungreifbares,
> Schwebendes und Unbegrenztes, vermischt mit Angst und Sehnsucht:
> all dies findet im Rehhaften seinen Ausdruck. Dieses Gazellen-
> wesen ist in der Art wie Kinder gehen, spürbar: "Es liegt die
> Erwartung unbegrenzter Möglichkeiten darin." (A 150) . . . In
> ihrer Unbestimmtheit und Unbegrenztheit bildet die Tochter des
> Geisterkönigs den Gegensatz zu den durch das Schicksal einge-
> schränkten Menschen: zum Einäugigen, Einarmigen, Buckli-
> gen . . . . (18)

Those qualities aside which express physical characteristics or personality traits, such as grace or shyness, the significant features which Kobel describes are "Unbestimmtheit" (lack of definition) and "Unbegrenztheit" (boundlessness, infinitude). Both of these qualities seem also to be expressed through the multitude and variety of the kinds of creatures into which the Empress is capable of changing. She carries within herself an infinitude of possibilities. There is, however, a negative side to this state in which she finds herself: she has realized none of the possibilities open to her. She is, consequently, nothing.

Hofmannsthal was early critical of the inability of people to restrict themselves and thereby to become someone and accomplish something. The following commentary and quotation from his essay "Das Tagebuch eines Willenskranken:

THE TEXT OF THE FRAU OHNE SCHATTEN

Henri-Frédéric Amiel, 'Fragment d'un journal intime' "exhibits this attitude:

> Initiative Anfangskraft fehlt. "Ich warte immer auf die Frau,
> auf das Werk, gross genug, meine Seele zu erfüllen und mir
> Ziel zu werden." Das ist das ewige, symbolische Warten, der
> grosse Trugschluss aller Raphaels ohne Hände, der "Künstler"
> von Gotthold Ephraim Lessings Gnaden.
> Dieser Ueberreichtum ist eigentlich Mangel; dieses Alles-
> wollen nichts als die hilflose Unfähigkeit, sich zu beschränken.
>
> (P I 31.)

Hofmannsthal implies here that it would be far better to attempt something - and
fail if need be - than wait for a lifetime and accomplish nothing.

Hofmannsthal uses the animal symbols, which suggest both unity with the
world and also boundlessness and infinity, in a positive fashion in the libretto and
the narrative. Within a child or a young girl the aspect of this quality which implies
a unity between the self and the world seems to counterbalance the inability to
achieve realization of any one of the possibilities present. Yet Hofmannsthal's criticism of Amiel cited above definitely suggests that somewhere and at some time it
is appropriate to choose a possibility and to create a reality out of that possibility.

Talisman

The Empress possessed as a child and a young girl a Talisman, the source
of the magic which enabled her to change form. At the instant when the Emperor was
about to plunge a spear into her while she was in the shape of a white gazelle, she
changed into her true form as a fairywoman. In the ensuing hour of love, "in der
Trunkenheit der ersten Stunde" (D III 153), she lost the Talisman. Because the Talisman conferred upon her the ability to transform herself into any creature of the
world, its loss symbolizes that the fairy is no longer a true fairy being. Moreover,
with the loss of the Talisman she has lost both her sense of unity with the world and
also her non-reflective manner of experiencing life. This change in her character is
consistent with Hofmannsthal's views on the significance of the first meeting between
people:

> Jede neue bedeutende Bekanntschaft zerlegt uns und setzt uns
> neu zusammen. Ist sie von der grössten Bedeutung, so machen wir
> eine Regeneration durch.
>
> (A 27.)

The exterior fact of her inability to transform herself thus reflects an interior
change of personality. She is no longer what she was, and this may be directly at-
tributed to her association with the Emperor. The Empress has taken the first step
toward the realization of one of the possibilities inherent within her.

THE TEXT OF THE FRAU OHNE SCHATTEN

The Emperor does not, however, further this process which he has initiated; the mutual change wrought at the very core of their beings occurred only once instead of becoming a continuing process:

> Der Sinn der Ehe ist wechselseitige Auflösung und Palingenesie.
> Wahre Ehe ist darum nur durch den Tod lösbar, ja eigentlich
> auch durch diesen nicht.
>
> (A 29.)

Neither the Empress nor the Emperor develops as a result of their mutual association. The Emperor is not only incapable of calling forth any growth on the part of the Empress, he also prevents her from meeting another individual who might perform this catalytic function. In the first scene the Nurse, presumably upon orders from the Emperor, sends the servants away before the Empress even has the opportunity to see them. On the other hand, the threat of turning to stone which hangs over the Emperor is evidence of the Empress' inability to transfigure him, petrification being in this instance the opposite of regeneration ("Palingenesie").

In both the libretto and the prose version this impasse is broken by the intervention of the Falcon. In the libretto the Falcon speaks, intoning before the Empress the fate which is about to befall the Emperor. In the prose narrative he returns the Talisman to the Empress; engraved upon its surface are the words of the curse which the Empress reads aloud.

With the return of the Talisman, and presumably with it her fairy powers, the Empress might possibly return to her former life, abandoning the Emperor to his fate. This possibility, which seems uppermost in the mind of the Nurse, seems not to occur to the Empress. Immediately upon reading the curse, she demands that the Nurse help her to find a shadow. In this manner she rejects the way of life which the Talisman symbolizes, which might be characterized as change without growth. She chooses instead a process which will transform her to the very depths of her being.

Tag

As the Empress decides to enter the world of men in order to obtain a shadow, day begins to dawn. When she cannot be dissuaded from her resolution by the Nurse, dawn gives way to the bright light of day. This is the first time that the Empress has actually experienced a true day. Previously, she has been sleeping days and staying awake nights when the Emperor is home:

> Nurse: Seine Nächte sind ihr Tag,
>   Seine Tage sind ihre Nacht. --
>   (D III 151.)

Even her prior life as a fairy-child was experienced in a place where the very name implies a half light - Mondberge.

60

THE TEXT OF THE <u>FRAU OHNE SCHATTEN</u>

Moonlight had a special significance for the young Hofmannsthal. The entire verse drama <u>Das kleine Welttheater</u>, or <u>Die Glücklichen</u> as he subtitled it, takes place in the evening twilight. The playlet, consisting of a series of monologues, demonstrates both the feeling of unity which each of the speakers feels with the world and also the facility with which each is able to approach other people. The sense of unity demonstrated here is akin to the Empress' experience of being at one with the world during the time when she, the being of light, was able to turn herself into the creatures of the air, the earth, or the water. The ease with which the Empress and the Emperor approach each other may be observed both in the initial encounter and also in the regularly occurring love nights. Moonlight, therefore, sets the stage for an easy coming and going in relationships, or negatively seen, for a lack of commitment to another. By contrast, the bright light of the sun separates things and people from each other and requires acts and commitments to overcome this separation.

The Empress takes the first step in leaving this world of magical relationships when she marries the Emperor. She takes the second step when she determines to leave the palace in search of the shadow which will save the Emperor. For the first time in her life she demonstrates a commitment to another individual. At this point she joyously greets the new day:

> Ein Tag bricht an!
> Führ mich zu ihnen:
> ich will!
> (D III 160.)

In a 1911 letter to Hofmannsthal, Rudolf Borchardt expressed his belief that it was necessary for artists to become fully human. Like Hofmannsthal in the <u>Frau ohne Schatten</u>, he related this task to the dawn of a new day:

> Was ich darin [in Rosenkavalier] dem Geiste nach begrüsse, ist
> der freie Stolz, menschlich zu sein, dem nur die wahre innere
> Grösse zugänglich und die selbstische Affengrösse, die sich den
> ganzen Tag die Hände wäscht, um ja rein zu bleiben, auf ewig
> feind ist. . . . Es ist seine [Stefan Georges] wohlbekannte
> Manier, sich dem Leben grundsätzlich nicht zu stellen, und durch
> seine Feuerproben nicht zu schreiten, wobei es denn leicht ist
> sich siegermässig aufzutun. Die grosse Feuerprobe durch die er
> damals hätte gehn müssen und durch die alle tapferen Menschen
> seiner Generation, Sie vorauf, gegangen sind, war der Uebergang
> in Mannesalter. . . . . Wie an einem nebeligen Frühsommermor-
> gen die Entscheidung ob der Tag heiter oder wolkig sein soll erst
> möglich wird wenn das über dem Nebel liegende höhere Himmels-
> gewölk durch den verziehenden Rauch sichtbar wird, wie gegen den
> bis Nachmittag währenden Kampf zwischen Sonne und Haufenwolken
> das morgendliche Spiel von Lichtblicken Verschleirungen,

zartem Gold und zartem Grau kaum mehr als ein Präludium bedeutet, so wird auch unser Tag erst sichtbar wenn er ein Tag,
ein voller Tag zu sein beginnt, wenn der volle Bogen geschrit-
ten wird, den die Menschheit gestern und vorgestern und vor
Jahrhunderten von Osten bis in den Zenith und ab nach Westen
sich hat erkämpfen müssen. . . . .
Eines Tages schien eine neue Sonne, und die alten selbstge-
rechten Ideale der Impeccabilität und der Vollkommenheit als
einziger Existenzberechtigung des Kunstwerkes hatten ein
verblichenes und fadenscheiniges Ansehen; der Glanz über allem
was uns bisher geglänzt hatte, hatte ein steriles, undurchsich-
tiges Email; dass unsere alte Liebe unglücklich gewesen war,
hatten wir immer gewusst - wehe dem Jüngling der glücklich
liebt! Dass sie unfruchtbar war sahen wir nun; nur unsere unbe-
wusste willenlose Seele hatte empfangen und geboren; nun griff
unser Wille nach der Menschheit wie nach einer Geliebten um zu
befruchten und zu erzeugen; und die Menschheit sagte, "sei zu-
erst ein Mensch, zu irren und dich zu wagen, zu leiden zu wei-
nen zu geniessen und zu freun Dich und der Götzen nicht zu
achten, wie wir". (19)

Hofmannsthal replied to Borchardt in the following words:

Nun kommt Ihr Brief [23. VII. 1911.] und spricht mir in unver-
gleichlicher Weise aus, dass ich von Ihnen - und ich muss mir
sagen: wie könnte es anders sein? - verstanden bin, wo verstanden zu sein ein selten zu Teil werdendes und höchst ersehntes
Glück ist: in dem dunklen, gewundenen Wege meiner notwendigen
Entwicklung. (20)

The Empress, like the artists in the quotation above, enters into the bright light of
day in order to become fully human. The self-serving ideal of perfection, in which
state she had lived in the <u>Mondberge</u> and in the palace, is recognized as sterile. In
order to become fruitful she turns to mankind; she will become apprenticed to one of
them.

The new day which breaks forth symbolizes not only the dawn of the first
true day for the Empress, that is, the day of her first true commitment to another
being; it also represents an externalization of her inner courage to face the unknown.
In a note written in 1919 Hofmannsthal related courage to light:

Mut ist das innere Licht in jedem Märchen, darum ist die Kaiserin so leuchtend und mutig - und wirft sich, wo ihr schaudert,
mit erhobenen Flügeln, wie ein Schwan, dem Fremden und Ge-
heimnisvollen entgegen.
(A 196.)

THE TEXT OF THE FRAU OHNE SCHATTEN

The dawn of the new day thus signifies that the Empress has courageously determined to overcome her fear of men in order to fulfill her newly-discovered commitment to the Emperor. The symbolism of the new day is not, however, exhausted
at this point. Another occurrence, which is concomitant with the dawn of the day
and with the Empress' expression of commitment, takes place. A feeling of being
grasped by an external power overcomes her:

> Weh, was fasst mich
> grässlich an!
> (D III 162.)

The following comment from Hofmannsthal's prose writings may aid in making the
meaning of this passage clear:

> Indem er [the hero of the short story "Der Engelwirt, eine Schwa-
> bengeschichte" by Emil Strauss] sein Glück zu fassen meint, be-
> kommt sein Schicksal ihn zu packen, und während wir atemlos dem
> Verlauf eines Abenteuers zuzusehen meinen, entfaltet sich uns ein
> menschliches Wesen.
> (P I 313-14.)

Whereas the Empress had thought that through her decision to descend to earth she
was consciously directing her own actions, what actually occurs is that her personal
fate, emanating from the depths of her personality, takes over the direction of her
life. The following quotations, expanding as they do upon Hofmannsthal's conception
of fate, also help to clarify these verse lines:

> Die mögliche Tat geht aus dem Wesensgrund, aus dem Geschick
> hervor.
> (A 237.)

> Schicksal auf sich zu ziehen, anderer Schicksal zu werden, ist
> edelste Lebenskraft; sie ist an die Auserwählten verteilt, an
> den Knaben wie an den Greis.
> (P III 141.)

The acts which emanate from the depths of one's personality must take place among
men, for actions cannot take place in isolation (see Tat, pp. 65-66); they will lead
to a fulfillment of the individual's fate ("Schicksal auf sich zu ziehen") and to the fulfillment of the fates of others ("anderer Schicksal zu werden"). Hofmannsthal used
the word Schicksal, or fate, therefore, to designate the achievement of a true relationship to others. Only by participating in the activities of life, that is, only by living in the day as opposed to the night, can this be realized.

Hofmannsthal's use of the word Tag, therefore, encompasses all of these
possibilities: 1) day is the time for commitment to another, in contrast to the dreamy
occurrences of the Mondberge and of the palace; 2) day is the time when an individ-

dual must courageously exchange a quiet, sheltered life for a life of exposure to squalor, rancor, and filth, for only then can relationships to others develop; 3) day is the time for the actualization of one of the many possibilities which the Talisman symbolizes, the time for the realization of one's fate.

<u>Dienst</u>

"Sie tut die Dienste einer Magd." say the Unborn Children of the Empress and the Emperor to the Emperor. (E 320.) Into this category of service are gathered most of the activities of the Empress in the home of Barak. To these acts belong a symbolical significance, even if in this case Hofmannsthal employs no word in the libretto as a specific literary symbol. These actions symbolize an inwardly held attitude of respect and concern for others and thus constitute one of the more important symbols of the entire fairytale.

Not surprisingly, these actions are most apparent – to the reader, at least – from the prose narrative, where no gesture remained unwritten or was left to the discretion of the actors and actresses. The Empress' first significant act expressing concern for another takes place in the Dyer's home; she protects the Wife from the Efrit or Youth conjured by the Nurse. This occurs on the first day of her service to Barak and the Wife:

> Der Efrit hatte die Färberin um die Mitte gefasst, er wollte sie
> mit sich fortziehen, es schien, als söge er mit der Nähe der Ge-
> fahr einen doppelten frechen Mut in sich. Er war bereit, seine Beute
> hoch in der Luft über den Köpfen der Eindringenden hinwegzutragen,
> und er war schön in seiner knirschenden Ungeduld. Die Kaiserin
> trat ihm in den Weg. Ihr Mut war dem seinen gleich, sie legte beide
> Arme um die Frau, der Efrit wandte ihr sein Gesicht zu, das loderte
> wie ein offenes Feuer; durch seine zwei ungleichen Augen grinsten
> die Abgründe des nie zu Betretenden herein, ein Grausen fasste
> sie, nicht für sich selber, sondern in der Seele der Färberin, dass
> diese in den Armen eines solchen Dämons liegen und ihren Atem
> mit dem seinen vermischen sollte. Sie wollte die Färberin an sich
> ziehen, sie achtete es nicht, dass es ein menschliches Wesen war,
> um das sie zum ersten Male ihre Arme schlang.
> (E 290-91.)

Another signilficiant action expressing the Empress' concern for another's needs takes place on the second day of service:

> Die Kaiserin lief hin zur Leiter und lautlos die Sprossen hinauf;
> sie fand auf dem flachen Dach den Färber, der noch keuchte, und
> dem der Schweiss mit blauer Farbe vermischt von der Stirne
> rann, und sie wischte ihm mit ihrem Tüchlein das Gesicht ab. . . .
> (E 329.)

At the end of this same day, according to the libretto, she gathers Barak's scattered tools together, replying to his query of who is there: "Ich, mein Gebieter, deine Dienerin!" (D III 201.) On the third day of her service, according to the prose narrative, the Empress lies at the feet of Barak in an attitude of extreme humility:

> Zu des Färbers Füssen lag eine weibliche Gestalt hingestreckt,
> an der Erde, sie hatte das Gesicht an den Boden gedrückt, mit
> unsäglicher Demut reckte sie den Arm aus, ohne ihr Gesicht zu
> heben, bis sie mit der Hand die Füsse des Färbers erreichte,
> und umfasste sie.
>
> (E 345.)

The Empress has courageously left the protected world of the palace and has acted in the world of men only to discover that to act means to transgress upon another's being: "Dir - Barak - bin ich mich schuldig!" (D III 201.) Awareness of this transgression elicits humility and respect for Barak. The initially callous attitude which governed her actions - "Ich will den Schatten küssen, den sie wirft!" (D III 170) - has changed to one of caring for Barak and the Wife:

> Gepriesen sei, der mich diesen Mann finden liess
>   unter den Männern,
> denn er zeigt mir, was ein Mensch ist,
> und um seinetwillen will ich bleiben unter den Menschen
> und atmen ihren Atem
> und tragen ihre Beschwerden!
>
> (D III 204.)

The actions which are cited above of the Empress in her guise as a serving maid reflect an attitude of concern and respect for the lives of others. From the Veronica-like act of wiping Barak's face to her prostration at his feet there is an awareness of the physical needs and emotional concerns of another. Her acts of service constitute the physical expression of an inwardly held attitude of respect for others: "Die Zeremonie ist das geistige Werk des Körpers." (A 49.)

Tat

The time which the Empress has spent in Barak's home has prepared her for an ultimate deed (Tat): she must either save the Emperor from his stony fate at the expense of Barak, or she must deny the Emperor her help in order to spare Barak. The choice which she must make will be detrimental to someone, no matter what she decides.

The act or deed represents for Hofmannsthal the means whereby an individual establishes a connection with the exterior world. It symbolizes the end of a purely individual existence and the beginning of a relationship to others:

> . . . in beiden [Elektra und Jedermann] wird gefragt, was bleibt
> vom Menschen übrig, wenn man alles abzieht? - in beiden geant-
> wortet: was, wodurch sich der Mensch der Welt verbinden kann,
> ist die Tat oder das Werk.
>
> (P III 354.)

The decisive act of the Empress is the rejection of the Wife's shadow,
which constitutes a refusal to harm Barak. The fact that her deed is a <u>refusal</u> to act
does not alter Hofmannsthal's conception of the act as a positive deed accomplishing
relationship. Commenting upon a similar renunciation of self-assertion, the Beggar's refusal to destroy a society in the <u>Salzburger Grosses Welttheater</u>, Hofmannsthal says:

> . . . eben dieses Nicht-Tun sei die grosse entscheidende Tat
> seines Lebens: es sei wieder im Niederfahren eines Blitzes
> aus einem Saulus ein Paulus geworden.
>
> (A 298.)

Like the Beggar, the Empress' refusal to harm another for her own gain may be
characterized as the "decisive act" of her life. By means of this refusal she establishes a positive relationship to Barak and the Wife.

It is, therefore, through her own efforts that the Empress achieves a relationship to men. Neither the Emperor, who willed to maintain her as a beautiful
crystal decorative piece, nor the Nurse, whose magical efforts to coerce others the
Empress comes to reject, is able to achieve this for her. Moreover, the Empress'
commitment to a positive relationship to Barak is so great that in the third act she
feels that her place is among men:

> Nun zeig mir den Platz
> der mir gebührt
> inmitten derer,
> die Schatten werfen.
>
> (D III 232.)

With this speech she claims for herself a place among those who throw shadows, a
place among those whose lives encompass suffering and ultimately death. The Empress' willingness to become human encompasses, therefore, all aspects of hu-
manness, including death. There can be, according to Hofmannsthal, no greater tie:
"Das Geheimnis der Verbundenheit ist Todesgemeinschaft . . . . " (A 205.)

Prüfung, Gericht

Hofmannsthal differentiated between <u>Prüfung</u> and <u>Gericht</u> by using the word
<u>Prüfung</u> to refer to that period which the Empress spends in Barak's home. The

word Gericht he reserved for the Empress' final decision of whether or not to harm Barak. For example, as she approaches Keikobad's residence where she will be called upon to make this decision, she states:

> Aus unsern Taten
> steigt ein Gericht!
> Aus unserm Herzen
> ruft die Posaune,
> die uns lädt.
>
> (D III 222.)

The relationship to John of Patmos' vision of the Last Judgment of Christianity, which is described in Revelations (see especially Chapter VIII), is unmistakable, particularly in its use of the word "Posaune."

A further distinction between Prüfung and Gericht may be discerned in the different kinds of time which are ascribed to each one. Prüfung takes place in time: "Alles ist an eine Zeit gebunden, sonst wären es keine Prüfungen." (E 256.) Those acts occurring in time are revocable according to the poet. For this reason Barak can say of the Wife:

> und ihre Reden sind gesegnet
> mit dem Segen der Widerruflichkeit
>
> . . . .
>
> (D III 188.)

The underlying thought apparently is that angry speeches can be cancelled by later words and deeds of love. By contrast, the words of the Empress as she comes to the time of judgment (Gericht) take place in the eternal moment: "Vergisst sich in Aeonen ein einziger Augenblick?" (Ariadne auf Naxos, L III 31.). The Unborn Children emphasize this eternal moment as they talk to the Empress:

> "Merke, Frau", rief der erste, "alle Reden unserer Mutter
> [der Färberin] geschehen in der Zeit, darum sind sie wider-
> ruflich - aber deine", fiel der zweite ein, "deine wird gesche-
> hen im Augenblick und sie wird unwiderruflich sein: so ist dein
> Los gefallen." "Von welchem Augenblick redet ihr?" rief die
> Kaiserin. "Von dem einzigen!" rief das kleine Mädchen und
> flammte heran. "Was muss ich tun?" fragte die Kaiserin und
> heftete ohne Atem ihre Augen auf die drei Kinder. "Im Augen-
> blick ist alles, der Rat und die Tat!" rief ein kleiner breiter
> Mund . . . .
>
> (E 362.)

Any act committed at this point cannot be later revoked. The eternal moment, which is that moment encompassing both the deed and also the judgment upon the deed, has arrived.

THE TEXT OF THE FRAU OHNE SCHATTEN

Symbols Pertaining to the Emperor

Jäger, Lieber (Abenteurer)

The Emperor is most frequently characterized by his two primary activities of hunting and loving:

> . . . es war seine Gewohnheit, zeitig vor Tag zur Jagd aus-
> zureiten und seine Gemahlin noch schlummernd zurückzulas-
> sen, abends aber erst spät heimzukehren, wenn schon Fackeln
> auf den Absätzen der Treppe brannten und das Schlafgemach von
> den neun Lampen einer Ampel sanft erleuchtet war. Immerhin
> hatte er noch keine einzige Nacht dieses Jahres, dessen zwölf-
> ter Monat eben zu Ende gegangen war, bei seiner Frau zu ver-
> bringen versäumt.
>
> (E 256-57.)

> Die Amme: Er ist ein Jäger
> und ein verliebter,
> sonst ist er nichts!
>
> (D III 151.)

Hofmannsthal portrayed the hunter many times throughout his life; the Young Hunter of the Kleines Welttheater as well as the aging King Basilius of the Turm are representatives of this type. Two primary aspects of the Hunter seem to have engaged Hofmannsthal's attention. First, the hunter is involved in an active search for his game and thus stands in the midst of life. This engagement with life contrasts with character types like Claudio of the Tor und der Tod, whose relationship to life is that of a bystander. Hofmannsthal tended to portray this involvement positively, apparently considering it an improvement upon isolation from life's activities. Second, there is a frantic artificiality attached to the hunter's life, which seeks excitement in the daily recurrence of the chase. Since the entirety of nature, as individualized in various animals, is his goal, the hunter is not committed to any one person or thing. Hofmannsthal condemned this lack of commitment in many works, among them the Tor und der Tod and the Turm. The contrast in his portrayal of the Young Hunter and of Basilius suggests that Hofmannsthal believed that a time arrives in everyone's life when commitment to one other person is necessary and when the frantic chase must be ended.

Hofmannsthal utilized the word Abenteurer to suggest an attitude toward life similar to that symbolized by the hunter. Like the hunter, the adventurer stands in the midst of life but is unable to commit himself totally:

> Gerade hier drang alles tief in ihn, er war im Bereich seines
> ersten Abenteuers mit der geliebten Frau. Jene unvergessliche
> erste Liebesstunde war ihm nahe, sein Blut war bewegt, dass

er die seltsame Grabeskühle kaum fühlte, die aus den Wänden
des Berges und von unten auf ihn eindrang. Für ein neues Abenteuer wäre kein Platz in ihm gewesen - oder doch? wer hätte
es sagen können. - -

(E 303.)

Hofmannsthal qualified the statement that there would be no room within the Emperor for a new adventure with ''- - oder doch? wer hätte es sagen können.'' He
thus implied that the Emperor could very easily forget the Empress in order to en-
joy another adventure.

The word Abenteuer, which is employed in the above quotation in conjunc-
tion with the Emperor, recalls other adventurer figures which are antecedent to the
Emperor in Hofmannsthal's works, such as Florindo in the early comedy <u>Christinas
Heimreise</u> and Baron von Weidenstamm in the transitional drama the <u>Abenteurer und
die Sängerin</u>. These portrayals of the adventurer and lover were developed from Hofmannsthal's study of the memoirs of Casanova in the late 1890's. In this type of person the poet apparently sensed that he had discovered a character who was fully engaged in life with its demanding relationships. Although Hofmannsthal in general
portrayed the adventurer-lover positively, he did not seek to make this type of individual into a hero for emulation, for he also included in his portrayal the weakness
of this character as he saw it - the affirmation of a long succession of affairs, to the
exclusion of commitment to any one person.

The following diary entry by Hofmannsthal, dated approximately six weeks
following the premiere of the <u>Frau ohne Schatten</u> demonstrates the close association
between the hunter and the lover which apparently existed in his mind:

> Fremd und geheimnisvoll sind solche Nächte, wie alle
> Geschenke des Himmels, aber darum sind sie heilig, und sie
> durchleben ist ein heiliger Dienst - in dem darf man nicht zittern.
> Das Erschütternde ist da, der dunkle schauerlich süsse Abgrund
> ist da - aber du darfst nicht hineinstürzen - seine Nähe ist nur
> eine Heiligung mehr.
> Alles ist heilig und schön - jede Sekunde : küsse die
> Augen und heilige sie und dann lass sie alles in sich trinken, das
> Oben und das Unten und die wunderbare Mitte, die süssen beweg-
> ten Arme und die süssen ruhenden Brüste, die Lippen und das
> Haar.
> Verbirg nichts - wo das Verbergen ist, da ist die Hast
> und die Glut der Jagd, da ist der Kaiser und der tödliche Pfeil
> und die Gazelle; wo alles sich darbringt, da ist die nächtliche
> Feier, der Tempel und die Sterne.
> Gib dich sanft und festlich, du Süsse, und erschüttere
> den, der selig wird durch dich, mit deinen zarten Händen - wie
> du eine Harfe erschütterst -, dann ist die Erschütterung von dir
> genommen, und was du empfängst, ist die Musik. - Zittere nicht,

69

denn was wird aus dem Tempel, wenn die Priesterin zittert!
Wirf dich in den Abgrund, aber nur weil unten die goldene
Treppe ist, die zu den Sternen führt.
    Sei die süsse Herrin und nicht das scheue Mäd-
chen, - giess dich aus in Augen, Hände und Mund, behalte
nichts von dir in dir, dann wirst du leicht sein und schwe-
ben, Zauberin auf ihrem Zauberbette - Verwandlerin, selber
verwandelt, unfindbar allen ausser dem einen, den du ver-
zauberst.

(A 196.)

The Empress' description of the hunt from the prose narrative appear to be
directly related to the above diary entry: "seine Augen waren rot von der Hast und
Wildheit der Verfolgung, und seine Züge waren gespannt. . . ." (E 258.)

Höhle, Gewölbe, zu Stein werden

One other aspect of the hunter and lover which Hofmannsthal sketched into
the Emperor's portrait is egotism; this is first evidenced in the libretto by the isolation which the ruler imposes upon the Empress. It becomes even more apparent in
the prose narrative at the time when the Emperor becomes ragingly jealous of Barak
upon learning that Barak has succeeded in turning the Empress into a human being, a
feat which he has been unable to do. The protective jealousy which he exhibits in
these two instances appears to be symptomatic of his inability to commit himself.
Certainly a more appropriate attitude where a mutual commitment has taken place
is trust. The physical isolation, which his entrance into the grave-like cavern depicts visually, symbolizes an internal isolation from other people.

This isolation also manifests itself in indifference and cruelty toward
others. When the Emperor first makes an appearance in the prose narrative, he
completely ignores the Nurse, treating her as he might a piece of furniture:

Der Kaiser trat leichten Fusses über den Leib der Amme hinweg,
die ihr Gesicht an den Boden drückte. Er achtete ihrer so wenig,
als läge hier nur ein Stück Teppich.

(E 256.)

Furthermore, at the time of the search for the Falcon the Emperor threatens the
Falconer with death, should they be unsuccessful:

"Auf deinen Kopf, sagte er [der Kaiser] leise, "dass wir in diesem
Revier den roten Falken finden und ihn wiedergewinnen, wir beide,
du und ich."

(E 298.)

In these and also in other associations with people the Emperor never takes the role
of the listener or of the one who exists solely for another. He is always the one who
gives orders or who is capable of cruelty, as reflected in the fears of his subordi-
nates that their hands might be cut off. (E 302.) He continues to behave in this self-
centered manner throughout the fourth chapter of the prose narrative, wich portrays the banquet given by the Unborn Children for their father the Emperor. Although
he is delighted with the charm and grace of the Children, it never occurs to him to
serve them or to treat them as his equal. Instead he desires to own them as he might
any object which pleases him.

> Die Lust des Besitzenwollens durchdrang ihn von oben bis unten,
> er musste sich beherrschen, sie nicht anzurühren.
>
> (E 308.)

Concurrently with the desire to "own" the children, the Emperor experiences a
feeling of coldness: " . . . . ein Gefühl der Kälte, das von seinen Füssen und Händen ausging, drang ihn bis ans Herz. " (E 308.) The desire to own the children is
paralleled by his turning to stone. The exterior reality symbolizes the internal quality of his personality: from the point of view of others the Emperor is cold and harsh,
an unfruitful object in the midst of life. His turning to stone within the cave symbolized among other things life for him (22); but because the Emperor is a statue,
and his egotistical isolation.

Wasser des Lebens (Teich), Schwelle des Todes.

Hederer speaks of Hofmannsthal's use of water as a symbol in the following
comment:

> Zeitlebens hat Hofmannsthal mit Wasser ein Aeusserstes ge-
> nannt, Symbol der geliebten Erde und dessen, was die Seele
> mit ihr verbindet, und ein Reines, Ueberwirkliches, das uns
> zuweilen aus der Höhe erreicht. (21)

For Hofmannsthal the phrase "Wasser des Lebens" embraces the relationship of
one's innermost being to the activities of life ("Symbol der geliebten Erde und des-
sen, was die Seele mit ihr verbindet"). This relationship and these activities are
further characterized by a purity which is transcendent. The Emperor, in approaching the spring, Hofmannsthal's symbol for the most significant activities of life,
measures himself against this ideal. In his failure to fulfill the ideal lies the transformation of the "Water of Life" into the "Threshold of Death. " Because he is unable to live in fruitful relationships to others, the "Water of Life" is deadly to him.

In the prose narrative the Emperor is described in his petrified state as
"ein mitten in den Teich gebautes Grabmal aus Erz. " (E 365.) Hofmannsthal thus
envisioned the Emperor as yet a part of life, for Teich with its aspect of water symbolized among other things life for him (22); but because the Emperor is a statue,
Hofmannsthal envisioned him as immobile, cold and unchanging, which are qualities
of a grave monument.

THE TEXT OF THE FRAU OHNE SCHATTEN

In contrast to the Emperor's failure, the Empress is able to withstand the test; she maintains a respect bordering on awe for the lives of others and thereby establishes fruitful relationships. In the exchange which takes place between the Empress and the Unborn Children of the Dyer pair, Hofmannsthal stressed the respect which she has learned:

> Die Kaiserin holte tief Atem. ''Ich hab mich vergangen'', sagte
> sie. Sie senkte die Augen und richtete sie gleich wieder auf ihn,
> der mit ihr sprach. Das Wesen horchte, antwortete nicht so-
> gleich. Die Seele trat in seine Augen; er schien die Worte zu
> liebkosen, die aus ihrem Mund kamen. ''Das muss jeder sagen,
> der einen Fuss vor den andern setzt. Darum gehen wir mit ge-
> schlossenen Füssen.'' Der Hauch eines Lächelns schwebte in
> seiner Stimme, als er das sagte; aber sein Gesicht blieb ernst,
> und in nichts glich er dem Färber mehr als in diesem tiefen
> Ernst seiner Miene. ''Kann ich ungeschehen machen?'' rief
> die Kaiserin. Ihre Augen hingen an seinem Mund, ihre Ehr-
> furcht vor ihm, der so mit ihr sprach, war nicht geringer als
> die seine vor ihr.

(E 361)

The sincere respect which the Empress exhibits in her interactions with others is that quality which ultimately brings about the solution to her dilemma. In contrast to her the Emperor fails.

Falke

Probably no other symbol is more closely identified with the activities of the Emperor than the Falcon. The Falcon is instrumental in helping the Emperor capture the Empress when she is in the form of the White Gazelle:

> Der Kaiser: Denn als sie [die Gazelle] mir floh
> und war wie der Wind
> und höhnte meiner -
> und zusammenbrechen
> wollte mein Ross -,
> da flog er [der Falke]
> der weissen Gazelle
> zwischen die Lichter -,
> und schlug mit den Schwingen
> ihre süssen Augen!
> Da stürzte sie hin
> . . . .

(D III 153.)

THE TEXT OF THE FRAU OHNE SCHATTEN

In his relationship to the Falcon the Emperor first becomes conscious of transgression against another being: "Denn ich habe mich versündigt gegen ihn / in der Trunkenheit der ersten Stunde. . . ." (D III 153.) In the libretto the Falcon is responsible for making the Empress aware of the curse by intoning it to her; in the prose narrative he accomplishes this goal in the following manner:

> Der Falke schwebte mit einem einzigen Flügelschlag in einem
> sanften Bogen nach oben und seitwärts, dann liess er sich jäh
> niedergleiten, ein Sausen schlug an den Gesichtern der beiden
> Frauen vorbei, in einem Nu war der Vogel wieder hoch oben in
> der Luft, auf dem Gewande lag der Talisman; die Schriftzeichen,
> die in den fahlweissen flachen Stein gegraben waren, glommen
> wie Feuer und zuckten wie Blicke. "Ich kann die Schrift lesen",
> sagte die Kaiserin und verfärbte sich. Die Amme schauderte,
> denn ihr waren die Zeichen undurchdringlich wie eh und immer. . . . .
> "Fluch und Tod dem Sterblichen, der diesen Gürtel löst, zu
> Stein wird die Hand, die es tat, wofern sie nicht der Erde mit
> dem Schatten ihr Geschick abkauft, zu Stein der Leib, an den
> die Hand gehört, zu Stein das Auge, das dem Leib dabei geleuch-
> tet - innen der Sinn bleibt lebendig, den ewigen Tod zu schmecken
> mit der Zunge des Lebens - die Frist ist gesetzt nach Gezeiten
> der Sterne."
>
> (E 261.)

In the libretto the Falcon leads the Emperor to the Imperial Falconer House, where he observes the Empress' disobedience to his command that she remain distant from people. Finally, as the Emperor enters the cavern where he turns to stone, the Falcon cries out mournful warnings. The Falcon thus symbolizes that quality within the Emperor which leads him steadily towards the fulfillment of his potential as a human being, for in all cases the Falcon leads him either to another being or to a deeper insight into life, at the end protesting against his isolation within the cavern.

The incipient fate toward which the Falcon guides the Emperor is not to be understood as pre-determined. The scene at the Falconer House (IIii) establishes the freedom of choice available to him. In observing the Empress' deceit, the Emperor might have confronted her in the role of a judge similar to the manner in which Barak confronts the Wife in IIv. This action by Barak precipitates the first moment of mutual respect and love which the Dyer pair experience. Had the Emperor acted in a like manner at this point, a similar experience for himself and the Empress might have occurred. He does not, however, and the opportunity for a true relationship through his initiative is lost. His decision to avoid the confrontation with the Empress becomes one step more in the direction of total isolation.

One other example of the Falcon as symbolical of the Emperor and the fulfillment of his potential as a human being occurs in the final description of the prose narrative:

THE TEXT OF THE <u>FRAU OHNE SCHATTEN</u>

Hoch über dem Fluss kreiste der Falke. Der Blick des
Kaisers hing an ihm lieber als an dem Prachtschiff. Höher ins
Unersteigliche riss sich der Vogel empor, leuchtende Himmels-
abgründe enthüllte sein Flügel; des Kaisers Blick war über die
Trunkenheit erhöht, so waren seine Glieder übertrunken von der
Nähe der herrlichen Frau, in deren Arme er sich drückte. Ober
ihm und unter ihm war der Himmel.

(E 374-75.)

The juxtaposition of the Falcon with the water of the river symbolizes the return of
the Emperor to life's activity of establishing fruitful human relationships. The Emperor is now a part of life, as the image in the water suggests, even though by reasons of his position and power he is immeasurably above ordinary life in his freedom and capacities, as the flight into the heavens suggests.

Symbols Pertaining to the Wife

Traum

The symbol which most frequently occurs in relationship to the Wife is the
dream. Her reaction to the vision of wealth and slaves conjured by the Nurse is:
"O Welt in der Welt! O Traum im Wachen!" (D III 173.) She confesses to having
day-dreamed about a handsome young man, just for the sake of dreaming:

und des ich gedachte
heimlich, zuweilen,
um Träumens willen!

(D III 185.)

She criticizes Barak for having ruined her dream when he interrupts her first
meeting with the Efrit:

Und wer von der Schüssel der Träume kostete,
zu dem treten Tiere
und halten ihm den Wegwurf hin
vom Tisch des Glücklichen,
und er hat nichts
wohin er sich flüchte,
als in seine Tränen!

(D III 188.)

These examples suggest that the Wife is searching outside the perimeter of her life
for the love and beauty which she is unable to find within it; incapable of creating
beauty within her life, she escapes into a dreamworld. This flight from reality is
indicative both of the youth of the Wife and also of her lack of commitment to another
person or thing.

74

THE TEXT OF THE FRAU OHNE SCHATTEN

The playlet Idylle (1893), subtitled Nach einem antiken Vasenbild: Zentaur mit verwundeter Frau am Rand eines Flusses, demonstrates clearly the relationship between the youth, dreaming, and lack of commitment. The Wife in this story is given to dreaming the beautiful stories which she learned as she watched her father, a potter, decorate his works with stories of the gods. The Husband remonstrates with her, urging her to distinguish between her life and that of the gods; otherwise she may learn like Semele, sadly and too late, what is appropriate for her. When a handsome young centaur comes and requests that the Husband, a blacksmith, repair a spear, she determines to leave with the centaur:

Die Frau:	Wie konnt ich Gatten, Haus und Kind verlassen hier?
Der Zentaur:	Was sorgst du lang, um was du schnell vergessen hast?
Die Frau:	Er kommt zurück, und schnell zerronnen ist der Traum!
Der Zentaur:	Mitnichten, da doch Lust und Weg noch offensteht. Mit festen Fingern greif mir ins Gelock und klammre dich, am Rücken ruhend, mir an Arm und Nacken an!

(GLD 63-64.)

The Wife climbs upon the back of the Centaur, but as they leave, the blacksmith returns, carrying the Centaur's spear. He throws the spear at the Wife and kills her.

It is apparent from this playlet that Hofmannsthal regards the dreamer as one who is immature, as demonstrated by his lack of a commitment to another person. It is also clear that the dreamer is not excused from participating in life, from establishing ties to other people, for a judgment awaits those who seek to escape from life. The judgment which Hofmannsthal places upon the Woman in Idylle is unquestionably stern, but there is no hint within the story that this judgment is anything other than just.

Hofmannsthal also criticized the dreamer both for his failure to be imaginative and loving enough to find beauty in his own life and also for compensating for this lack by retreating to a land of unreal beauty:

Es gibt unzählige Dinge die für uns nichts sind als Triumphzüge und Schäferspiele der Schönheit, inkarnierte Traumschönheit, von Sehnsucht und Ferne verklärt, Dinge, die wir herbeirufen, wenn unsere Gedanken nicht stark genug sind, die Schönheit des Lebens zu finden, und fortstreben, hinaus nach der künstlichen Schönheit der Träume. [Italics mine.]

(P I 157.)

75

Hence the tendency of the Wife in the <u>Frau ohne Schatten</u> to dream symbolizes both her youth and her lack of commitment to Barak; these qualities make her susceptible to the persuasions of the Nurse. Because of her dreams she is blind to the beauty and dignity of Barak's behavior toward others; the Youth of her dreams seems far preferable.

<u>Spiegel</u>

The interest of the Wife in maintaining her beauty is manifested by her stage actions with a mirror. She is obviously very engrossed in the outward aspects of her person, so engrossed in fact that it does not occur to her to question whether the price she will have to pay - the loss of the shadow - is too high for the eternal beauty which she has been promised. She merely exults: "und der Kaufpreis ist herrlich / und ohnegleichen!" (D III 207.) The symbols of the dream and the mirror thus reinforce each other in their portrayal of an immature, egocentric woman who has not yet committed herself to anyone.

<u>Speech</u>

There is no greater contrast between the Empress and the Wife than the one made evident by the frequency of occurrence and the length of their verse lines. Although this is not a symbol in the sense that the words <u>Spiegel</u> and <u>Traum</u> are symbols, Hofmannsthal employs this means to convey something far greater than the speeches themselves impart. In this sense the speeches become symbols. This is especially evident from the following comments about speech made by Hofmannsthal:

> Es handelt sich um ein Zu-viel im Reden, ein Uebertreiben -
> und in diesem Zu-viel ist eine Spaltung - ein Teil des Ich begeht was der andere nicht will. . . .
> (A 230.)

It is apparent from these comments that the Wife does not possess an integrated personality. Her frequently contradictory acts and speeches stem from the lack of a solid inner core. The anxiety, for example, which the Wife feels about Barak when she learns that the Nurse has given him a sleeping potion gives way to derision after she has awakened him and has assured herself that he is still alive. She will forego motherhood and yet she says of a child:

> Schmutzig ist ein kleines Kind und sie müssen es dem Haushund
> darreichen, um es rein zu lecken; und dennoch ist es schön wie
> die aufgehende Sonne; und solche sind wir zu opfern gesonnen.
> (E 337.)

The Wife often gives the impression that she is speaking in order to gain time and to delay having to take any definitive action. This procrastination provides evidence once again of her lack of purpose and commitment.

Efrit (der Jüngling)

The Youth which is conjured by the Nurse fascinates the Wife. She is attracted by his physical beauty and yet repulsed by him, as this passage from the stage directions of the libretto indicates:

> Sie [die Frau] beugt sich über ihn [den jungen Mann], will
> sanft die Hände von seinem Gesicht lösen; sein Blick trifft
> sie, seine Hand zuckt, die ihrige festzuhalten. Sie fährt mit
> einem Schrei zurück.
>
> (D III 197.)

The ambiguity which she exhibits toward the Efrit demonstrates Hofmannsthal's concept of the "world-demon": "Die Welt will einen jeden aus ihm selbst herausreissen und wieder zu ihm bringen." (A 39.) The demon thus represents those elements in the world which tempt a person to desert his true development of himself. In the final analysis, however, these negative elements serve both to make him fully conscious of his fulfillment through relationships to others and also to bring about his commitment to another person. The necessity for confrontation with one's demon if one is to become aware wherein his fulfillment lies is stressed by Günther Erken: "So erscheint Tyche als notwendige Voraussetzung der Selbstfindung und Schicksalsfindung und doch 'immer als ein unerträglicher Dämon' (A 222)."(23)

Hofmannsthal's concept of the Efrit as world-demon seems to be developed from Goethe's concept of "Tyche, das Zufällige":

> Bei der Erziehung, wenn sie nicht öffentlich und nationell ist,
> behauptet Tüche ihre wandelbaren Rechte. Säugamme und Wär-
> terin, Vater oder Vormund, Lehrer oder Aufseher, sowie alle
> die ersten Umgebungen, an Gespielen, ländlicher oder städti-
> scher Lokalität, alles bedingt die Eigentümlichkeit durch frü-
> here Entwicklung, durch Zurückdrängen oder Beschleunigen
> . . . . Allein Tüche lässt nicht nach und wirkt besonders auf
> die Jugend immerfort, die sich mit ihren Neigungen, Spielen,
> Geselligkeiten und flüchtigem Wesen bald da -, bald dorthin
> wirft und nirgends Halt, noch Befriedigung findet. (24)

Goethe's description of the "seducing Tyche" seems to be particularly closely related to the Efrit:

> . . . der Mensch scheint nur sich zu gehorchen, sein eigenes
> Wollen walten zu lassen, seinem Triebe zu frönen, und doch sind
> es Zufälligkeiten, die sich unterschieben, Fremdartiges, was
> ihn von seinem Wege ablenkt; er glaubt zu erhaschen und wird

gefangen, er glaubt gewonnen zu haben und ist schon verloren.
Auch hier treibt Tüche wieder ihr Spiel, sie lockt den Verirr-
ten zu neuen Labyrinthen, hier ist keine Grenze des Irrens:
denn der Weg ist ein Irrtum. (25)

This passage from Goethe's works, written over one hundred years before the <u>Frau
ohne Schatten</u>, very accurately describes the Efrit's subtle alienation of the Wife
from any commitment to Barak while concurrently creating the impression that she
is exercising her own will.

The close relationship between the temptation which the Efrit represents
and the fulfillment of the Wife's fate through her relationship to Barak is made apparent in Act II scene iii; in this scene she turns away from the Youth and goes immediately to the drugged Barak:

> Sind die Toten lebendig,
> so sind wohl die Schlafenden tot!
> Wach auf, mein Mann!
> Ein Mann ist im Haus!
> Ich will! wach auf! zu mir!

Sie eilt zu Barak hin, rüttelt ihn, bespritzt ihn mit Wasser; die
Kaiserin ist bei ihr, hilft ihr.

(D III 197.)

The Efrit is the primary force which causes the Wife to turn to Barak.

Symbols Pertaining to Barak

Barak

The most obvious symbol which Hofmannsthal gave to the Dyer is the name -
Barak. The name itself, in the form "Baraka," designates saintliness among the
Berbers, (26) but this meaning does not exhaust the symbolism of the name. Possibly of greater importance is the fact that the librettist gave a name to the Dyer while
designating all other characters by generic names. In this manner he indicated that
Barak is truly an individual, whereas the other characters have yet to attain a realization of the many possibilities open to them. Barak is, therefore, a mature person
while the Empress, the Emperor, and the Wife have yet to discover wherein their
fulfillment lies; he already has learned that his individuality lies in selfless devotion
to others, as indicated in one of his first speeches:

> Speise für dreizehn,
> wenn es nottut,
> schaff ich auch
> mit diesen zwei Händen!

78

> Gib du mir Kinder, dass sie mir hocken
> um die Schüsseln zu Abend,
> es soll mir keines hungrig aufstehn.
> Und ich will preisen ihre Begierde
> und danksagen im Herzen,
> dass ich bestellt ward,
> damit ich sie stille.
>
> (D III 166.)

Vater

In Barak's first appearance, Act I scene ii, he answers the Wife's demand that he throw his brothers out of the house with a speech claiming their dependence upon him:

> Hier steht die Schüssel
> aus der sie sich stillen.
> Wo sollten sie herbergen
> wenn nicht in Vaters Haus?
>
> (D III 165.)

In this speech Barak visualizes himself as father and provider. Nor is he the only one to see himself in this role. When he and the brothers come home carrying the food for the feast in II iii, the Beggar Children and the Three Brothers all refer to him as "O unser aller Vater!" (D III 189.)

Barak's view of himself as a father is so fundamental to his self-image that it even colors his attitude toward his occupation. In Act II scene iii when Barak has presumably fallen asleep and somehow spilled the glue needed for his work, he laments:

> Ich höre und weiss nicht, was eines redet,
> und habe vergossen den Leim, da ich hinfiel –
> und mir ist bange um mein Handwerk,
> und dass ich nicht werde nähren können,
> die meinen Händen anvertraut sind.
>
> (D III 199-200.)

Even his prodigious physical labor is obviously motivated by his desire to be father and provider.

The aspect of fatherhood which provides for the physical needs of others was emphasized by Hofmannsthal in his characterization of Barak, as the examples quoted immediately above demonstrate. He also gave depth to the father image by writing lines for Barak which call to mind qualities associated with the caring aspect of God the Father and God the Son. One line which relates Barak to the latter is

"Fürchte dich nicht. " (D III 214.) In the opera this line is sung by the imprisoned Barak as an expression of his changed attitude toward the Wife. No longer does he feel himself to be her judge; instead he wishes to dispel her fear of him. These lines are a direct rephrasing of Jesus' reassurance to his disciples as he walked to them on the water: "Fürchtet euch nicht. " (Matthew 14: 27.) The lines "Wo sollten sie [die Brüder] herbergen / wenn nicht in Vaters Haus?" (D III 165) call to mind the line spoken by Jesus in John 14: 2 (Biblia Germanica, 1545): "In meines Vaters Hause sind viel Wohnungen. " The similarity of the line spoken by the Brothers and the Beggar Children, "O unser aller Vater," to the first line of the Lord's Prayer "Unser Vater in dem Himmel" (Matthew 6:9) is obvious. All of these verses, which in style or vocabulary relate to Jesus' sayings, give depth to the poet's characterization of Barak as a caring, loving individual.

These specific words and phrases are not the only indication of similarity between Barak and Jesus. The transfiguration of Jesus - including the fear of imprisonment and of death, the feeling of desertion by friends, the acceptance of death, and the consequent illumination - depicts a transcendence arising from suffering. The parallel to this, although to a lesser degreee, in the Dyer's suffering at the hands of the Wife and in his ability to forgive her is obvious:

> Barak: Ihre Zunge ist spitz, und ihr Sinn ist launisch,
> aber nicht schlimm -
> und ihre Reden sind gesegnet
> mit dem Segen der Widerruflichkeit
> um ihres reinen Herzens willen
> und ihrer Jugend.
>
> (D III 188.)

Perhaps it is both Barak's patient acceptance of his suffering and also his forgiving attitude toward the Wife, the source of his grief, which justifies his name.

Knoten des Herzens

Barak's transcendence of suffering through a forgiving acceptance of it teaches the Empress what it means to be human:

> Die Kaiserin: Gepriesen sei, der mich diesen Mann finden
> liess unter den Männern,
> ·denn er zeigt mir, was ein Mensch ist,
> und um seinetwillen will ich bleiben unter den
> Menschen
> und atmen ihren Atem
> und tragen ihre Beschwerden!
>
> (D III 204.)

More than once she emphasizes his suffering and the godliness which his acceptance of it implies:

80

THE TEXT OF THE FRAU OHNE SCHATTEN

> Sieh - Amme - sieh
> des Mannes Aug, wie es sich quält!
> Vor solchen Blicken liegen Cherubim
> auf ihrem Angesicht!
>
> (D III 201.)

The Empress thus recognizes ''der Mensch ist dazu da, durch die Unreinheit, der er zugehört, ins immer Reinere zu streben.''(27)

Because of her contact with Barak, the Empress begins to sense man's capacity to behave with goodness and decency toward others under the most difficult circumstances. These qualities enable Barak to accomplish what the Emperor has been unable to do - untie the ''knots of the Empress' heart''; the Unborn Children make this clear to the Emperor as he is turning to stone:

> ''Du hast den Knoten ihres Herzens nicht gelöst! das ist es, worüber wir weinen müssen. So muss sie von dir genommen werden und in dessen Hände gegeben, der es vermag, den Knoten ihres Herzens zu lösen.''
>
> (E 319.)

Richter

In the final scene of Act II Barak takes upon himself the role of judge and executioner. In the face both of the Wife's declaration of her infidelity and also of her renunciation of the Children, he determines to punish her with death:

> Hat sie solch eine Hurenstirn
> und sieht lieblich darein
> und schämt sich nicht?
> Heran, ihr Brüder, einen Sack herbei
> und hinein von den Steinen,
> dass ich dies Weib
> ertränke im Fluss
> mit meinen Händen!
>
> (D III 208.)

The Wife accepts his judgment and is willing to die at his hand: ''Barak, so töte mich, / schnell!'' (D III 211.) Barak later (IIIi) expresses remorse for the attempted execution, but there is never any indication that he was wrong in his judgment. This is consistent with Hofmannsthal's views on justice as expressed both in the playlet Idylle (see p. 75) and also in the short story ''Gerechtigkeit.'' In this prose narrative a Messenger of God appears and speaks with two persons, one a young child and the other a young man. The child may approach the Messenger without fear of a negative judgment upon him, the young man may not. The child and the young man appear to represent two different ages of the same person - with that person holding the same attitudes toward life and behaving similarly at both ages. The lack of meaningful relationships which is so obvious in the lives of both the child and the young man appears to be the key to this differentiation. The Messenger does not expect them of the child, but he does of the adult. Because these relationships are lacking, the Messenger sternly brushes aside the young man's lame excuse of not having understood life with: "Gerechtigkeit ist alles." (P I 121.) Barak's judgment is thus a concrete portrayal of Hofmannsthal's concept that individual lives are subject to judgment and that judgment will be stern and merciless.

Esel, Tier

The Wife in her scorn for Barak likens him to an animal:

> Es gibt derer, die bleiben immer gelassen,
> und geschähe, was will, es wird keiner jemals
> ihr Gesicht verändert sehen.
> Tagaus, tagein
> gehen sie wie das Vieh
> von Lager zu Frass,
> von Frass zu Lager
> und wissen nicht, was geschehen ist,
> und nicht, wie es gemeint war.
> (D III 205.)

Nor does she cease her name-calling by labeling him a dumb beast; she even calls him an ass:

> Ein Handwerk verstehst du sicher nicht,
> wie du's von Anfang nicht verstanden,
> sonst sprächest du jetzt nicht von dir
> und diesem Mörser.
> Geschah dir das, was dir eben geschah,
> dein Herz müsste schwellen vor Zartheit,
>
> . . . .
> Aber es geht ein Maulesel
> am Abgrund hin,
> und es ficht ihn nicht an
> die Tiefe und das Geheimnis!
> (D III 199.)

Although caution must be exercised in accepting any of the Wife's strident criticisms of Barak, there is some truth in this characterization. Barak does not regard the Wife as an individual in her own right. For him she is solely the mother-to-be of his children; her youth and beauty are non-existent in his eyes. Nor does he approach her with awe and with respect for the mystery of human life. As a consequence, he resembles the Emperor in that he is unable to establish a deeply satisfying relationship with the Wife; he is, therefore, unable to help the two of them attain a true marriage wherein each aids the other in a continuing growth process: "Der Sinn der Ehe ist wechselseitige Auflösung und Palingenesie."(A29.)

Symbols Pertaining to the Nurse

Hündin

Early in the libretto Hofmannsthal associates the word "dog" with the Nurse; in fact, the Nurse refers to herself as "like a dog" when she speaks with the Emperor in Act II:

Der Kaiser	(tritt in die Tür des Gemaches):
	Amme! Wachst du?
Die Amme:	Wache und liege
	der Hündin gleich
	auf deiner Schwelle!

(D III 152.)

In this particular episode the Nurse takes upon herself the qualities of watchfulness, loyalty, and protectiveness which are traditionally associated with the dog. In the prose narrative these characteristics are strongly emphasized as the Empress attempts to persuade the Nurse to help her obtain a shadow:

"Du hast mich nie im Stich gelassen", rief sie und drückte heftig die Arme um den Leib der Alten zusammen, "hilf mir, du Einzige! Du hast mir alles verziehen, nachgewandert bist du mir von unserer Insel, bist über die Mondberge geklettert, drei Monate bist du in den Städten und Dörfern herumgezogen, bis du erfragt hattest, wo ich hingeraten war, unter den Menschen hast du gewohnt, vor denen es dich schauderte, hast mit ihnen gegessen und geschlafen, ihren Atem über dich ergehen lassen, und alles um meinetwillen, hilf mir du, dir ist nichts verborgen, du findest die Wege und ahndest die Mittel, die Bedingungen sind dir offenbar, das Verbotene weisst du zu umgehen! Hilf mir zu einem Schatten, du Einzige!"

(E 262.)

Superficially, this devotion seems akin to the devotion of the Empress to the Emperor; rather than desert the Empress when the Empress escapes her watchful care, the Nurse searches three long months for her charge, even looking among men, whom she despises. The similarity between the Empress' devotion and the devotion of the Nurse ends, however, upon closer inspection. The Empress in the third act is unwilling to allow her loyalty to the Emperor to cause further detriment to Barak and the Wife and consequently renounces any claims which she might legally have had upon the shadow. She will not allow her loyalty to the Emperor to cause unhappiness and pain to others. The Nurse, on the other hand, delights greatly in increasing the

83

misery which Barak and the Wife experience as a result of the quest for the shadow:

> Wer schreit nach Blut
> und hat kein Schwert,
> dem wird von uns
> die Hand bewehrt!
> Und fliesst nur schnell
> das dunkle Blut,
> wir haben den Schatten,
> und uns ist gut!

(D III 209.)

The Nurse exhibits no allegiance to an over-riding principle of respect for others and for the mystery of life which the very existence of people represents. The Empress, on the other hand, comes to know such a principle during the course of the opera and demonstrates an allegiance to it. The Nurse's loyalty is thus shown to be perverse and idolatrous. She merely exhibits a dog-like devotion which is neither restricted nor supported by an ethic based upon respect for others.

Nachtvogel

In the prose version Hofmannsthal associates the <u>Nachtvogel</u> (nightbird) with the Nurse: "Die Amme allein, deren Augen, wie eines Nachtvogels, jede Finsternis durchdrangen. . . ." (E 345.) Inasmuch as birds of the night are primarily birds of prey, such as owls, Hofmannsthal implies here that the Nurse preys upon others, such as Barak and the Wife. This particular bird of prey, the Nurse, loses her way after having returned to the realm of the spirits:

> Der Fluss rann tief unten ohne Rauschen hin, nirgends war ein
> Zeichen, sie musste sich eingestehen, dass sie den Weg ver-
> loren hatte. Sie rief gellend den Namen ihres Kindes, nichts
> antwortete, nicht einmal ein Widerhall. Nur ein Nachtvogel kam
> auf weichen Flügeln zwischen dem Gestein hervor, stiess gegen
> ihren Leib und taumelte gegen die Erde. Da warf auch sie sich zu
> Boden und drückte das Gesicht gegen den harten Stein.

(E 357-58.)

Hofmannsthal chose this manner to depict the Nurse's complete loss of orientation with regard to her existence. The denunciation by the Empress and the consequent separation of the Nurse from her former charge have removed all sense of purpose from the Nurse's life. In contrast to the Empress, who shows a desire to live among people and to establish relationships with them when she has been separated from the Emperor - the object of her loyalty, the Nurse experiences only isolation. Although in the opera Keikobad decrees banishment to the world of people for the Nurse, this change from the isolation on the rocky mountain is not significant. In both cases alienation from others as a result of her own activities characterizes the

84

Nurse's life.

Schlange

In the opera libretto the Wife calls the Nurse a snake:

Ich will nicht in deinen Händen sein,
und dass du ausspähest
all mein Verborgenes,
du alte weiss und schwarz gefleckte Schlange!
(D III 194.)

Hofmannsthal adds detail to this characterization in the prose narrative by describing the Nurse as having a toothless mouth and thin lips (E 274), eyes without lashes (E 275), and a forked tongue (E 264). The following quotation clarifies the underlying symbolism:

Mephistopheles: Staub soll er [Faust] Fressen, und
mit Lust,
Wie meine Muhme, die berühmte Schlange! (28)

Hofmannsthal thus associated the Nurse with the demonic and specifically related her to the Mephistopheles of Goethe's Faust. Words spoken by the Nurse herself make the relationship even more explicit: "Muhme nennen sie mich / und Mutter gar!" (D III 161.) The poet has thus chosen to use two symbols - Schlange and Muhme - with strong ties to Goethe's Mephistopheles in an attempt to express the demonic element of the Nurse's character. Other incidents occurring in the tale develop the similarity between them. She grasps the cooking herbs out of the air with black claws (E 276); she mixes a sleeping potion for Barak (E 329-30) as Mephistopheles had done for Gretchen's mother; she initiates a pact with the Wife (D III 175-76), the price of which is the Wife's soul; other people specifically call her a (Hexe) (E 340); she engages in magic, as in the conjuring of the Youth (D III 184-85).

Perhaps of greater significance than all of these parallels is the inability, common to both the Nurse and Mephistopheles, to discern anything good about men. In Faust Mephistopheles characterizes men in the following words:

Er scheint mir, mit Verlaub von Euer Gnaden,
Wie eine der langbeinigen Zikaden,
Die immer fliegt und fliegend springt
Und gleich im Gras ihr altes Liedchen singt. (29)

The Nurse expresses her contempt for them in these terms:

Der Tag ist da,
der Menschentag, -
ein wildes Getümmel,
gierig - sinnlos,
ein ewiges Trachten
ohne Freude!
    (Wild und hasserfüllt)
Tausend Gesichter,
keine Mienen -
Augen, die schauen,
ohne zu blicken -
Kielkröpfe, die gaffen,
Lurche und Spinnen -
uns sind sie zu schauen
so lustig wie sie!

(D III 161.)

Mephistopheles and the Nurse also possess one other common trait: both have a quick tongue and a ready wit. Faust, as a total work, gains immeasurably from Mephistopheles' repartee, such as "Für einen Leichnam bin ich nicht zu Haus: / Mir geht es wie der Katze mit der Maus."(30) Hofmannsthal has endowed the Nurse with a similar ability, although her speeches tend to be more proverbial:

Schnell dreht sich der Wind,
und wir rufen dich wieder!

(D III 197.)

"Ein krummer Nagel" antwortete die flinke Zunge der Alten, "ist noch kein Angel, es muss erst ein Widerhaken daran."

(E 289.)

The skill which the Nurse possesses in making clever remarks demonstrates the third higly distinctive approach to speech which Hofmannsthal utilized in the Frau ohne Schatten. The first consists predominantly of silence and is exhibited by the Empress; the second consists of excessive speaking and is exhibited by the Wife. Hofmannsthal utilized this third approach, repartee, to emphasize the lack of respect for others which characterizes the Nurse.

Summary

The relationships of the five principal characters of the Frau ohne Schatten to each other represent a many-faceted mirroring of the same problem: how to establish a deeply satisfying human relationship. As the fairy-tale opens, this kind of relationship - a mutually rewarding commitment of two mature individuals to each other, a commitment wherein each exhibits awe for the mystery which the other represents - does not exist. Barak in his selfless devotion to his work, which occurs

86

because he so strongly feels his position as the family provider, comes most closely to achieving this kind of relationship; he does not succeed, however, because he is unable to look upon the Wife with the wonder and respect which would cause her to view him, with trust and love. The Wife typifies youth's lack of commitment to others and is, therefore, very distant in the relationship which she is called upon to fulfill. Being an egotistical dreamer, she stands to the side in the relationships which are open to her rather than participating.

The counterpart of the Wife in the Emperor-Empress relationship, in the sense of being the more negative partner, is the Emperor. His egotism would prevent the Empress from learning that to be human means to establish relationships with other people; this lack of respect for others characterizes his entire behavior.

The Empress, because of her isolation in the palace, has no conception of how to establish a fulfilling human relationship and in her naivete turns to the Nurse as a guide. The Nurse, for her part, exhibits as much devotion to the Empress as does Barak to his family, but she lacks the attitude of respect for others which is basic to a mature human relationship. She tends, moreover, to treat the Empress as a child so that a mature relationship cannot occur between them without a change in the Nurse's behavior. None of the characters has achieved, therefore, a deeply and mutually satisfying relationship to another individual at the end of the first act.

The Empress' commitment to the Emperor, as represented by her decision to obtain a shadow in order to prevent the curse from falling upon the Emperor, sets into motion a series of events which changes this status quo. First of all, as the Empress observes the selfless devotion of Barak to others, she develops respect for others. Second, her interference in the lives of Barak and the Wife brings a threat to Barak's happiness through the deepening estrangement from the Wife which the Nurse occasions. Third, the Wife senses an opportunity for permanent escape into a dream world, an escape from the responsible acceptance of a partnership in a human relationship. Fourth, the change in the relationship between the Empress and the Emperor, which the Empress' grasping of the initiative, represents, reduces the Emperor to a status of total isolation. Unable to confront the Empress honestly with evidence of her deceit, he withdraws totally from any attempt to establish a fruitful relationship with her.

The Empress in her devotion to the Emperor, unlike the Nurse in her devotion to the Empress, is not willing, however, that her commitment should destroy the happiness of another - Barak. Respect for others becomes a guiding principle as she selflessly denies her own happiness for the sake of Barak. The magical fairytale realm in which the story takes place allows for the intervention of superior powers into this potentially tragic situation. The Empress is rewarded for her respect for others with an Emperor to whom life has been restored. The Wife and Barak are reunited so that the two of them, who experienced a true commitment to each other at the time when Barak threatened to kill the Wife, may now live out that commitment.

THE TEXT OF THE FRAU OHNE SCHATTEN

When the Emperor returns to life, he sings lines of praise which express his joy in life:

> Nirgend Ruhe, still zu liegen,
> nirgend Anker, nirgend Port,
> nichts ist da - nur aufzufliegen
> ist ein Ort an jedem Ort.
>
> (D III 239.)

In the prose narrative a similar thought finds expression in the line: "Ober ihm und unter ihm war der Himmel." (E 375.) Hofmannsthal expressed here two different ideas. The first is a negatively tinged one: quietness and peace can only be achieved in the twentieth century upon the insecurity of the shifting, sliding underpinnings of modern life: "Nichts lässt sich im Weltlichen befestigen." (A 230.) The second idea which the poet conjured forth is similar to the Dionysian joy of the poem "Lebenslied," the joy of total involvement in experience to the exclusion of contemplative reflection:

> Den Erben lass verschwenden
> An Adler, Lamm und Pfau
> Das Salböl aus den Händen
> Der toten alten Frau!
> Die Toten, die entgleiten,
> Die Wipfel in dem Weiten -
> Ihm sind sie wie das Schreiten
> Der Tänzerinnen wert!
>
> Er geht wie den kein Walten
> Vom Rücken her bedroht
> Er lächelt, wenn die Falten
> Des Lebens flüstern; Tod!
> Ihm bietet jede Stelle
> Geheimnisvoll die Schwelle;
> Es gibt sich jeder Welle
> Der Heimatlose hin.
>
> Der Schwarm von wilden Bienen
> nimmt seine Seele mit;
> Das Singen von Delphinen
> Beflügelt seinen Schritt:
> Ihm tragen alle Erden
> Mit mächtigen Gebärden.
> Der Flüsse Dunkelwerden
> Begrenzt den Hirtentag!

THE TEXT OF THE FRAU OHNE SCHATTEN

> Das Salböl aus den Händen
> Der toten alten Frau
> Lass lächelnd ihn verschwenden
> An Adler, Lamm und Pfau:
> Er lächelt der Gefährten. -
> Die schwebend unbeschwerten
> Abgründe und die Gärten
> Des Lebens tragen ihn.
>
> (GLD 12-13.)

The unity between self and world, which the Empress experienced in the Mondberge, returns - but with distinct differences. There is a definite commitment to one other individual and a concurrent diminishing of self-assertion; the principal attitude is an awe-filled respect for every other person.

Footnotes

(1) Suzanne Langer, Feeling and Form: A Theory of Art Developed from "Philosophy in a New Key" (New York: Charles Scribner's Sons, 1953), p. 306.

(2) From the "Vorrede auff den Psalter," Biblia: Das ist: Die ganze Heilige Schrift / Deutsch / Auffs new zugericht, trans. Martin Luther (Wittenberg: Hans Lufft, 1545, facsim. ed., Stuttgart: Württembergische Bibelanstalt, 1967).

(3) Philip Wheelwright, Metaphor and Reality (Bloomington, Indiana: Indiana University Press, 1962), p. 19.

(4) Philosophy in a New Key: A Study in the Symbolism of Reason, Rite, and Art (Cambridge, Mass.: Harvard University Press, 1942), p. 26.

(5) Wheelwright, p. 26.

(6) Langer, New Key, p. 43.

(7) Ibid., p. 61.

(8) Poetic Diction: A Study in Meaning (London: Faber and Gwyer Ltd., 1928; reprint ed., New York: McGraw-Hill Book Co., 1964), p. 131. Barfield's italics.

(9) Wheelwright, p. 51.

THE TEXT OF THE FRAU OHNE SCHATTEN

Footnotes

(10) George R. Marek, who is quoted on page fifteen of this paper, criticized Hofmannsthal for employing symbols in his opera libretti. When symbols are considered as language's method of negotiating new insights, however, this criticism becomes a call for a sterotype.

(11) Wheelwright, p. 164.

(12) Herbert Weisinger, The Agony and the Triumph: Papers on the Use and Abuse
of Myth ([East Lansing]: Michigan State University Press, 1964), p. 263.

(13) Wheelwright, p. 98-99.

(14) Richard Strauss - Hugo von Hofmannsthal: Briefwechsel, ed. Willi Schuh,
4th ed., Gesamtausgabe (Zurich: Atlantis Verlag, 1964), Hofmannsthal to
Strauss, 30. VIII. 1926.

(15) Wheelwright, p. 54.

(16) The book is not identified in Hofmannsthal's text. A note by the editor adds
that the article was at one time given the title "Das Buch von Peter Altenberg."

(17) Hugo von Hofmannsthal (Frankfurt: S. Fischer Verlag, 1960), p. 249.

(18) Hugo von Hofmannsthal (Berlin: Walter de Gruyter & Co., 1970), pp. 270-71.

(19) Hugo von Hofmannsthal - Rudolf Borchardt: Briefwechsel, ed. Marie Luise
Borchardt and Herbert Steiner (Frankfurt: Fischer, 1954), pp. 47-51, Borchardt to Hofmannsthal, 23. VII. 1911.

(20) Ibid., p. 54 Hofmannsthal to Borchardt, 27. VII. 1911.

(21) Hederer, p. 264.

(22) George C. Schoolfield, "The Pool, the Bath, the Dive: the Water Image in
Hofmannsthal," Monatshefte, XLV (November, 1953), 380-81.

(23) Hofmannsthals dramatischer Stil: Untersuchungen zur Symbolik und Drama-
turgie, Hermaea: Germanistische Forschungen: Neue Folge, v. 20 (Tübingen:
Max Niemeyer Verlag, 1967), pp. 143-44.

(24) Johann Wolfgang Goethe, "Commentary on the 'Urworte. Orphisch,'"
Gedenkausgabe der Werke, Briefe, und Gespräche, ed. Ernst Beutler,
24 vols. (Zurich: Artemis Verlag, 1950), II: 618.

Footnotes

(25) Ibid., pp. 618-19.

(26) Norman Del Mar, Richard Strauss: <u>A Critical Commentary on His Life and Works</u>, 3 vols. (Philadelphia: Chilton Book Co., 1969), II:158.

(27) <u>Hofmannsthal - Borchardt Briefwechsel</u>, p. 51, Borchardt to Hofmannsthal, 23. VII. 1911.

(28) Goethe, <u>Faust</u> in <u>Gedenkausgabe</u>, V: 151.

(29) Ibid., V: 150.

(30) Ibid., V: 151.

CHAPTER IV

TABLE OF ANALYSIS

     The Table of Analysis delineates the significant features of the opera. The text, the music, important gestures, and stage effects are all included, for it is only in this totality that the opera exists. The analysis also seeks to establish the relationship of these various parts to each other. For example, a speech which evidences a lessening of momentum in its final lines is examined in its setting to discover if a <u>ritardando</u> or similar device in the music parallels and enhances this quality in the libretto. This part of the analysis necessarily proceeds from the text to the music and deals ultimately with the question of how Strauss fulfilled Hofmannsthal's intent. Preceding the analysis is the "Introduction to the Table of Analysis," which seeks 1) to establish Hofmannsthal's general desires for the musical setting of the <u>Frau ohne Schatten</u>, 2) to indentify the major stylistic techniques which Hofmannsthal employed in writing the text, and 3) to determine what means Strauss used to structure the opera.

Introduction to the Table of Analysis

<u>The Text of the Frau ohne Schatten</u>

     Hofmannsthal desired four principal qualities for the musical setting of his libretto the <u>Frau ohne Schatten</u>. First, he perceived an analogy between his <u>Frau ohne Schatten</u> and W. A. Mozart's Zauberflöte (1); by means of this perception he envisioned a definite musical style as an appropriate setting for the libretto. Second, he desired that the musical setting of the text should allow comprehension of significant verse lines (2). Third, he expected Strauss to develop the musical characterizations of the principal figures in a manner which would be consistent with the characterizations begun in the libretto (3). Fourth, he expected, or at least hoped, that Strauss would perceive the forms of the speeches and set them with music appropriate for their structure (4).

     The relationship to the <u>Zauberflöte</u> which the poet desired to foster may be discerned from the following comments which he made upon the occasion of the 150th anniversary of Beethoven's birthday:

     Aus den Tiefen des menschlichsten der deutschen Stämme hervor-
     gestiegen, trat sie [Mozarts Musik] vor Europa hin, schön und fass-
     lich wie eine Antike, aber eine christliche, gereinigte Antike, un-
     schuldiger als die erste. Aus den Tiefen des Volkes war das Tiefste
     und Reinste tönend geworden; es waren Töne der Freude, ein heiliger,
     beflügelter, leichter Sinn sprach aus ihnen, kein Leichtsinn; seliges
     Gefühl des Lebens; die Abgründe sind geahnt, aber ohne Grauen, das
     Dunkel noch durchstrahlt von innigem Licht, dazwischen die Wehmut
     wohl - denn Wehmut kennt das Volk -, aber kaum der schneidende
     Schmerz, niemals der Einsamkeit starrendes Bewusstsein.

                  (P IV 7-8.)

TABLE OF ANALYSIS

Hofmannsthal's deceptively simple statement that as he envisioned the Frau ohne Schatten an analogy to the Zauberflöte existed can be rephrased according to this speech: one of the primary qualities which he desired for the completed Frau ohne Schatten was a transcendence of the dark aspects of life by means of light, or a transcendence of pain, sorrow, and death by means of a vital and joyful serenity. No matter how violently opposed the protagonists might become, the conflicts were to be overcome by a unity of content and style wherein the accent was to be on lightness and deftness of touch.

That the poet was concerned with the uniting of conflicting forces is indicated by his interest at this time in John Keats' poem "A Song of Opposites." His copy of Keats' works has this notation in the margin beside this poem: "Für den Kaiser / was er der Kaiserin vorenthalten hat."(5) The motto and first stanza of the poem are:

>   "Under the flag
>   Of each his faction, they to battle bring
>   Their embryon arms."

>   Welcome joy, and welcome sorrow,
>   Lethe's weed and Hermes' feather;
>   Come to-day, and come to-morrow,
>   I do love you both together! (6)

Another quality in Mozart's operas for which Hofmannsthal expressed admiration was the significance accorded to the arias, the "Nummern" (7). From the time when the collaborators began work on Ariadne auf Naxos the two of them had been attempting to employ a musical style which differentiated between the dialogues and the more purely musical numbers. In fact, included in the early discussion of Ariadne was Hofmannsthal's comment that this small work would prepare them for the Frau ohne Schatten in the opportunity which it would afford for working with arias. (8)

It can also be deduced that Hofmannsthal admired Mozart's style of characterizing different figures by means of the melodic line. (9) The following quotation suggests that the poet was here indicating a preference for characterization by means of the vocal line over a characterization by means of symphonic melody, color, rhythm, or harmony. The librettist wrote this description of the kind of setting which he felt would be appropriate for the Aegyptische Helena:

. . . wenn sich, als ein neuer Stilversuch, nicht absteigender Kräfte, sondern gesteigerter Kunsteinsicht, zu einem Weniger von Musik gelangen liesse, wenn die Führung, die Melodie etwas mehr in die Stimme gelegt werden und das Orchester, mindestens auf grosse Strecken, begleitend und nicht sich in der Symphonie auslebend, sich der Stimme subordinieren würde (nicht in bezug auf Klangstärke, sondern in

anderer Verteilung des ''Führenden'') - so wäre, für ein Werk
dieser Art, der Operette ihr Zauberring entwunden, mit dem
sie die Seelen der Zuhörenden so <u>voll</u> bezwingt! (10)

In addition to his desire to develop a certain similarity in style to Mozart's
operatic style, Hofmannsthal was also eager to ensure that much of the text be comprehended. In an attempt to achieve this end he wrote the following lines to Strauss
on April 22, 1914:

> Ich hörte unlängst eine Oper [''Notre Dame''] hier, von einem bis-
> her Unbekannten, Franz Schmidt. Ich kann darüber kein Urteil ab-
> geben, es schien mir aber weit über all dem Zeug von d'Albert,
> Schreker etc. , ja auch Schreker, trotz seines Talentes. Das Merk-
> würdige an der Oper von Schmidt, weshalb ich hier davon spreche,
> war mir dies, dass ich beim ersten Hören fast alles von dem (übri-
> gens absurden) Text verstand, und doch war es keine dünne melo-
> dramartige Musik - aber wenn die Singstimme vorwiegen soll, so
> war alles andere so zurücktretend, und - ich kann mir nicht helfen,
> ich hatte einen <u>sehr</u> schönen Eindruck davon, trotzdem der Text,
> wie gesagt , albern war. Ich sage <u>das ja</u> nicht um <u>meines</u> Textes
> willen, so weit kennen Sie ja jetzt mich schon, sondern ich will
> in ganz inkompetenter Weise damit sagen, dass es doch Möglich-
> keiten geben muss, manchmal das Wort absolut vorwalten zu lassen
> und dass mir <u>viel gewonnen</u> schiene, wenn das auf Ihrem Wege läge,
> diesmal. (11)

At the time when this letter was written, Strauss had just begun work on the <u>Frau
ohne Schatten;</u> the relevance of the poet's comments to this work is thus apparent.
Nor was this attempt by Hofmannsthal to achieve comprehension of the text an isolated instance. He arranged for the Munich premiere of the <u>Aegyptische Helena</u> to
be performed with the house lights partially on so that the audience would be able
to follow the printed text. (12)

Besides these two desires - that the text be comprehended and that the
opera be composed in a style analogous to Mozart's operatic style, the poet also
expected Strauss to develop the musical characterizations of the principal figures
in a manner consistent with the characterizations which he had begun in the libretto.
Not infrequently did he give Strauss instructions which were designed to maintain
consistency in this area, as for example:

> Der Geist der Musik für diese Szene wird sich mit dem der Dich-
> tung decken, wenn Sie dem Ganzen etwas Leichtes, Fliessendes,
> Gehauchtes geben - trotz der Gegensätze darin: diese Gegensätze
> haben nicht die Schwere der Kontraste der irdischen Sphäre; sie
> sind durch ein gemeinsames Geisterhaftes versöhnt.
> Der Kaiser ist von den fünf Hauptfiguren des Stückes die mindest

hervortretende: sein märchenhaftes Geschick, zu Stein und
wieder erlöst zu werden, ist ein stärkster Zug im Bilde - seine
Physiognomie ist minder individuell als typisch: der Jäger und
der Liebende (siehe Anmerkungen). Die Musik wird ihm das
wahrhaft Musikhafte mehr als das scharf Charakteristische mit-
zugeben haben; er soll eine süsse, schöngeführte Stimme in dem
Ganzen sein. Von der dreifachen Natur der Kaiserin, die am
Dasein von Tier, Mensch und Geist Anteil hat, kommen in diesem
Teil nur das Tierhafte und das Geisterhafte, beide zusammen das
Fremdsein ausmachend, in Erscheinung; in der Mitte klafft die
Lücke, das Menschliche fehlt: diese zu gewinnen, ist der Sinn des
ganzen Stückes - so auch in der Musik: erst im dritten Akt wird die
Stimme der Kaiserin ihren vollen menschlichen Klang annehmen -
die tierhaft geisterhaften Elemente werden dann in einem höheren
Medium zu einer neuen Wesenheit verschmolzen erscheinen. Ueber
das Doppelgesicht der Amme, die zwischen dem Dämonischen und
dem Grotesken schillert, finden Sie Gelegentliches dem Text bei-
geschrieben. (13)

Hofmannsthal also sought to predetermine the course of the music by the
manner in which he structured the text. This goal was the subject of a letter which
he wrote to Strauss on September 24, 1913:

Nicht der dramatische Aufbau - in diesem kann die "Frau ohne
Schatten" es mit jedem existierenden Musiktext aufnehmen - aber
die unnachahmliche Vortrefflichkeit, mit der in der Ausführung
[der Wagner-Textbücher] der Musik vorgewaltet ist - die uner-
reichbare Qualität: dass, wie die Flussläufe eine Landschaft be-
stimmen - so hier die poetische Landschaft durch die vom Dichter
schon gewussten Ströme und Bäche der Melodie figuriert ist -,
das hatte mich wirklich niedergeschlagen. (14)

An analysis of the text reveals his attempts to predetermine the flow of the music.
For example, the following speech exhibits a tendency to relax its momentum as it
comes to a close, obviously prefiguring a ritardando in the music:

Alles, du Benedeite, alles
zahlen begierige Käufer, du Herrin
wenn eine Unnennbare deinesgleichen
abtut ihren Schatten und gibt ihn dahin!
Ei! Die Sklavinnen und die Sklaven,
so viele ihrer du verlangest,
und die Brokate und Seidengewänder,
in denen du stündlich wechselnd prangest,
und die Maultiere und die Häuser
und die Springbrunnen und die Gärten

95

TABLE OF ANALYSIS

und deiner Liebenden nächtlich Gedränge
und dauernde Jugendherrlichkeit
für ungemessene Zeit
dies alles ist dein,
du Herrscherin,
gibst du den Schatten dahin!

(D III 172.)

The average number of syllables per line for the first twelve lines is 9.75; this average drops to 5.75 for the last four verse lines. These statistics confirm the intuitive feeling which occurs with a reading of the speech.

Hofmannsthal also attempted to prefigure the flow and style of the music by devising textual styles which differentiated between a) text which convey information, the comprehension of which is necessary if the plot is to be followed, and b) text which conveys an emotional state and consequently serves primarily as a vehicle for the expression of feeling in the music. These two textual styles will henceforth be respectively referred to as conversational text and lyrical text. The following lines from Act I of the <u>Frau ohne Schatten</u> exemplify what is meant by the term conversational text:

Amme: Herr, wenn du anstellst
ein solches Jagen –
leicht bleibst du dann fern über Nacht?
Kaiser: Kann sein, drei Tage
komm ich nicht heim!

(D III 154.)

The last two of these five lines convey the information that the Emperor will be absent from the royal household for three days. His absence becomes convenient for the purposes of the Empress – as she later determines them; hence, this information is significant as far as plot development is concerned. Important information of this kind characterizes conversational text, as do short sentences and a simple vocabulary. Often, too, a particularly significant line may be monosyllabic.

The following lines exemplify speeches of a lyrical nature:

Denn meiner Seele
und meinen Augen
und meinen Händen
und meinem Herzen
ist sie die Beute
aller Beuten
ohn Ende!

(D III 154-55.)

TABLE OF ANALYSIS

All of the primary characteristics of lyrical passages may be observed here: 1) the speech, which may be characterized as a love song to the Empress, contains no information which must be understood in order for the plot to be followed; 2) parallel grammatical structure, as in the first four lines, is a frequent occurrence; 3) long sentences, often with relatively complex syntax, commonly occur; 4) intensification by means of delay, which occurs in this sentence because the subject of the sentence does not arrive until the fifth line, is also frequent.

This example ("Denn meiner Seele") and the immediately preceding one ("Herr, wenn du anstellst") represent the extreme ends of one long continuum. Little of the libretto so obviously represents these two different styles; much of it falls on a mid-point of the continuum and consists of a mixture of lyrical and conversational lines.

The following verse lines of the Nurse and the Messenger demonstrate a sudden shift from lyrical to conversational text and back again to lyrical text:

Die Amme:	Konnt ich einem Vogel
	nach in die Luft?
	Sollt ich die Gazelle
	mit Händen halten?
Der Bote:	Lass mich sie sehn!
Die Amme:	Sie ist nicht allein:
	Er ist bei ihr.
	Die Nacht war nicht
	in zwölf Monden,
	dass er ihrer nicht hätte begehrt!

(D III 151.)

In this dialogue the librettist placed the significant line introducing the Emperor, "Er ist bei ihr," in the midst of a long lyrical speech by the Nurse. This lyrical passage is broken by the demand of the Messenger that he be allowed to see the Empress and by the Nurse's response that the Empress is not alone. To highlight the line Hofmannsthal employed two specific techniques. First, he simplified the line as far as vocabulary and length is concerned: where previously there was talk of a gazelle and of a bird with each sentence encompassing a minimum of two verse lines, there is now an unadorned single verse line - "Er ist bei ihr." Second, he used only monosyllabic words for the line, perhaps thinking that these were more likely to be comprehended when sung than polysyllabic words. Immediately following this line, which constitutes the first mention of the Emperor in the opera text, the lyrical style is resumed.

Hofmannsthal is, of course, responsible not only for the stylistic differences to be observed between various speeches, but also for the structure of the opera libretto: for the relationship of speeches to other speeches within a scene, of scenes to other scenes and of each act to the other acts. These relationships are

97

often very important as far as plot development or lyrical expression is concerned; they, as well as the structure and style of individual speeches, will be analyzed in the table which constitutes the greater part of this chapter.

The Music of the Frau ohne Schatten

The structure of the music of the late nineteenth century avant-garde, which Strauss so whole-heartedly embraced, is characterized by two devices. 1) A literary program, such as a poem or a prose description, determines the overall structure of the work. 2) Short melodic ideas, called motives, are attached to the more important characters and situations in an opera as musical labels, giving the orchestra and the singers the ability to comment upon a person or thing in its absence and without mentioning it specifically. More importantly, this use of the motive confers structural unity upon a composition. Whereas the traditional sonata form gives unity to a composition by requiring a return of the melodic material to the opening key, the music-drama accomplishes the same purposes by utilizing recurrent motives. Symmetry of keys within an act, as might be found in an opera by Mozart, does not exist as a structural principle for the music-drama, although key centers often provide a unifying factor for shorter sections within an act. Strauss accepted and used for the Frau ohne Schatten both of the principles of structure described here: that of organization by means of an extra-musical program (in an opera this must, of course, be the libretto) and that of organization through the use of melodic and harmonic motives.

Strauss's use of musical motives in his operas was not absolutely dependent upon extra-musical associations; often, in fact, musical considerations appear to have been of greater importance. This may be best demonstrated by observing the various contexts in which the following motive occurs:

26. Blessedness (I ii: 39-40)

pp subito

15

Strauss first used this motive to accompany Barak's Blessedness Song (Act I):

Barak: Aus einem jungen Mund
        gehen harte Worte
        und trotzige Reden,
        aber sie sind gesegnet
        mit dem Segen der Widerruflichkeit.
        Ich zürne dir nicht
        und bin freudigen Herzens,
        und ich harre
        und erwarte
        die Gepriesenen,
        die da kommen.   (D III 168.)

In this setting the motive may be designated the Blessedness Motive. It next occurs as an accompaniment to Barak's last lines in Act I (Act I scene ii, rehearsal number 129): "Hörst du die Wächter, Kind, und ihren Ruf?" (D III 180.) Here the motive might be termed the Patience or Goodness Motive. Perhaps it makes its most pronounced appearance in the Empress' Nightmare Scene (Act II scene iv, rehearsal number 150), where it could aptly be called the Nightmare Motive. This apparent change in referential content demonstrates both the freedom with which Strauss used motives and also the near impossibility of giving a motive an appropriate name. In spite of this difficulty, the motives will be assigned names as well as numbers in the Table of Analysis, because names more readily recall musical examples than numbers. No claim is intended that these names exhaust the possible references which could be given, or even that the motives must have an external referent.

Strauss used one additional means of structuring a work other than the programmatic and motivic ones which he accepted from his predecessors. This was a personal one which tended to equate different keys with different feeling-states: "Strauss' Musik muss im Zusammenhang mit dem Stimmungs- und Symbolcharakter der Tonarten gewürdigt werden, wenn man ihr gerecht werden will. "(16) Accordingly, the following correspondences are established:

E-dur:	erotische Erregtheit
F-dur:	heiter, sorglos
B-dur:	Jagd
e-moll:	Unbehagen, Ekel
G-dur:	Kindlichkeit, Naivität
Des-dur:	Feier
Fis-dur:	Verzauberung, Märchen
As-dur:	weiche, träumerische, abendliche Stimmungen
a-moll:	vollendetes Schicksal
e-moll:	Vernichtung des Lebenswillen
es-moll:	Kampf mit Schicksal, Tod
c-moll:	heroische Auflehnung
fis-moll:	Schmerz (17)

(E major:	erotic agitation
F major:	serene, carefree
B♭ major:	the hunt
e minor:	uneasiness, loathing
G major:	childlikeness, naivity
D♭ major:	celebration, ceremony
F-sharp major:	enchantment, fairy-tale
A♭ major:	gentle, dreamy, evening-like moods
a minor:	the fulfillment of fate
e minor:	annihilation of the desire to live
e♭ minor:	struggle with fate, death
c minor:	heroic rebellion
f-sharp minor:	pain, sorrow)

TABLE OF ANALYSIS

As a consequence, there are two reasons for calling attention to the significant key areas of the Frau ohne Schatten: 1) in spite of the lesser function of key relationships as a force for structural unity in a Strauss opera as compared to an opera by Mozart, key areas do provide some structural unity; 2) Strauss's personal equation of keys to different feeling-states provides insight into his understanding of the characters and the plot of the libretto.

Strauss utilized, therefore, two primary means of organizing the Frau ohne Schatten other than the libretto. He gave structure to the composition through the use of a great many harmonic and melodic motives. These are identified in the following table; notation of the motives is given in the appendix. The second means of organization which he used was a personal one; he employed different keys to express different feeling-states. These keys, whenever they appear to be significant, either as a unifying factor or as indicative of certain feelings, will also be pointed out in the table.

Summary

The following table gives an analysis of the opera, pointing out the significant structural and stylistic details of the text, such as the prefiguring of a ritardando, or the differentiation between conversational and lyrical passages in the text. This textual analysis is presented in the left-hand column. Other significant occurrences, such as gestures, pantomime, and changes in lighting and stage sets, are indicated in the center column.

The important musical developments are detailed in the right-hand column. Here the music is examined not only for the structure accorded it both by key centers and also by motives but also for its relationship to the text and to relevant stage occurrences. The following points are considered: the location of principal melodic themes and motives - whether in the orchestra or in the vocal line; the correspondence between the musical characterization and the textual characterization; the differentiation in the music between the stylistically distinguished conversational and lyrical texts; the accord between textual devices, such as intensification or ritardando and their musical settings; the probability of audience comprehension of the text because of its vocal setting and its accompaniment. These many facets of the opera are not of equal importance for the setting of every speech; in some cases one aspect predominates and in other cases a different one. In the interest of conserving space only the more significant aspects of the various verse lines and their settings are discussed.

100

TABLE OF ANALYSIS

Footnotes

(1)   Richard Strauss - Hugo von Hofmannsthal: Briefwechsel, ed. Willi Schuh, 4th ed., Gesamtausgabe (Zurich: Atlantis Verlag, 1964), Hofmannsthal to Strauss, 20. III. 1911.

(2)   Ibid., Hofmannsthal to Strauss, 22. IV. 1914.

(3)   Hofmannsthal not infrequently instructed Strauss concerning the intent of his characterizations. See, for example, Briefwechsel, 28. XII. 1913.

(4)   This desire is not explicitly stated in any of Hofmannsthal's letters, but it may be deduced from this letter: Briefwechsel, Hofmannsthal to Strauss, 24. IX. 1913.

(5)   Quoted from Michael Hamburger, "Hofmannsthal and England," Hofmannsthal: Studies in Commemoration, ed. F. Norman, Institute of Germanic Studies, vol. 5 (London: Institute of Germanic Studies, 1963), p.20.

(6)   Complete Poems and Selected Letters, ed. Clarence DeWitt Thorpe (New York: Odyssey Press, 1933), p. 211.

(7)   Briefwechsel, Hofmannsthal to Strauss, 20. III. 1911.

(8)   Ibid.

(9)   Ibid., Hofmannsthal to Strauss, 1. VIII. 1916.

(10)   Ibid., 26. VII. 1928.

(11)   Ibid.

(12)   Ibid., Strauss to Hofmannsthal, 29. IX. 1928.

(13)   Ibid., 28. XII. 1913.

(14)   Briefwechsel.

(15)   Die Frau ohne Schatten, Oper in drei Akten von Hugo Hofmannsthal [sic.], Musik von Richard Strauss, Op. 65. (Copyright 1919 by Adolph Fürstner: copyright assigned 1943 to Boosey and Hawkes Music Publishers Ltd., London, for all countries except Germany, Danzig, Italy, Portugal and the U.S.S.R.), Act I scene ii, rehearsal number 39.

(16)   Willi Schuh, Hugo von Hofmannsthal und Richard Strauss: Legende und Wirklichkeit (Munich: Carl Hanser, 1964), p. 17.

(17)   Ibid., pp. 17-34, passim.

TABLE OF ANALYSIS OF THE OPERA
THE FRAU OHNE SCHATTEN[1]

Text	Visual Effects[1]	Music
	The scene opens with the Nurse crouching in the dark upon a flat roof above the Emperor's gardens. At the side is the entrance into the penthouse. A light which appears in the distance approaches; finally the Messenger, surrounded by blue light, emerges from the darkness.	There is no overture; a two measure introduction, which contains what one later learns to be the motive directly associated with Keikobad, occurs in A♭ minor. (See musical example #1 in the appendix.) Following three statements of the Keikobad Motive, new melodic material employing wide leaps and irregular rhythms occurs in F minor, the key center for the scene between the Nurse and the Messenger. This motive, the Nurse Motive, sounds in the orchestra as the curtain rises to expose the Nurse on the stage. (See musical example #2.)

The light which appears on stage is commented upon by the Nurse. In her opening words Hofmannsthal begins to establish an association between light and the spirit world of Keikobad:
 	
Licht überm See--
ein fliessender Glanz--
schnell wie ein Vogel!
Die Wipfel der Nacht
von oben erhellt--
eine Feuerhand
will fassen nach mir--
bist du es, Herr?
Siehe, ich wache
bei deinem Kinde
nächtlich in Sorge und
    Pein!
        (D III 149.)
	The Nurse shows fear.	Apparently inspired by Hofmannsthal's use of words denoting light and brightness, Strauss wrote rapid passages for the upper register. An extreme contrast thus occurs between the heaviness with which the Keikobad Motive first appeared and the lightness with which Strauss characterized the Messenger from the spirit world.

This opening speech of the Nurse is conceived breathlessly: no pause occurs until the significant line "bist du es, Herr?" Structurally, all preceding lines lead to this one. It is emphasized by 1) the change to a monosyllabic line, 2) the use of words with full stops such as b, d, and t as contrasted to the previous softness of m, n, s, f, v, w, and 3) a change in metrical pattern from a basic ∪∪∪ (with ∪ representing the unaccented syllables and / the accented syllables) to a more stable ∪∪/. The unsettled feeling which the more irregular line imparts tends to give the regular line of "bist du es, Herr?" a feeling of arrival. This line is also accentuated by the first use in the opera of a present tense verb and the concomitant change from commentary to direct address which this entails. These changes		As the Nurse begins to sing, the orchestra gives a programmatic representation of the light which is appearing on stage by means of its high register, a tremolo in the strings, and rapidly paced scale passages. There is a tendency for the orchestra to cover the words, but the stage action will convey their meaning. The lack of audience comprehension of the text because of the orchestral accompaniment will be likely to change when the line "bist du es, Herr?" is sung; the vocal melody is simplified and the orchestra is reduced to a soft tremolo in the strings at this point. Instead of the expected interval of a fourth from bist to du, there is the tritone interval. The drop of the extra one-half step seems to be an indication in the music of the Nurse's fear of Keikobad. It may also be interpreted as symbolic of the

[1]Lighting, stage sets, gestures, and pantomime are all discussed in this column.

TABLE OF ANALYSIS (continued)

Text	Visual Effects	Music

demonstrate a shift from lyrical to conversational text. The audience will benefit from being able to comprehend this line and also the two following ones because the relationships between several of the major characters are delineated here.

In the Messenger's answer to the Nurse the name Keikobad appears for the first time in the libretto:

Nicht der Gebieter,
Keikobad nicht,
aber sein Bote!
(D III 149.)

The Messenger recounts how many messengers have visited the Nurse and numbers himself the twelfth:

Ihrer [Boten] elf
haben dich heimgesucht,
ein neuer mit jedem schwindenden Mond.
Der zwölfte Mond ist hinab:
der zwölfte Bote steht vor dir.
(D III 149.)

It is important that the audience comprehend that the twelfth month is past, that a year with its connotation of a time for completion of a task is over.

The Messenger inquires if the Empress throws a shadow:

Genug: ich kam
und frage dich:
Wirft sie einen Schatten?
Dann wehe dir!
Weh uns allen!
(D III 150.).

"Wirft sie einen Schatten?" is one of the key lines in this conversation between the Nurse and the Messenger. Hofmannsthal treated it in a manner typical for him of lines which he considered to be

demonic aspects of the Nurse's character. Generally, the Nurse's vocal line is characterized by wide intervals and frequent modulations.

The primary melodic theme of this exchange between the Nurse and the Messenger does not occur in the voices, but appears solely in the orchestra. It is hereafter called the Messenger Motive. (See musical example #3.)

As with the Nurse's question above ("bist du es, Herr?"), the orchestra is subdued for the Messenger's answer, interjecting the Keikobad Motive after the verse lines "bist du es, Herr?" and "Nicht der Gebieter." Strauss apparently considered the verse line "Kerkobad nicht" to be very important; the voice alone carries the motive without orchestral accompaniment of any kind. The composer added musical interest after "Keikobad nicht, / aber sein Bote!" by setting orchestral counterpoint against the vocal line.

At the verse line "der zwölfte Bote steht vor dir" the orchestral accompaniment is simplified:
1) it doubles the vocal line; 2) it is chordal;
3) it is set in a low register. (The previous lines are contrapuntally accompanied with the orchestra playing in a middle to high register.) This line ("der zwölfte Bote . . .) is set to ten beats plus upbeat as compared to six beats for the preceding line; the syllable count is eight for this line as contrasted to seven for the preceding one. This represents a considerable broadening.

At this significant line ("Wirft sie einen Schatten?") Strauss simplified both the orchestral accompaniment and also the vocal line: the orchestra pulses on a single low note, doubling the nearly monotone setting of the verse line. The motive which is associated with the shadow occurs in the orchestra after the words have been sung. (See musical example #4 for the Shadow Motive)

103

TABLE OF ANALYSIS (continued)

Text	Visual Effects	Music
significant: it is delayed in that other less important lines by the same speaker precede it; it is couched in the simplest possible words and syntax. (For a discussion of the symbolic significance of the shadow see the discussion of the Empress in Chapter III.) There is a problem in staging a shadowless heroine. Although a diffuse lighting may help the imagination somewhat, the essence of the lack of the shadow must be carried by the words. This line must be comprehended if the audience is to understand the plot. The answer to this question ("Wirft sie einen Schatten?") is given once and then repeated twice: Keinen! Bei den gewaltgen Namen! Keinen! Keinen! (D III 150.) This repetition serves two purposes: audience comprehension and aesthetic intensification.		Strauss emphasized the significance of the words here by structuring the music so that the orchestra ebbs and flows in inverse ratio to the vocal line. After this information ("Keinen!") has been conveyed, the musical elements of the opera take precedence over the words for the Nurse's characterization of the Empress. The intensification of the answer "Keinen!" is achieved by the repetition of the melodic material on a pitch one-half step higher. This also provides a convenient modulation to B major and thence to the key of F# major, the key of the Nurse's characterization of the Empress and of Strauss's fairy-tale key.
Hofmannsthal emphasized the lack of the Empress' shadow by utilizing the words Licht and gläsern in the Nurse's description of her: Durch ihren Leib wandelt das Licht, als wäre sie gläsern. (D III 150.)	.	The lightness and airiness of the Empress' nature is portrayed by Strauss through the use of the very bright key of F# major and the use of a high register in the orchestra. The melodic motive of the Empress, the Empress Motive is used here for the first time. (See musical example #5.) Other means by which Strauss characterized the Empress were 1) a solo violin obligato above the Nurse's vocal line, 2) parallel thirds in the accompanying violins, and 3) a cantabile motive in a rising configuration.
The Nurse mentions the inclination of the Empress which led her to associate with people: Von der Mutter her war ihr ein Trieb übermächtig zu Menschen hin! (D III 150.)		Following the verse line which mentions people ("übermächtig zu Menschen hin"), Strauss introduced a new orchestral motive (the Dissension Motive) which probably can be said to represent the dissension typically found among people. It consists of an augmented fourth, a perfect fourth and a diminished fourth, all restlessly rising. (See musical example #6.) This motive, given a vehement reading, prefigures the later evidenced antipathy of the Nurse to people.

TABLE OF ANALYSIS (continued)

Text	Visual Effects	Music
As the Messenger and the Nurse cease speaking of the Empress in order to talk of the Emperor, the text is momentarily simplified: Amme: Konnt ich einem Vogel nach in die Luft? Sollt ich die Gazelle mit Händen halten? Bote: Lass mich sie sehn! Amme: Sie ist nicht allein: Er ist bei ihr. Die Nacht war nicht in zwölf Monden, dass er ihrer nicht hätte begehrt! (D III 151.) Following the use of a lyrical style in the characterization of the Empress, the sense-meaning of the words once again comes to the foreground with the lines: "Lass mich sie sehn! / Er ist bei ihr!" Significant structural aspects of these lines are: 1) the first use of the present tense since "Wirft sie einen Schatten?" 2) the monosyllabic lines; 3) the shift from characterization of the Empress to direct address. These changes constitute a movement from lyrical style to conversational style and back again. Hofmannsthal characterized the Emperor through the Nurse's words by means of his relationship to the Empress: Amme: Er ist ein Jäger und ein Verliebter, sonst ist er nichts! (D III 151.) Although the words must carry the action because there is nothing happening on stage to inform the audience, the relative importance of the words to music recedes in those sections of the opera which like this one serve characterization.		Strauss simplified the vocal line at "Lass mich sie sehn!" The orchestra, however, still plays the primary contabile line against which the vocalist sings a syllabic setting of the text. At the important introduction of the Emperor ("Er ist bei ihr!"), the vocal line is above the orchestra and the word "Er" is emphasized by means of its relatively longer duration. Apparently the composer intended to differentiate conversational text from lyrical text. Strauss characterized the Emperor, like the Empress, with a flowing cantabile motive. Also as with the Empress' characterization, the primary accompanimental instruments are the strings. An apparent indication of the dependence of the Emperor upon the Empress occurs with the intertwining of his motive, the Emperor as Lover Motive with her motive. (See musical example #7.) The irregular rhythms of the characterization, wherein both 3/4 and C occur, bring a sense of uneasiness into this lyrical passage, which is perhaps indicative of the fate which awaits the Emperor. The key for this characterization of the Emperor is E major, the erotic key for Strauss. Divergences from the F minor key center of the exchange between the Nurse and the Messenger are, therefore, up one-half step to F# major for the characterization of the Empress and down one-half step to E major for the characterization of the Emperor.

105

TABLE OF ANALYSIS (continued)

Text	Visual Effects	Music
The Messenger announces the fate which will descend upon both the Empress and the Emperor, if at the end of three days the Empress still does not throw a shadow: Bote: Zwölf lange Monde war sie sein! Jetzt hat er sie noch drei kurze Tage! Sind die vorbei:--- sie kehrt zurück in Vaters Arm. Amme: Und ich mit ihr! O gesegneter Tag! Doch er? Bote: Er wird zu Stein! Amme: Er wird zu Stein! (D III 151-52.) In the midst of a conversational passage where the greatest importance rests with the sense-meanings of the words, Hofmannsthal provides a line which is primarily a vehicle for the expression of emotion: "O gesegneter Tag!" This represents the introduction of a lyrical verse line into a passage which is generally conversational in style. The lines which follow this outburst (Amme: "Doch er?" Bote: "Er wird zu Stein!") are character-ized by simplicity of vocabulary and monosyllabicity. They must be comprehended if the audience is to follow the plot. The line "Er wird zu Stein!" is repeated once after its initial appearance, Hofmannsthal apparently desirous that this line should not escape the comprehension of the audience. The words must carry the action for this verse line; it is doubtful that any other lines in this exchange between the Nurse and the Messenger are more important to the ensuing action. The Emperor, like the Nurse, characterizes himself by means of his relationship to the Empress. Almost all of his entire monologue is one long reference to the Empress. The words serve primarily as an expression of his fervent love for her and are,	The Messenger departs; the Emperor, dressed in hunting clothes, makes his initial appearance as the orchestra plays the Stone Motive. Darkness begins to recede as morning nears.	The beginning of this part of the conversation ("Zwölf lange Monde / war sie sein!") contains a complex orchestral accompaniment which utilizes the Dissension Motive, the Shadow Motive, and the Emperor as Lover Motive. In contrast to the orchestral density, the Messenger's vocal line is quite simple with frequent repetition of notes. This simplicity, plus the relatively high baritone range and the long note values of the important words "drei" and "Tage", may overcome the complexity of the orchestral counterpoint. The accompaniment for the significant lines "Sind die vorbei: / sie kehrt zurück / in Vaters Arm" are free of this complexity; the orchestra either remains silent or plays a cadential formula. The joyous exclamation of the Nurse ("O gesegneter Tag,") is given full expression in both the vocal line and in the orchestra. Strauss then gradually reduced the intensity of the joyous feeling in order to give emphasis to the unaccompanied "Doch er?" The verse line "Er wird zu Stein!" is set with startling effect: Strauss used a tritone drop from C# to G. Since the passage begins in C# minor, the G minor orchestral chord which sets the word "Stein" represents an alien element and very effectively suggests a total change in the being of the Emperor. (See musical example #8 for the Stone Motive.) The Stone Motive is, therefore, a harmonic one as well as a melodic one. The two repetitions of this line are set identically each time, giving the audience three opportunities to comprehend the meaning of the words. (Notice that Strauss apparently repeated this line one time more than Hofmannsthal.) Long flowing lines characterize the Emperor, as do also sustained strings in the accompaniment. There are, moreover, irregular rhythms in the setting of the verse lines; for example, the word "heute" is given one entire measure, while the immediately following line of text

TABLE OF ANALYSIS (continued)

Text	Visual Effects	Music

therefore, not important—with the exception of the story of the hunt for the white gazelle, which gives significant background information. Hofmannsthal used monosyllabic lines in an attempt to make this story clear. They are interspersed throughout a much longer and more elaborate passage:
 	
Denn als sie [die Gazelle] mir floh
und war wie der Wind
und höhnte meiner—
und zusammenbrechen
wollte mein Ross—,
da flog er
der weissen Gazelle
zwischen die Lichter—,
und schlug mit den
    Schwingen
ihre sussen Augen!
Da sturzte sie hin
und ich auf sie
. . . .
da stieg Zorn in mir auf
gegen den Falken,
. . . .
Und in der Wut
warf ich den Dolch
gegen den Vogel
und streifte ihn,
und sein Blut tropfte nieder.— [Italics added
    to emphasize the monosyllabic lines.]
 	
(D III 153-54.)
 	
The audience is here given a more detailed version of the story of the hunt of the white gazelle than that which was first told by the Nurse. Comprehension of this story is necessary because it tells how the Empress and the Emperor met each other and lays the groundwork for the curse upon the Emperor. Enmeshed within the story of the white gazelle is the tale of the Red Falcon; an understanding of the role of the Falcon is as important as an understanding of the role of the white gazelle, inasmuch as the Falcon assumes the part of a protagonist. (See the discussion of the Emperor in Chapter III.) The dense interweaving of persons and things which is exemplified by the story of the white gazelle is typical of the entire tale, for Hofmannsthal created a story in which every being and thing relates to every other being and thing.
 	
Hofmannsthal structured the Emperor's speech so that there is movement away from the purely conversational
	As the Emperor sings, servants gather to listen.	"streif ich bis an die" is compressed into one measure. This gives the characterization a sense of restlessness; throughout the aria this quality is maintained. The key center is E♭ major, with one extended divergence to E major, Strauss's erotic key.
		The story of the hunt of the white gazelle is set to a somewhat elaborate accompaniment which is contrapuntal in nature. The more significant parts of the story are set to pianissimo markings in the accompaniment, but the vocal line is still covered and it is doubtful if the words can be understood. For example, the orchestra doubles the beginning of the important line "Wollte Gott, dass ich heute/meinen roten Falken wiederfände," but when the falcon is mentioned the striking Falcon Cry Motive is introduced. (See musical example #9.) This motive probably covers the word "wiederfände".
		
		Some of the accompaniment may, however, allow comprehension. Orchestral doubling occurs on the verse line "Da flog er/der weissen Gazelle/zwischen die Lichter." The following lines are unaccompanied: "ihre süssen Augen"; "da stürzte sie hin"; "da riss sich's in Angst—"; "meinen Armen rankte ein Weib." On the whole, the audience probably will not be able to comprehend enough of the words to follow the plot without the aid of either a summary of the plot or a copy of the libretto.
		
		In agreement with the Nurse's characterization of the Emperor as a "hunter and lover" Strauss used two primary motives for the Emperor. The first, the Emperor as Lover Motive (#7), with its easy expansion into the Empress Motive seems to exemplify him as a lover. The second, with its use of the perfect fourth in a hunting call apparently refers to the Emperor as Hunter. (Example #10.) Strauss used the harmonic Stone Motive to set two different ideas in the Emperor's aria: 1) "Wollte Gott, dass ich heute / meinen roten Falken wiederfände"; 2) "der mir damals / meine Liebste fing". This close association between Emperor and his fate, the Empress, and the Falcon is an excellent example of the interrelatedness through music which Hofmannsthal sought to achieve. (See Chapter II.)
		
		Strauss followed the general outline of the Emperor's speech which Hofmannsthal gave to him. The vocal lines

Text	Visual Effects	Music

"Amme, wachst du?" of the beginning to a lyrical passage recounting past events. This is broken by another short conversational passage:
 	
  Amme: Herr, wenn du anstellst
      ein solches Jagen--
      leicht bleibst du dann fern übernacht?
  Kaiser: Kann sein drei Tage
      komm ich nicht heim!
        (D III 154.)
 	
The lyrical element then comes to the fore again, this time with a love song addressed to the absent Empress. This second section of the speech, in contrast to the first, is in the present and future tenses, bringing the focus back to the current happenings on stage and away from past events.
 	
Hofmannsthal employed two obvious structural techniques in the final section of the Emperor's aria. First, there is a four-fold repetition of grammatical structure which builds intensity both through the repetition and also because each repetition delays yet once more the expected subject of the sentence. Second, he wrote a ritardando into the final lines by decreasing the number of syllables used in the last two lines:
 	
  Denn meiner Seele
    und meinen Augen
    und meinen Händen
    und meinen Herzen
    ist sie die Beute
    aller Beuten
    ohn' Ende!
    (D III 154-55.)
	The Emperor exits. Although there are no explicit stage directions to this effect, it is appropriate that upon his	dominate in the conversational passages while the orchestral lines tend to dominate in the lyrical ones.
		
		Generally speaking, Strauss utilized the structural devices as they seem to have been intended: the climax of the musical passage is delayed until the end of the aria and a lessening of momentum occurs once the climax is reached.
		
		Strauss gave the Emperor's aria a feeling of musical completion and of independence from the rest of the opera by alluding to and developing both the Hunter Motive and the themes which seem intended to suggest the love of the Emperor and the Empress for each other. These Love Themes #1 and #2 first occur in the orchestra following the lines "und in meinen Armen / rankte ein Weib!--" (See musical example #11.) They provide the musical material for the close of the Emperor's aria and also for the short orchestral interlude which accompanies his exit.
		
		As the Emperor leaves the stage, the orchestra is dominated by themes associated with his love for the Empress. These melodic ideas are shortly super-seded by the Stone Motive, thereby characterizing

TABLE OF ANALYSIS (continued)

Text	Visual Effects	Music
	departure the Nurse cast aside her servile demeanor and gloat with pleasure at the thought of his turning to stone.	the Nurse's true feelings toward the Emperor.
The Nurse orders the servants to leave: Fort mit euch! Ich höre die Herrin! Ihr Blick darf euch nicht sehn! (D III 155.) These lines are obviously conversational in style.	After the Emperor's exit, the Nurse usurps his role and orders the servants who have gathered to leave for she hears the Empress. The Empress is thus effectively identified before she appears.	The Nurse is accompanied by a tremolo in the string section and bird calls in the woodwinds which suggest the approach of dawn. Underlying the bird calls is a melodic motive which is associated with the Emperor but which is later used to set the Empress' words "O, dass ich mich nimmer verwandeln kann!" (D III 155.) This motive is an inversion of the Emperor as Lover Motive. This tracing to the Emperor of the Empress' inability to grow or change is an example of Strauss' realization of those possibilities for inter-relation-ship which are inherent within a musical work.
The opening lines which Hofmannsthal wrote for the Empress emphasize the lack of relationship to others which characterizes her entire being. She will dream—a person who dreams avoids the world and its necessary interaction with others. She wants to transform herself—a being without definite shape cannot relate to other persons and things. (See the discussion of the Empress in Chapter III for a more detailed discussion of her character.) This initial speech characterizes the Empress primarily by means of lyrical verse lines. Only a few lines are conversational in style, such as those announcing the arrival of the Red Falcon: Ist mein Liebster dahin? Was weckst du mich so früh? Lass mich noch liegen! Vielleicht träum ich mich zurück In eines Vogels leichten Leib oder einer jungen weissen Gazelle! Oh, dass ich mich nimmer verwandeln kann! (D III 154.)	The Empress appears and dawn brightens the sky.	Strauss emphasized brightness and lightness in his characterization of the Empress by using 1) a high tessitura for the vocal line, 2) a high solo violin obligato line, 3) an accompaniment which is set without employment of the lower range, and 4) the very bright key of F# major, his fairy-tale key.
During the course of the Empress' aria Hofmannsthal repeats the line from the Emperor's aria which stresses the strong erotic attachment of each for the other: "in der Trunkenheit der ersten Stunde". (D III 155.)		Strauss did not utilize this opportunity to repeat the melodic line which sets this line of text in the Emperor's aria. This does not mean that he neglected to relate the two principals to each other; he used 1) the cantabile Love Theme #1, which was introduced in connection with the Emperor, to set the Empress' line "oder einer jungen/weissen Gazelle" (D III 155) and 2) an inversion of the Emperor as Lover Motive to set several of the Empress' lines.

Text	Visual Effects	Music
Hofmannsthal was apparently eager that the idea of the Empress' ability to transform herself be understood by the audience. This idea occurs at three different places in the monologue: 1) "Vielleicht träum' ich / mich zurück / in eines Vogels leichten Leib"; 2) "Oh, dass ich nimmer verwandeln kann!"; 3) "Oh, dass ich den Talisman verlieren musste".		This particular aspect of the Empress' personality—her ability to transform herself—receives attention by means of a vocal line and an instrumental accompaniment which intimates something of the beings into which the Empress desires to change herself. Strauss seemed mainly interested, however, in giving an overall impression of the Empress. That aspect of her which is her most salient characteristic—her lack of a shadow, her lightness and airiness—is the one which he emphasized. This he accomplished by means of those techniques listed on page 137.
Hofmannsthal has carefully constructed the Empress' speech in order to give maximum impact to the appearance of the Falcon and to his prophecy. An emotional intensity is imparted by the broken lines: Und wäre so gern das flüchtige Wild, das seine Falken schlagen—Sieh!— da droben, sieh!— Da hat sich einer von seinen Falken— sieh—verflogen! Oh, sich doch hin, der rote Falke, der einst mich mit seinen Schwingen— ja, er ists! O Tag der Freude für meinen Liebsten und für mich! Unser Falke, unser Freund! Sei mir gegrüsst, schöner Vogel, kühner Jäger! Er hat uns vergeben, er kehrt uns zurück. Oh, sieh hin, er bäumt auf! (D III 155-56.) A change from a lyrical to a conversational style is apparent with the first use of the word "sieh!" The use of enjambment ("der einst mich / mit seinen Schwingen—") and parallel grammatical structure ("Unser Falke / unser Freund!")	The appearance of the Falcon is customarily represented on the stage by a light which intermittently brightens and dims.	Strauss emphasized the change from what might be termed lyrical characterization of the Empress to action precipitating a crisis by a sudden key change at "sieh! / da droben" from C# minor to G major. He returned to a more melodic style at "der rote Falke"; here the cantabile Love Theme #1 re-enters. This more melodious type of vocal line reverts to a more word-oriented type of setting at "Oh, sieh hin, er bäumt auf!" (D III 156.) The composer also made allowance for the change of purpose indicated here in the text by the shift from a lyrical style to a conversational style by simplifying the accompaniment for the line "Da hat sich einer / von seinen Falken—". There is a shift from G major to G minor as the Empress sings of the Falcon's tears. This key is maintained throughout the Falcon's prophecy and the subsequent Talisman section. Strauss introduced several new melodic or harmonic motives into this aria. One characterizes the magic of the Talisman—the Talisman Motive. (See musical example #12.) Another is a drooping motive which sets the word "Tränen"—the Tears Motive. (See musical example #13.) The melodic upward sweep of musical example #14 becomes here associated with the Falcon—the Falcon Motive. The Hunter Motive, which first occurred in the Emperor's aria, also occurs here. Incorporated from the Emperor's aria is the melodic line which sets the Emperor's line "und sein Blut tropfte nieder". (D III 154.) It occurs in the orchestra as the Empress sings "von seinem Fittich / tropft ja Blut". (D III 156.) Strauss gave Hofmannsthal's delay of the speech of the Falcon an added emphasis by relatively slowing down the momentum of the music just prior to the prophecy. He also ritards the action by inserting a short orchestral passage which employs

TABLE OF ANALYSIS (continued)

Text	Visual Effects	Music

indicate a reversion to lyrical style. The mono-syllabicity and simplicity of "Oh, sieh hin / er bäumt auf!" signal a conversational style once again. The report by the Empress of the Falcon's return, of his settling into the tree, of his bleeding, and of his crying delays and intensifies the Falcon's speech when it finally occurs.
 	
The verse lines of the Falcon are identical rhythmically:
 	
Wie soll ich denn nicht
  weinen?
Wie soll ich denn nicht
  weinen?
Die Frau wirft keinen
  Schatten,
  der Kaiser muss versteinen!
    (D III 156-57.)
 	
It is absolutely essential that the prophecy of the Falcon be understood if the plot is to be followed.
 	
The introspective, sad mood established by the Falcon's prophecy continues as the Empress reacts to the words of the Falcon; she reflects upon the pro-phecy and recalls that she knew it once for it was engraved upon her Talisman. The gloom deepens as the Nurse, the Falcon, and the Empress reiterate various lines of the prophecy:
 	
Kaiserin: Dem Talisman,
den ich verlor
in der Trunkenheit der ersten Stunde,
ihm war ein Fluch
eingegraben--
gelesen einst,
vergessen, ach!
Nun kam es wieder:--
Des Falken Stimme: Die Frau wirft keinen Schatten,
der Kaiser muss versteinen!
Wie soll ich denn nicht weinen?
Amme: Die Frau wirft keinen Schatten!
Kaiserin: Der Kaiser muss versteinen!
    (D III 156.)
		the Falcon Cry Motive before the singing of the prophecy.
		
		Strauss seized upon the uniform rhythm provided him by Hofmannsthal and set the first three lines of the prophecy identically, not only rhythmically but also melodically. The setting of the fourth line is similar to the preceding three, but added emphasis is given to the word "Kaiser" by means of a lengthened note value and a one-half step rise in pitch. An extraordinary effect is achieved in the vocal setting of the first three lines where 1) each syllable is set on the same pitch--except for the penultimate one in each line; 2) each note except for the last is preceded by a grace note; 3) the penultimate note is raised one-half step and lengthened. The accompaniment consists of soft strings with the characteristic Falcon Cry Motive in the woodwinds. The words will be compre-hended if the dynamic marking of pianissimo for the accompaniment is strictly observed and if the singer's diction is good.
		
		Strauss employed the Talisman Motive as the principle melodic material for his setting of the Empress' reflection upon the curse. (This section of the aria is henceforth referred to as the Talisman section.) The quietness of the motive is appropriate to the sense-meanings of the words which are set here. Strauss repeated for the various lines of the prophecy the same melodic and harmonic settings with which the lines first occurred. Momentum is very slow in this section, establishing congruence between the text and the music. Tension is contained in the final chord which is a widely spaced tone cluster of C, C#, D. Eb; this adds a sense of foreboding to the close of the Talisman section.

111

Text	Visual Effects	Music
Hofmannsthal apparently intended these particular verses to convey a point of quiet repose before the emotional outbursts and dramatic conflicts of the remainder of the scene. The introspective reminiscence of the Empress and her companions is broken by this outburst from the Empress: Amme, um alles, wo find ich den Schatten? (D III 157.) The verse "wo find' ich den Schatten" must be considered one of the more significant lines in this particular scene because it demonstrates resolution on the part of the Empress, a characteristic which she has not previously exhibited.		The change from lyrical introspection to emotional outbreak is accomplished by 1) a sudden shift in register—the Empress' vocal line moves from a low soprano register to a high one, 2) a sudden quickening of tempo, and 3) a key change to Bb minor. The verse lines are also compressed into relatively short time units; the final line of the introspective Talisman section spans approximately three measures of 4/4 time in a slow tempo while the first line of the emotional outburst is compressed into only one measure of a rapid 6/8 (2/4) meter. The verse line "wo find' ich den Schatten?" is set to a variation of the Shadow Motive. The line achieves a climax on a high Bb, giving it great dramatic impact. Strauss left the line unaccompanied, so it may possibly be understood. Unfortunately, the high dramatic interest which finds expression in the high register and the rapid tempo may interfere.
Demonstrating her character, the Nurse avoids giving the Empress a direct answer and enlarges upon the nature of the pact which was made when the Emperor and the Empress married: Er hat sich vermessen, dass er dich mache zu seinesgleichen— eine Frist ward gesetzt, dass er es vollbringe. Deines Herzens Knoten hat er dir nicht gelöst, ein Ungebornes trägt du nicht im Schoss, Schatten wirfst du keinen. Des zahlt er den Preis! (D III 157-58.) This speech culminates in the last two lines where a shift from a lyrical style to a conversational style is evident, especially in the monosyllabicity of the last line. Here for the first time there is mention of the Unborn Children, who serve as symbols of the attaining of humanity on the part of the Empress. (See the discussion of the Empress in Chapter III for a more detailed analysis.)		Strauss attempted to make the words of the Nurse comprehensible by using an orchestral accompaniment which ebbs and flows in inverse relationship to the vocal line; while the Nurse sings, a low, quiet tremolo sounds in the strings, and when she is silent, the orchestra sounds various motives at the forte and fortissimo levels. The motives which are used are the Nurse Motive, the Shadow Motive, and the Keikobad Motive. The Nurse's vocal line exhibits a gradual upward tendency: the high point of the first line is C, of the second C#, of the third D, of the fourth E#, of the fifth Bb, and of the sixth F. The final line begins at the high point and descends, reversing the pattern of the previous lines, but it does contain the highest note—G—of this particular solo of the Nurse. This ascending, culminating type of structure emphasizes the verse line "des zahlt er den Preis!" which is set to the Stone Motive.

TABLE OF ANALYSIS (continued)

Text	Visual Effects	Music

The Empress refuses to be satisfied with the devious answer of the Nurse, stating:
 	
   Doch stärker als andre
   noch bin ich!
       (D III 158.)
 	
With these lines, which form part of a longer speech, the Empress' courage begins to surface. This is the first evidence of this characteristic.
		While there is a great deal of orchestral motion (sixteenths in the strings) and noise (forte and fortissimo) throughout the passage which encompasses both the Nurse's solo ("Er hat sich vermessen") and the Empress' reply, Strauss silenced the orchestra for these verse lines. A striking modulation from Ab minor to E major further emphasizes them.

		Following the Empress' answer ("Weh, mein Vater!" to "noch bin ich") to the Nurse's recounting of the marriage contract, the two sing a short duet, the Empress imploring the Nurse to help her and the Nurse trying to avoid giving her consent to help. The words are unavoidably lost, but audience comprehension will not suffer because nothing new takes place.

The Empress senses that the Nurse's resistance to the proposed task is weakening and in unmistakable words orders the Nurse to do her will:
 	
   zeig mir den Weg,
   und geh ihn mit mir!
       (D III 159.)
 	
The monosyllabicity and simplicity of the language in these verses are an indication of the importance with which Hofmannsthal regarded them.
		Strauss apparently did not place as much importance upon these lines as Hofmannsthal did. At least, the lines are not unaccompanied. He did, however, momentarily interrupt the duet by silencing the Nurse.

The Nurse responds to the Empress with a tirade against mankind about which there is some question as to the order of the lines of the text. It appears in the Steiner edition as follows:
 	
   Bei den Menschen!
   Grausts dich nicht?
   Menschendunst
   ist uns
5 Todesluft.
   Dies Haus, getürmt
   den Sternen entgegen,
   emporgetrieben spielende Wasser
   buhlend um Reinheit
10 Uns riecht ihre Reinheit
   nach rostigem Eisen
   und gestocktem Blut
   und nach alten Leichen!
15 Und nun von hier
   noch tiefer hinab!
       (D III 159.)
 	
Verse lines 6-10 are reversed with lines 11-14 in the
		Strauss imparted a frightening effect to the verse line "Bei den Menschen" by suddenly shifting keys from E major to D minor, the key center for the rest of this scene and also for the orchestral interlude between the two scenes of the first act. The entire passage contains the three different motives which Strauss consistently used to depict mankind in the opera. The first, the Dissension Motive (#6), was initially employed in the exchange between the Nurse and the Messenger. It seems admirably suited to portray inconsistency (no fourth sets the pattern for another), vacillation (no tonal center can be discerned), and perhaps aggression (it is blared out by the brass section). The second, the Traitor Motive, consists of a chromatic pattern and is ultimately set to the Nurse's words "Ein Verräter Wind schleicht sich heran". (D III 160.) (See musical example #15.) The third, the Beating Motive, receives its most characteristic use in the second scene of the first act where it appears to depict the rhythmic beating of one brother by another. (See musical example #16.) One other motive which occurs here is the Descent to Mankind

113

TABLE OF ANALYSIS (continued)

Text	Visual Effects	Music
score. The speech as a whole is primarily lyrical in style.		Motive. (See musical example #17.) The three motives relating to people and the Descent Motive are employed primarily in the orchestra which tends to overpower the vocal line here.

As the Nurse continues her tirade against mankind, intensification follows intensification until a climax is reached with "ihnen dienen!"
 	
    Dich ihnen vermischen,
    hausen mit ihnen,
    handeln mit ihnen,
    Rede um Rede,
    Atem um Atem,
    erspähn ihr Belieben,
    ihrer Bosheit dich schmiegen,
    ihrer Dummheit dich bücken,
    ihnen dienen!
    Grausts dich nicht?
              (D III 159-60.)
 	
The style is lyrical until the final line is reached.
		Strauss followed Hofmannsthal's structural pattern here. Generally speaking, the melody ascends in pitch; the verse "ihnen dienen" is unaccompanied, as well as being the one which is highest in pitch, so that full attention is focused on the vocal part.

The Nurse's second attempt to dissuade the Empress is unsuccessful, for the Empress reiterates her desire to obtain the shadow:
 	
    Ich will den Schatten!
    Ein Tag bricht an!
    Führ mich zu ihnen:
    ich will!
              (D III 160.)
 	
Of significance in this speech are: 1) only two words are not monosyllabic; 2) the emphasis lies on the word "will" (want, intend). The Empress is no longer a dreamer.
	The first direct rays of light brighten the stage.	The Empress' first line "Ich will den Schatten!" contains a variation on the Shadow Motive. Another variation on this motive also occurs in the orchestra. Strauss attempted to make the verse line comprehensible by placing the accompaniment in a low register. (This is in direct contrast to the immediately preceding passage ["Bei den Menschen!"] where the orchestra provides counterpoint to the Nurse's vocal line, much of which is higher than the Nurse's line.) Strauss gave the line "Ein Tag bricht an!" significance by 1) leaving it unaccompanied and 2) introducing a new motive, the New Day Motive, here. (See musical example #18.) This motive merges with Love Theme #1 in the orchestra, giving the audience an insight into the reason for the Empress' strong resolution: she loves the Emperor.

The Nurse attempts for a third time to dissuade the Empress, fully disclosing her hatred and contempt for mankind. Hofmannsthal accomplished this by having the Nurse take up the Empress' line "Ein Tag bricht an!" and distort the meaning so that the glorious dawn becomes associated with the shadow, the dark side of man:
 	
    Ein Tag bricht an
    ein Menschentag.
    Witterst du ihn?
    Schauderts dich schon?
		Although Strauss began setting these verse lines in a vein which is similar to the Empress' setting, even using the love theme for a short while, he shortly had the Nurse drop all pretense and launched her into a parody of the Empress' melody. Blaring brass underline her solo, so that the new day is given the quality of a nightmare.

114

TABLE OF ANALYSIS (continued)

Text	Visual Effects	Music
Das ist ihre Sonne! der werfen sie Schatten! (D III 160.) (For a fuller discussion of the shadow, see the section on the Empress in Chapter III.) As the Nurse continues her tirade against mankind, the demonic element of her personality becomes more and more evident: Diebesseelen sind ihre Seelen— so verkauf ich einen dem andern! Eine Gaunerin bin ich unter Gaunern, Muhme nennen sie mich und Mutter gar! Ziehsöhne hab ich und Ziehtöchter viel, hocken wie Ungeziefer auf mir! Warte, du sollst was sehn! (D III 161.) These lines of the Empress, along with part of the Nurse's preceding speech, are frequently omitted in performance: Weh, was fasst mich gässlich an! Zu welchem Geschick reisst mich hinab? (D III 162.) (Hofmannsthal's concept of fate is discussed in the section on the Empress in Chapter III.) The Empress replies to the Nurse's question as to whether or not she is afraid: Mich schaudert freilich, aber ein Mut ist in mir, der heisst mich tun, wovor mich schaudert! (D III 162.) (See the discussion of the Empress in Chapter III for insights into Hofmannsthal's concept of "Mut".) Faced with such determination on the part of the		While the Nurse sings her condemnation of mankind, the Empress reiterates the Falcon's prophecy. The singing on the part of the Empress of the Falcon's prophecy is apparently Strauss's idea alone; it does not appear in the Steiner edition. The complexity of the score in combination with the duet makes any comprehension of words very unlikely. At this point Strauss's main goal seems to have been to write an effective end to the scene rather than to give the words an opportunity to be understood. Strauss has interrelated the characters by tying the Empress' fate ("Geschick") both to Keikobad and also to the Emperor by means of the Stone Motive and the Keikobad Motive. Hofmannsthal's concept of fate is thereby expressed in the music. (See Chapter III.) The cut which is frequently made here is apparently a customary one, for it occurs in both of the recordings which have been made of the opera (Deutsche Grammophon 2711005; Richmond 64503). Considering the length of the opera, the lack of forward action at this point, and the slight, but obvious flagging of musical inspiration occurring here, this is probably a justifiable decision. Strauss related the Empress' courage to her concern for the Emperor by setting the words "Mut ist in mir" to the Stone Motive.

115

TABLE OF ANALYSIS (continued)

Text	Visual Effects	Music
Empress, the Nurse consents to help her obtain a shadow. The Empress and the Nurse conclude the scene with speeches in which each expresses part of her inner being. The Empress shows a newly found concern for someone other than herself and the Nurse exhibits a delight in deceiving mankind: Kaiserin: Und kein Geschäfte ausser diesem, das wert mir schiene besorgt zu werden! Hinab mit uns! Amme: Hinab denn mit uns! Die Geleiterin hast du dir gut gewählt, Töchterchen, liebes, warte nur, warte! Um ihre Dächer versteh ich zu flattern, durch den Rauchfang weiss ich den Weg, und ihrer Herzen verschlungene Pfade, Krümmen und Schlüfte, die kenne ich gut. The musical interludes which serve as bridges between the scene of the opera were planned by Hofmannsthal early in the conception of the opera: "--die Übergänge von einer Welt in die andere, siebenmal, erfüllen mich mit einer Art Neid auf den Komponisten, der sie ausfüllen darf, wo ich sie leer lassen, nur das Jenseits und Diesseits in ihnen in der Idee geniessen darf." (Briefwechsel, Hofmannsthal to Strauss, 20. I. 1913.)	Full daylight first occurs with the Empress' utterance of the decisive "Hinab denn mit uns!" (See the discussion of the Empress in Chapter III for Hofmannsthal's views on moonlight and daylight.)	Strauss set these lines as a duet. This ensemble is not specified in the Steiner edition, but nothing in the text suggests that this is contrary to Hofmannsthal's wishes. The composer did, however, apparently find the Empress' lines too few for the duet, for he added one line from the Falcon's prophecy, "Der Kaiser muss versteinen," and repeated parts of "Hinab denn mit uns!" three different times. A musical interlude provides the bridge between the world where the Empress has been isolated in a castle and the world where ordinary people live. As the interlude begins, the orchestra utilizes primarily the New Day Motive in combination with the Love Theme #1. Added later are the Dissension Motive, the Beating Motive, the Traitor Motive, the Descent Motive, the Stone Motive, and the Keikobad Motive. This change in the motives which are employed signifies a movement away from a cantabile melody to a fairly dissonant harmony. Strauss called upon the resources of the full orchestra, particularly using the percussion instruments, which had previously been silent, to portray the confusion, the noise, and the brutality of man's world. This is in great contrast to his use of the orchestra throughout the immediately preceding scene where the orchestra was used almost like a chamber orchestra.

TABLE OF ANALYSIS (continued)

Text	Visual Effects	Music
	Act I Scene ii	The key of the immediately preceding orchestral interlude and of the fighting at the beginning of Act I Scene ii is B♭ minor, the key of the Shadow Motive when it first appeared in Act I Scene i. A variation on this motive occurs repeatedly throughout this section. Strauss also employed a new motive in this passage, the Activity Motive. (See musical example #19.) Another motive, the first to be exclusively associated with the Wife occurs after the Hunchback finishes the line "bist doch unserm Bruder mit Lust zu Willen!" (D III 164.) It might best be termed the Irritability Motive. (See musical example #20.)
	The curtain rises on the interior of a poor home which also serves as a workshop for a dyer. The Three Brothers are fighting and calling each other names. The Wife throws a bucket of water upon them and they respond by ridiculing her.	
The opening verse lines of the second scene of Act I appear to have been designed as gestures; that is, they are not significant lines as far as understanding the plot is concerned. Instead, they express verbally through name-calling the physical fight which is occurring. This opening scene depicts one of the more ugly facets of men--in apparent fulfillment of the Nurse's characterization which occurred at the end of the first scene.		
Hofmannsthal differentiated between the palace world and the world of common men by means of his verse. The inhabitants of the palace in Scene i used a two-beat line when they spoke: Amme: Licht überm See-- ein fliessender Glanz-- schnell wie ein Vogel!-- Die Wipfel der Nacht von oben erhellt-- eine Feuerhand will fassen nach mir-- bist du es, Herr? (D III 149.) The poet utilized a four-beat line and a different vocabulary when he wrote lines for the inhabitants of the common world: Der Einäugige: Willst du uns schmähen, Hergelaufene! Du Tochter von Bettlern, wer bist denn du? (D III 164.)		Like Hofmannsthal, Strauss distinguished between the palace world and the world of men. Mellifluous melodic lines abound in Act I Scene i; on the other hand, Act I Scene ii is marked by a lack of melody except in the characterization of Barak. Strauss also employed a lighter orchestration for Act Ii, adding percussion and brass for Act Iii.

117

Text	Visual Effects	Music

The opening of Act I ii, the beating section, serves as a prelude to this important exchange between Barak and the Wife:
 	
   Frau: Sie aus dem Hause,
   und das für immer,
   oder ich.
   Daran will ich erkennen,
   was ich dir wer bin.
   Barak: Hier steht die Schüssel,
   aus der sie sich stillen.
   Wo sollten sie herbergen,
   wenn nicht in Vaters Haus?
     (D III 165.)
 	
In this conversation Hofmannsthal delineated the relationship between Barak and the Wife. The Wife does not feel valued by Barak; he shows more concern for children than he does for her.
 	
Barak's love for children is expressed in a short passage in a lyrical style:
 	
   Gib du mir Kinder, dass sie mir hocken
   um die Schüsseln zu Abend,
   es soll mir keines hungrig aufstehn.
   Und ich will preisen ihre Begierde
   und danksagen im Herzen,
	Barak enters as the Three Brothers are taunting the Wife and sends the tormenters outside.
	
	Barak works to the accompaniment of a short orchestral interlude.
		Strauss characterized Barak initially in a short orchestral interlude, employing a melody reminiscent of a folk-tune in its simplicity and steady rhythm. (See the Work Motice, #21.) The contrast in this scene between the number of melodies associated with Barak—five motives and one short song—and the number associated with the Wife—one—demonstrates both the difficulty Strauss had in characterizing the Wife and also the affinity he felt for Barak. (Briefwechsel, Strauss to Hofmannsthal, 16. VII. 1914.) The key center is F minor, the most frequently appearing key in the opera.
		
		Strauss set these significant lines in two different ways. The first four lines of the Wife's speech he treated as conversation; they are largely unaccompanied and rapidly paced. To the Wife's last line ("was/ich dir wert bin") and to Barak's speech he gave a more lyrical setting in a slower rhythm. This lyrical setting of the text has a simple orchestral accompaniment, consisting primarily of a doubling of the vocal line.
		
		The motive associated with children, the Children Motive, makes its first appearance as Barak remembers the Three Brothers as children. (See musical example #22.)
		
		Strauss followed Hofmannsthal's stylistic divisions here, giving the first part of the speech a primarily lyrical setting and setting the last two lines in a style where the words carry greater significance; here the accompaniment consists of two soft chords and the vocal line is melodically and rhythmically simple. The simplicity with which Strauss set these

Text	Visual Effects	Music
dass ich bestellt ward, damit ich sie stille. Wann gibst du mir die Kinder dazu? (D III 166.) This speech attains a climax with the words "Und ich will preisen ihre Begierde / und danksagen im Herzen." Thereafter, a ritardando is written into the lines "dass ich bestellt ward, / damit ich sie stille" where the syllable count drops to five and six per line from the previous average of slightly less than nine. A shift in style--from lyrical to conversational--is apparent in the last two lines. The Wife responds to Barak's touch with an emotional torrent of words expressing irritation. The breathlessness, the many syllables with relatively few accents suggest that this is an emotional outburst and that comprehension of the words is not the primary goal here: Frau: Mein Mann steht vor mit! Ei ja, mein Mann, ich weiss, ei ja, ich weiss, was das heisst! Bin bezahlt und gekauft, es zu wissen, und gehalten im Haus und gehegt und gefüttert, damit ich es weiss, und will es von heut ab nicht wissen, vorschwöre das Wort und das Ding! (D III 166-67.) Barak expresses joy at the thought that the Wife might be pregnant, while she denies that his superstitious activities have had any effect on her: Barak: Heia! Die guten Gevatterinnen, haben sie nicht die schönen Sprüche gesprochen über deinen Leib, und ich hab siebenmal gegessen von dem, was sie gesegnet hatten, und wenn du seltsam bist und anders als sonst--- ich preise die Seltsamkeit und neige mich zur Erde vor der Verwandlung! O Glück über mir und Erwartung und Freude im Herzen!	Barak touches the Wife gently, but she impatiently shakes his hand away.	lines makes it likely that the audience will comprehend the words, although the gestures on stage will probably convey a truer picture of the relationship between Barak and the Wife than either the words or the music. (See musical example #23, Barak's Desire for Children Motive.) Strauss set the Wife's tirade at a rapid pace and with an accompaniment which will probably cover the lines. The Wife's cantankerous nature is, however, portrayed in the angular movement of the melodic lines. Strauss combined these two speeches into a duet. (It is impossible to know from the Steiner edition whether Hofmannsthal planned a duet here or not. The thoughts expressed in both speeches, however, suggest that he did intend for Strauss to write an ensemble here.) The audience will probably be confused by Barak's joyful response to the Wife's bad temper; the duet covers the words with the result that they will be unlikely to comprehend that Barak interprets her foul mood as a sign of pregnancy. Strauss ended the duet just prior to the line "ich preise die Seltsamkeit", focusing attention thereby upon Barak's joy at his approaching fatherhood. The solo attains a climax with the final line "und Freude im Herzen!" by means of the high range of the vocal line and by a modulation to the key of

TABLE OF ANALYSIS (continued)

Text	Visual Effects	Music
Frau: Triefäugige Weiber, die Sprüche murmeln, haben nichts zu schaffen mit meinem Leib, und was du gegessen hast vor Nacht, hat keine Gewalt über meine Seele. (D III 167.) Barak's speech moves gradually from a long line of ten syllables to one of six. A slower tempo is implied by this drop in the number of syllables. Intensification occurs in the last three lines; "und Freude im Herzen" receives the heaviest accent because of the repetitive nature of the preceding two lines.		D major. This key serves as the key center for the succeeding section of dialogue between Barak and the Wife. The closing section of Barak's solo contains two new motives: 1) the Happiness Motive (see musical example #24); 2) the Joy Motive (see musical example #25).
	Barak kneels to work again.	Strauss's apparent great interest in the figure of Barak led him to insert another orchestral interlude here which serves primarily to characterize the Dyer. The Joy Motive, one of the motives with which Barak ended his solo, provides the principal melodic material.
The Wife exhibits a more gentle side of her personality in this speech where she states her sorrow at not having any children: Dritthalb Jahr bin ich dein Weib-- und du hast keine Frucht gewonnen aus mir und mich nicht gemacht zu einer Mutter. Gelüsten danach hab ich abtun müssen von meiner Seele: Nun ist es an dir, abzutun Gelüste, die dir lieb sind. (D III 167-68.) This speech contrasts with her previous ones; here the lines are shorter and the sense-meanings more direct. Loquacity being a result of her evasion of interpersonal relationships, these lines represent an attempt to bridge the gap between herself and Barak.		Strauss completely changed the manner in which he had been setting the Wife's verse lines. Previously he had employed a rapid pace and utilized wide leaps; he set these lines in very nearly a monotone and at a very slow tempo.
Barak's reply to the Wife serves more as a vehicle to display a conciliatory manner toward the Wife than as a means to communicate important information either to her or to the audience: Aus einem jungen Mund gehen harte Worte und trotzige Reden,		Strauss gave Barak a melody to sing--in contrast to the Wife's near monotone--and surrounded it with an accompaniment of lush string sound. A new motive is introduced, the Blessedness Motive. (See musical example #26.) This motive is utilized to give emphasis to the word "gesegnet."

120

Text	Visual Effects	Music
aber sie sind gesegnet mit dem Segen der Widerruflichkeit. Ich zürne dir nicht und bin freudigen Herzens und ich harre und erwarte die Gepriessenen, die da kommen. (D III 168.) In spite of the lack of significance of these lines--as far as conveying information is concerned--these lines contain what are probably the two most beautiful lines in the entire opera: "aber sie [trotzige Reden] sind gesegnet / mit dem Segen der Widerruflichkeit."		Strauss set all of these lines except for the last two with a contrapuntal accompaniment, so they probably will not be understood. The setting of the last two lines, again in nearly a monotone, was apparently suggested to Strauss by the immediately preceding stage note by Hofmannsthal: "fast tonlos". Perhaps this note also influenced Strauss in the setting which he wrote for the immediately preceding speech of the Wife. The quiet point of the entire opera is reached in the last two lines of this speech, quiet in the sense that there is almost no movement or sound in either the accompaniment or the vocal line.
The Wife states again that there are not going to be any children; that someone is more likely to leave than that someone might come: Es kommen keine in dieses Haus, viel eher werden welche hinausgehn und schütteln den Staub von ihren Sohlen. Also geschehe es, lieber heute als morgen. (D III 168-69.) These lines add nothing that the audience has not already learned and serve, therefore, primarily to characterize the Wife.	Barak packs to go to market.	Movement gradually picks up in the orchestral interlude which follows the Wife's monotone song and leads directly to Barak's Market Song.
Hofmannsthal stressed Barak's roots among the common folk by giving him a proverb to say: Trag ich die Ware mir selber zu Markt, spar ich den Esel, der sie mir schleppt! (D III 169.)	Barak staggers out the door, carrying a heavy load to market. The Wife sits down.	Strauss gave the proverb a setting which is reminiscent of a folk-tune: 1) the rhythm of both verse lines is identical (Strauss deleted the word "mir" in the first line in order to achieve this); 2) with the orchestral repetition of the tune considered an integral part of the melody, the harmony is I to V and V to I in D major. (See musical example #27.)
	The stage lighting dims and then flashes brightly, signifying the approach of the Empress and the Nurse. As	Strauss utilized strings in a high register and sweeping arpeggios on the harp to depict the flight of the Empress and the Nurse into the room.

121

TABLE OF ANALYSIS (continued)

Text	Visual Effects	Music
The Wife asks what these two strange beings want: Was wollt ihr hier? Wo kommt ihr her? (D III 169.) The questions are rhetorical from the point of view of the audience, for they already know why the Nurse and the Empress have come.	the lights flash, the new-comers are standing inside the Dyer's hut without having come in through the door. The Empress is disguised as a serving maid; the Nurse wears a garment of black and white patches. The Wife, startled, jumps up.	Strauss gave the audience maximum opportunity to compre-hend the first question by leaving it unaccompanied. The orchestra answers the question by playing the motive which comes to be associated with the renun-ciation of motherhood. (See musical example #28, the Renunciation of Motherhood Motive.) The second question is unlikely to be understood because Strauss set the accompaniment at a pitch level which covers the words.
Provided that the audience has previously compre-hended the Nurse's low regard for mankind, her flattery of the Wife will not be misunderstood: Ach! Schönheit ohnegleichen! Ein blitzendes Feuer! Oh! Oh! Meine Tochter, vor wem stehen wir? Wer ist diese Fürstin, wo bleibt ihr Gefolge? Wie kommt sie allein in diese Spelunke? (D III 169.) The physical posture of the Nurse, feigned humility before the Wife's beauty, conveys the tenor of her speech; the words themselves are not significant.	The Nurse falls to her knees in feigned humility before the Wife, signifying to the Empress to do the same.	Strauss utilized the Nurse's attempt to delude the Wife as an opportunity to write music which is ravishing in its sensual beauty. The primary motive which he employed is a rising major sixth played by obligato violin. (See the Flattery Motive, #29.) The accompaniment consists mainly of rapidly repeated chords. The entire exchange between the Wife and the Nurse is characterized by restless motion in both the accompaniment and the vocal line—possibly a repre-sentation of the Nurse's attempt to beguile the Wife with sensual pleasures and to exclude reflection. Arpeggios for the flute and the harp, scale passages for voice, and a trio written in close harmony for women's chorus are among the other means Strauss employed to achieve this end. The key center for this deception scene of the opera is B major.
In order to follow the dialogue the audience must understand these verse lines: Amme: War dieser einer von deinen Bedienten oder von deinen Botengängern, der Grosse mit einem Pack auf dem Rücken, solch ein Vierschrötiger, nicht mehr junger, mit gespaltenem Maul und niedriger Stirne! Frau: Du Zwinkernde, die ich nie gesehn und weiss nicht, wo du hereingeschlüpft bist-- dich durchschau ich so weit: Du weisst ganz wohl, dass dieser der Färber und mein Mann ist,	The Nurse, still showing awe before the Wife, gradually begins to rise from the floor.	Strauss set this question of the Nurse to various motives associated with Barak. It is doubtful that the audience will understand the words. On the other hand, he imparted significance to the Wife's answer; the key words ("Färber und mein Mann") are unaccompanied.

Text	Visual Effects	Music
und dass ich hier im Hause wohne. (D III 169-70.) This speech is important because it shows that the Wife is clever enough to see through the pretense of the Nurse. The wordy compliments of the Nurse are meant to flatter the Wife and to appeal to her baser emotions. Because the audience knows of the deceit which the Nurse is practicing, her behavior serves as a foil to that of the Empress. The simplicity and lack of pretense in the Empress' single verse line demonstrates her integrity: "Ich will den Schatten küssen, den sie wirft!" (D III 170.) Hofmannsthal considered the verse lines of the Empress to be very important (Briefwechsel, Hofmannsthal to Strauss, 25. VII. 1914); this is her first speech in the Dyer's hut. Flattery having been unsuccesful, the Nurse attempts to arouse the Wife's curiosity: Wehe, mein Kind, und fort mit uns! Diese weist uns von sich und will nicht unsre Dienste Sie kennt das Geheimnis und will unser spotten, fort mit uns! (D III 171.) The word "Geheimnis" becomes a key word for the passage which is here introduced by the Nurse, Hofmannsthal having employed the word five times within the space of eight verse lines.	The Nurse jumps up in astonishment when she learns of the Wife's relationship to Barak. The Wife responds to the overtures of the Nurse and the Empress by crying, apparently feeling that they are ridiculing her. This act demonstrates both her vulnerability and her capacity for gentleness. The Nurse feigns amazement and pretends to depart, pulling the Empress after her.	Strauss gave the Empress' vocal line pre-eminence by setting most of it above the accompaniment. Both the vocal line and the orchestra employ the Shadow Motive. Strauss seized upon the repetitions of the word "Geheimnis" and set them to a distinctive melodic line and harmonic progression. (See the Secret Motive, musical example #30.) The motive appears to have been partly designed with a programmatic intent, considering the surprising intrusion of the F major chord into the C# minor tonality. The orchestration--soft strings in a low register--and the lack of movement also emphasize the sense of mystery which Strauss apparently wished to impart. The low register and chordal nature of the accompaniment

Text	Visual Effects	Music
The Nurse answers the Wife's question "Welches Geheimnis?" with the following: Oh, meine Herrin, soll ich dir glauben, dass du deinen Schatten, dies schwarze Nichts hinter dir auf der Erde, dass dir dies Ding ohne Namen nicht feil ist— auch nicht um unvergänglichen Reiz und um Macht ohne Schranken über die Männer? (D III 171.) There is a sudden drop in the number of syllables per line in lines 2-4 of this passage. This change in structure emphasizes the shadow. Attention is also concentrated on the shadow by the three-fold mention of this object in three verse lines: 1) "dass du deinen Schatten"; 2) "dies schwarze Nichts"; 3) "dass dir dies Ding ohne Namen nicht feil ist—" If the audience is not to become hopelessly lost in this section of the opera, they will need to understand at least part of this speech. A minimum would be: ". . . soll ich dir glauben, / . . . . . / dass dir dies Ding ohne Namen nicht feil ist—" In order to follow the dialogue the audience will need to follow these lines of the Wife: Wer gäbe dafür auch nur den schmählichsten Preis? (D III 172.) Hofmannsthal structured the Nurse's answer to the Wife's question with significant lines both at the beginning and the end of the speech. An elaboration on the answer comprises the middle section: Alles, du Benedeite, alles zahlen begierige Käufer, du Herrin, wenn eine Unnennbare deinesgleichen abtut ihren Schatten und gibt ihn dahin! Ei! Die Sklavinnen und die Sklaven, so viele ihrer du verlangest,	The Wife turns to look at her shadow.	increase the likelihood that the words will be understood. The composer utilized the Shadow Motive in this particular section, alluding thereby to the shadow's intimate involvement with the secret. Strauss did not differentiate verse lines 2-4 from the rest of the text as did Hofmannsthal: they neither stand out from the preceding or the following lines as they are set. Also in contrast to his librettist, the composer emphasized the word "feil", giving it three beats while he gave, for example, the entire second verse line ("dass du deinen Schatten") only slightly more than two beats. Nor did Strauss utilize the three-fold mention of the shadow for intensification. The composer also altered the text slightly, omitting the word "um" in the verse line "und um Macht ohne Schranken." The words of the text are probably covered by the accompaniment with the possible exception of the word "feil". With the help of gestures on stage these lines will probably be comprehended, for Strauss set them in a moderately high range with an accompaniment consisting primarily of a doubling of the vocal line. Strauss repeated the word "Alles" at the beginning of the speech, effecting a key change with the repetition. The rise of one-half step in the vocal line emphasizes the word. The significant opening two lines of the Nurse's speech are set in a moderately high range, the accompaniment consisting both of a melodic line which parallels the vocal line rather closely and also of repeated chords in a low range. These qualities would probably not cover the words, but

Text	Visual Effects	Music
und die Brokate und Seidengewänder, in denen du stündlich wechselnd prangest, und die Maultiere und die Häuser und die Springbrunnen und die Gärten und deiner Liebenden nächtlich Gedränge und dauernde Jugendherrlichkeit für ungemessene Zeit dies alles ist dein, du Herrscherin, gibst du den Schatten dahin! (D III 172.) Being devious as usual, the Nurse stresses what the seller of a shadow might receive rather than who might buy a shadow, which was the question the Wife had asked. The last three lines of the speech contain a drop both in the number of accented syllables and also in the total number of syllables. This lessening of momentum emphasizes these last lines.		Strauss also wrote a contrapuntal line for obligato violin which if played with enough volume to be heard, will probably destroy comprehension. The vocal setting and the accompaniment are noticeably more complex for the remainder of the speech with the exception of the final line ("Gibst du den Schatten dahin!"), which is unaccompanied except for cadential chords. Strauss wrote descriptively for the middle part of the speech, depicting the rustling of the brocade and silk clothes, the walking gait of the donkeys, and the bubbling of the fountains. He also made an ironic comment upon the Nurse's speech by accompanying some of her lines with the Traitor Motive, thereby implying that the Nurse is a traitor. Strauss set the last three verse lines at a less rapid pace than he did the middle section of the speech, achieving thereby a similarity in style to the setting of the first four verse lines.
	The Nurse reaches into the air and produces a pearl hair ornament which she hands to the Wife. Flashes of lightning accompany the magic.	
The Wife's initial excitement upon receiving the hairband subsides, a dream world apparently giving way to reality: Dies in mein Haar? Du Liebe, du!-- Doch ich armes Weib, ich hab keinen Spiegel! Dort überm Trog mach ich mein Haar! (D III 172.) It is important that the audience understand the Wife's line: "ich hab keinen Spiegel!" This verse gives rise to the entire Pavilion scene which follows.	The Nurse produces a pavilion complete with slaves and leads the Wife--in a dressing gown and with the pearls in her hair--to a large metal mirror.	Strauss adapted his setting of the Wife's first two verse lines to the immediately preceding passage by the Nurse, suggesting how easily the Wife can be influenced. This similarity is dropped for the remainder of the setting which with its great simplicity implies impoverishment. It is as though the Wife has suddenly become sober after drinking deeply of the sensual draught offered by the Nurse. Comprehension of the significant line "ich hab keinen Spiegel!" is likely. The Pavilion section of the opera is a tour de force of Strauss's ability at instrumentation. A tremolo in the strings, rapid flute passages, arpeggios for the harp, and scale passages for the celeste co-ordinate to present a passage of ravishing beauty. Its object is, of course, to convince the Wife that she desires to

125

TABLE OF ANALYSIS (continued)

Text	Visual Effects	Music
The entire scene at the Pavilion focuses on the one speech of the Empress: Willst du um dies Spiegelbild nicht den hohlen Schatten geben? (D III 173.)	Gestures toward both the mirror and the shadow seem appropriate here. (No specific directions to this end are given in either Steiner or the score.)	exchange her shadow for the sensual life portrayed before her. Hofmannsthal apparently gave Strauss the cue for the setting of the slave voices with the stage direction: "sie rufen mit süssen, wie ein Glockenspiel ineinander klingenden Stimmen." (D III 173.) Strauss wrote descending scale passages for the slaves which he indicated were to be performed in a detached manner; the effect is not unlike that of a glockenspiel. The only distinctive motive which occurs in the entire passage is the Mistress Motive which appears approximately halfway through the scene in the orchestra. It occurs in the voices only in altered form. (See musical example #31.)
As though in answer to the Empress' question, a Youth sings: Gäb ich um dies Spiegelbild doch die Seele und mein Leben! (D III 173.)		Strauss prepared for the Empress' solo by silencing the chorus for several measures previous to her entrance. The verse lines are set to a flowing melody in a high tessitura which includes a high B. This high pitch level gives the lines great dramatic impact, but this gain will probably be offset by a concomitant loss of comprehension, since highly pitched vocal lines require a modification of vowels in order to be produced. Strauss set the lines for the Youth in a high tenor range and gave them a flowing melodic line. The Empress' melody ("Willst du um dies Spiegelbild / nicht den hohlen Schatten geben?") spans nine measures; the Youth's spans twelve. In every respect the answer of the Youth seems comparable to that of the Empress' question. It is doubtful that Hofmannsthal intended so much emphasis to be placed upon the Youth's lines. After hearing the first part of the opera, including this scene, he wrote to Strauss: . . . es war ein schwerer Fehler von mir . . . dass ich Sie nicht genug daran erinnerte, dass der "fremde Jüngling" ein Phantom ist, von einem Mimiker zartest zu spielen—und mit geisterhafter Stimme von irgendwoher (=aus dem Orchester) zu singen: nun haben Sie ihn leider Gottes anders aufgefasst, das macht mir schwere Sorgen, und ich bitte Sie herzlich, diesen Punkt nicht leicht zu nehmen. (Briefwechsel, 14. V. 1915.)
Hofmannsthal's text for the chorus in the Pavilion scene consists of one line: Dienerinnen: Ach, Herrin, süsse Herrin! Aah! (D III 173.)		In addition to the line written by Hofmannsthal, Strauss also utilized frequent repetitions of the word "Ha!" The nature of the melody and harmony which Strauss desired to use for the choir seems to be responsible for this change, for rapidly repeated

Text	Visual Effects	Music
The Wife reacts to the vision which the Nurse has conjured forth by saying: O Welt in der Welt! O Traum im Wachen! (D III 173.) Hofmannsthal often characterized the Wife by stressing her tendency to live in a dream world. These lines, therefore, give an important insight into her personality.	As the Wife sings, the vision begins to fade away.	notes are more easily sung to "Ha!" than to either "Ach!" or "Ah!" Strauss apparently interpreted the verse lines as an emotional outburst of excitement; he did not attempt to make them comprehensible but set them in the midst of a fairly dense contrapuntal fabric.
Hofmannsthal constructed a speech for the Wife which intensifies with each line until the climactic final one is reached: Und hätt ich gleich den Willen dazu-- Wie tät ich ihn ab und gäb ihn dahin-- den an der Erde, ihn, meinen Schatten? (D III 174.) The dependent clause of the first two lines both delays and also anticipates the independent clause of the third line. The third, fourth and fifth verse lines contain a pronoun without its antecedent, in this manner anticipating the final line where the antecedent is given.	The Pavilion vanishes from sight and the Dyer's hut replaces it. The pearl ornament in the Wife's hair also disappears.	A general and gradual rise in pitch distinguishes the setting of this speech: the high point of the first two lines is F, of the third is E♭, of the fourth is E, of the fifth is G, and of the sixth is A. The intensification which occurs in the text is thus parallelled by an intensification in the vocal line. The Shadow Motive occurs several times, both in the orchestra and in the vocal line.
The Steiner edition was printed with the answers which the Wife gives to the Nurse's questions prior to the questions. The following text, taken from the score, seems more logical: Amme: Hat es dich blutige Tränen gekostet, Frau: Nein, sag doch schnell, du Kluge, du Gute! Amme: dass du dem Breitspurigen keine Kinder geboren hast? Frau: Jetzt sag es, schnell, schnell, Amme: Und lechzt dein Herz darnach bei Tag und Nacht, dass viele kleine Färber durch dich eingehen sollen in diese Welt?	During the course of this exchange, the Wife shows impatience. The Nurse thereupon motions the Empress to approach more closely, as though she is to witness a significant occurrence.	Strauss left the first, second and fourth lines of the Nurse's speech largely unaccompanied. The vocal line is also fairly simple, so these verse lines will probably be comprehended. The entire speech is preceded by a fortissimo orchestral statement of the Renunciation of Motherhood Motive. This dynamic level in combination with the drama inherent within the motive itself tends to give this speech greater intensity than may be warranted, considering the relatively unimportant relationship of these words to the plot.

127

Text	Visual Effects	Music

Text column:

Soll dein Leib eine Heerstrasse werden
und deine Schlankheit ein zerstampfter Weg?
Und sollen deine Brüste welken
und ihre Herrlichkeit schnell dahin sein?   (D III 174-75.)

It is important that the audience comprehend at least part of the Wife's reply to the Nurse's prejudicial questions, for her answer anticipates the terms of the pact. The most significant lines appear to be: "Ich lebe hier im Haus, / und der Mann kommt mir nicht nah!" (D III 175.) Hofmannsthal gave these lines prominence by using three of his customary techniques for significant lines. 1) The lines are primarily monosyllabic. 2) The vocabulary is extremely simple. 3) Two verse lines precede the verse lines given, thereby delaying them.

The lines which complete the Wife's speech appear to have been written with an intention to lessen momentum, because there are in these lines both fewer syllables per line and also fewer accents per line:

So ist es gesprochen
und geschworen
in meinem Innern.
(D III 175.)

The correspondence between Hofmannsthal and Strauss reveals that they experienced difficulty in agreeing what the specific wording of this speech by the Nurse was to be (Briefwechsel, 5. VII. 1914 to 16. VII. 1914):

Abzutun
Mutterschaft
auf ewige Zeiten
von deinem Leibe!
Dahinzugeben
mit der Gebärde
der Verachtung
die Lästigen,
die da nicht geboren sind!
So ist es gesprochen
und so geschworen!
(D III 175.)

Hofmannsthal felt that the speech would be awkward and incomprehensible if it were to open with the line "Abzutun", as it is given here rather than with verse lines of this nature:

Music column:

Strauss utilized the Irritability Motive throughout the Wife's speech. The significant lines ("Ich lebe hier im Haus, / und der Mann kommt mir nicht nah!") are set in the middle range with a minimum of accompaniment. The final lines ("So ist es gesprochen / und geschworen / in meinem Innern.") gradually drop to the low soprano tessitura, effectively relaxing momentum.

Strauss apparently felt that he had a strong reason for using the passage as he desired. A study of the score reveals what this reason was. Strauss had devised a motive to set the words "Abzutun / Mutterschaft" which, for dramatic intensity, probably has no equal in the entire opera. The dramatic effect is heightened because the motive follows immediately, even abruptly, after the quiet, low-pitched words of the Wife. Any intermediate words would have diminished the dramatic effectiveness of the motive.

TABLE OF ANALYSIS (continued)

Text	Visual Effects	Music

Text column:

In deinem Innern,
o du Herrscherin,
dir gesprochen,
o du Seltene,
und beschworen!
                    (Briefwechsel, 8. VII. 1914.)

Strauss was just as adamant that the speech had to
open with "Abzutun / Mutterschaft." Ultimately,
Hofmannsthal had no choice, for Strauss had
already composed the passage as he desired it to
be. The insertion into the Steiner edition of the
lines "So ist es gesprochen / und so geschworen!"
after the line "die da nicht geboren sind!", two
verses which were never composed, seems to indicate
that the disagreement was never resolved.

The Nurse's speech continues with a blasphemous
variation on the annunciation to Mary. (See also
D III 172, where the Nurse refers to the Wife as
the Blessed One-- "Benedeite".) Thereafter, the
preliminary words to the actual pact are given:

Du Seltene du!
Du erhobene Fackel!
O du Herrscherin, o du Gepriesene unter den
          Frauen,
nun sollst du es sehn und es erleben:
angerufen werden
gewaltige Namen
und ein Bund geschlossen
und gesetzt ein Bann!
          (D III 175.)

The actual pact reads as follows:
Tage drei
dienen wir dir
hier im Haus,
diese und ich,
dies ist gesetzt!
Sind die vorbei,
dem Dienst zum Lohn
von Mund zu Mund,
von Hand zu Hand,
mit wissender Hand
und willigem Mund
gibst du den Schatten
uns dahin
und gehest ein
in der Freuden Beginn!

Music column:

Strauss set the Nurse's praise of the Wife in a short
melodic section wherein the orchestra carries the
primary musical interest.
The preliminary words to the pact are set with a
minimum of accompaniment.

Strauss set the words of the pact to a motive which
appears to be a transformation of the New Day Motive.
(See #18 for the New Day Motive and #32 for the Pact
Motive.) There apparently is no textural reason for
this relationship. One of the more salient characteristics of this passage is its rhythmic complexity:
the vocal line was written in C while the orchestral
accompaniment was set in a 6/4 meter.
Far from being silent for these important verse lines,
the orchestra plays contrapuntal lines against the
vocal line, part of them higher in pitch than the
vocal line. The essential lines of the pact are,
moreover, not distinguished from the non-essential
lines (lines 7-11, lines 16-18).
As a total effect, the pact itself does not carry
the dramatic impact that the immediately preceding

129

TABLE OF ANALYSIS (continued)

Text	Visual Effects	Music

Und die Sklavinnen und die Sklaven
und die Springbrunnen und die Gärten
und Gewölbe voll Tonnen Goldes—
(D III 176.)
 	
Lines 7-11 consist of a delay and are not significant from the point of view of meaning. Nor are lines 16-18 important to the pact. A shift to a lyrical style is here evident. The pact itself is marked by the fewest number of syllables per line of any lengthier passage in the entire opera. This suggests that Hofmannsthal envisioned a very deliberate setting for the speech.
 	
Because this speech by the Wife precipitates the magic which the Nurse practices at the end of the act, it is important that the audience comprehend at least a part of it:
    Die Frau: Still und verschwiegen!
    ich höre meinen Mann, der wiederkommt!
    Nun wird er verlangen nach seinem Nachtmahl,
    das nicht bereit ist,
    und nach seinem Lager,
    das ich ihm nicht gewähren will.
            (D III 176.)
 	
The Wife's lack of enthusiasm for the enterprise in which she is engaging is indicated by the stage direction "Fast tonlos", which precedes the final line of the speech.
 	
The Nurse, sensing the lack of resolution on the part of the Wife, hastily interjects her comments; she obviously desires to prevent the Wife from contemplating the terms of the pact:
    Du bist nicht allein:
    Dienerinnen hast du,
    diese und mich.
    Morgen zu Mittag
    stehn wir dir in Dienst:
    als arme Muhmen
    musst du uns grüssen,
    nach Mitternacht nur,
    indes du ruhest,
    für kurze Frist,
    das braucht niemand zu wissen!
    Jetzt schnell, was notut!
            (D III 176-77.)
		lines, those which are set to the Denial of Motherhood Motive, do. An analysis of the verse lines indicates that this emphasis at the expense of the pact ("Tage drei") was not intended by Hofmannsthal.
		
		Strauss set the first two lines of this speech to an octave tremolo in the strings. Provided that the orchestra follows the dynamic indication of piano, the lines will probably be comprehended. The vocal line carries the primary melody for the third verse line, while the accompaniment is generally without much movement and is inclined to parallel the vocal line. Comprehension of this line seems to be assured. This is not the case, however, with the remainder of the speech. As the orchestra repeatedly sounds one of the Barak motives (the Desire for Children Motive), the Wife completes her short solo with hesitation and with considerable loss of momentum, Strauss thereby evidencing the Wife's lack of resolution. These verse lines are set against contrapuntal lines in the orchestra which make comprehension somewhat problematic.
		
		Although Strauss indicated that the orchestra is to play pianississimo here, the contrapuntal lines in the orchestra tend to overshadow the vocal line, with the exception of the last one. This final line, "Jetzt schnell, was notut!", is set to a chord.

TABLE OF ANALYSIS (continued)

Text	Visual Effects	Music
Hofmannsthal considered this speech important because it prepares the audience for the appearance of the Empress and the Nurse at the Falconer House, the location of Act II, scenes ii and iv. (Briefwechsel, Hofmannsthal to Strauss, 14. VII. 1914.)		
The Nurse continues to assume the initiative in her relationship with the Wife, here working magic which seems designed to prevent the Wife from reflecting on the meaning of the pact: Fischlein fünf aus Fischers Zuber, wandert ins Öl, und, Pfanne, empfang sie! Feuer, führ dich! Hierher, du Bette des Färbers Barak! Und fort mit den Gästen, von wo sie kamen! (D III 177.) The actions on stage will carry the meaning of the words; comprehension does not seem necessary.	A darkening of the room, flashes of light, and sudden gusts of wind accompany the Nurse's magic. She claps her hands together silently, signaling the beginning of the conjuration. In response to her command fish fly through the air and land in the pan over the fire; the fire flares up. The bed separates into two parts, a curtain hiding the Wife's at the rear of the stage and Barak's appearing at the front of the stage. The Empress and the Nurse disappear silently without leaving through the door.	Strauss set the Nurse's words of conjuration in a manner expressive of command. The dramatic impact which this carries tends to give this speech greater significance than the actual pact ("Tage drei"). The elevated language of the pact seems to indicate that this was not Hofmannsthal's intention. Motives employed are the Keikobad Motive, and the Renunciation of Motherhood Motive.
	The Wife stares in amazement at what has occurred while the fire lights the room with its flickering.	The orchestra portrays the flickering of the fire. (See musical example #33, the Fire Flickering Motive.)
The Five Children's Voices call to the Wife: Fünf Kinderstimmen: Mutter, Mutter, lass uns nach Hause! Die Tür ist verriegelt, wir finden nicht ein, wir sind im Dunkel und in der Furcht! Mutter, o weh! Frau: Was winselt so grässlich aus diesem Feuer? Die Kinderstimmen: Wir sind im Dunkel und in der Furcht! Mutter, Mutter, lass uns ein! Oder ruf den lieben Vater, dass er uns die Tür auftu! (D III 178.)	The Wife shows fear at the supernatural quality of the experience she is having.	Strauss set the word "Mutter" to the Children Motive, thereby giving it considerable prominence, and utilized the Fire Flickering Motive for the accompaniment. The composer also used a variation of one of the Barak motives, the Desire for Children Motive, for a part of the text. The mourning of the children is expressed by means of chromaticism. It is doubtful if any of the text will be understood, with the possible exception of the word "Mutter", since the chorus is singing offstage.
The Wife expresses a desire to silence the fire with water:	The fire dies away at the Wife's words.	The Wife's lines are doubled in the orchestra, both at her pitch level and also an octave above. The

131

Text	Visual Effects	Music
O fänd ich Wasser, dies Feuer zu schweigen! Die Kinderstimmen: Mutter, o weh! Dein hartes Herz! (D III 178.)		higher pitch level of the orchestra may make under-standing her lines difficult.
	The Wife sits down on a bundle and wipes beads of sweat away from her forehead.	An orchestral interlude, dominated by Barak's Desire for Children Motive, separates the Children's Voices from the entrance of Barak, who begins his folksong "Trag ich die Ware" before he steps onto the stage.
	Barak enters; the Wife stands up and goes to her bed at the rear of the stage.	
In verse lines wherein the emphasis is upon convey-ing information Barak and the Wife converse: Barak: Ein gepriesener Duft von Fischen und Öl. Was kommst du nicht essen? Die Frau: Hier ist dein Essen. Ich geh zur Ruh. Dort ist jetzt dein Lager. Barak: Mein Bette hier? Wer hat das getan? Die Frau: Von morgen ab schlafen zwei Muhmen hier, denen richt ich das Lager zu meinen Füssen als meinen Mägden. So ist es gesprochen, und so geschieht es.		Strauss set these lines to assure comprehension by the audience. Although the orchestra does play between the verse lines, they are largely unaccompanied. The composer set the second and third lines of the Wife's speech ("Ich geh zur Ruh. / Dort ist jetzt dein Lager.") with rests breaking into the melodic line, thereby showing her lack of commitment to the terms of the pact. This manner of delivery contrasts greatly with the rapidity of her earlier speeches. The Wife's final four lines are completely spoken while the orchestra plays the Pact Motive in a low register. The audience will probably understand the entire exchange.
Hofmannsthal and Strauss strongly disagreed as to whether or not Barak should eat the fish which the Nurse had magically conjured forth. Strauss felt that the identification with the Unborn Children was so great as to make such behavior appear barbaric. Hofmannsthal finally yielded to Strauss, provided that Barak should sit and eat something, although not the fish; he desired that a different aspect of Barak's character be presented. (Briefwechsel, Hofmannsthal to Strauss, 12. VII. 1914.) The Steiner edition and the score do not reflect this agreement. In these sources the Wife says "Hier ist dein Essen"; customary performance of this line is "Hier ist kein Essen," reflecting what is probably a tradition leading back to Hofmannsthal and Strauss.		
Barak's reaction to the Wife's behavior is one of sadness. The speech is lyrical in style: Sie haben es mir gesagt, dass ihre Rede seltsam sein wird und ihr Tun befremdlich	Barak sits down on the floor, pulls a piece of bread out of his garment, and eats it.	Strauss set Barak's words in a flowing melodic style. The principle motive is the Children Motive, which provides an accompanimental figure in the orchestra for the solo.

TABLE OF ANALYSIS (continued)

Text	Visual Effects	Music

die erste Zeit.
aber ich trage es hart,
und das Essen will mir nicht schmecken.
    (D III 179-80.)
 	
In the score the reading of the second line is
"dass ihre Seele seltsam sein wird." Inasmuch as
Strauss's letter to Hofmannsthal on July 10, gives
the verse line as it is in the Steiner edition,
the reading in the score must be erroneous.
 	
Hofmannsthal utilized the Song of the Nightwatchmen
to summarize the meaning of marriage. (See the
discussions in Chapter III under Barak: "Knoten
des Herzens" and Empress: Shadow.) The verses
are significant in that they state the most impor-
tant ideas of the entire opera, but they are unim-
portant insofar as the plot can be followed without
comprehending them:
 	
Die Stimmen der Wächter in den Strassen: Ihr
    Gatten in den Häusern dieser Stadt,
liebet einander mehr als euer Leben
und wisset: Nicht um eures Lebens willen
ist euch die Saat des Lebens anvertraut,
sondern allein um eurer Liebe willen!
Barak: Hörst du die Wächter, Kind, und ihren Ruf?
Die Stimmen der Wächter: Ihr Gatten, die ihr
    liebend euch in Armen liegt,
Ihr seid die Brücke, überm Abgrund ausgespannt,
auf der die Toten wiederum ins Leben gehn!
Barak: Seis denn!
    (D III 180.)
	Barak listens, wondering if
	the Wife will answer him. On
	receiving no reply, he sighs
	and lies down to sleep.
	The curtain falls on the
	last chords.
		Strauss set the two strophes of the Watchmen's
		Song in Ab major, his evening key, for three male voices;
		the tessitura is the medium to upper baritone range.
		The number of singers, the tessitura, and the unison
		setting may allow the words to be understood, even though
		both verses are accompanied by a full string orchestra
		reinforced with horns and woodwinds and the first verse
		is sung off-stage.
		The Song is quite independent of the opera as a whole;
		the melodies appearing here do not recur at any other
		time.
		
		The act closes with the orchestra playing a melody
		derived from Barak's Joy Motive.

133

TABLE OF ANALYSIS (continued)

Text	Visual Effects	Music
	Act II scene i	
The second act is constructed so that the three days and the two nights of the pact's duration are portrayed; the first scene corresponds to the first day of the pact and takes place in the Dyer's Hut. The second scene depicts the first night and takes place outside the Emperor's Falconer House. The third scene takes place at the Dyer's Hut and portrays events of the second day. The fourth scene depicts the second night's happenings within the Falconer House. The fifth and final scene takes place at the Dyer's Hut and portrays the third day of the pact. In all the scenes which take place at the Dyer's Hut the words assume more importance than they do in the scenes which take place at the Falconer House. Hofmannsthal planned this differentiation early in his conception of the opera: "Ia [Ii] muss die Situation und den nicht so ganz elementar fasslichen Seelenzustand von Kaiser und Kaiserin völlig klar exponieren, so dass IIb und IId [IIii und IIiv] wirklich blosse lyrische Ausströmungen (als Ruhepunkte in der beständig fortschreitenden, irdischen Handlung IIa, IIc, IIe [IIi, IIiii, IIv]) bilden." (Briefwechsel, Hofmannsthal to Strauss, 3. VI. 1913.)	As the curtain rises in the middle of the orchestral introduction, Barak is getting ready to go to market; the Empress is helping him. The Three Brothers are ready to go and await him.	The second act opens prior to the raising of the curtain with a short orchestral introduction which contains the principal motives for the first scene. Among these motives is one which is specifically associated with the Youth. (See musical example #34.) Other motives which are first employed here are the Wife's Erotic Love Motive (#35), the Wife's Heart Motive (#36), the Nurse's Deception Motive (#37), and the Nurse's Hypocrisy Motive (#38). The great number of motives, five new ones within twenty-four measures, suggests that Strauss wrote the brief introduction after having composed the first scene. The key center for the first part of IIi is C major.
The Nurse's first words illustrate both her comtempt for Barak, whom the audience knows she despises, and also her willingness to deceive others in order to accomplish her own purposes: Komm bald wieder nach Haus, mein Gebieter, denn meine Herrin verzehrt sich vor Sehnsucht,	As Barak walks to the door, the Nurse rushes to open it and to make obeisance to him.	Strauss set the Nurse's words to the Deception Motive, one of the motives which was first employed in the orchestral introduction to Act II; he attached importance to the opening lines of the act by leaving the first verse line unaccompanied. The word "Sehnsucht" is given emphasis by means of i) its melismatic setting; 2) its relatively greater length in comparison with the

TABLE OF ANALYSIS (continued)

Text	Visual Effects	Music
Wenn du nicht da bist! (D III 181.) Although every speech which can be understood will enhance the audience's comprehension and their delight in the opera, this speech is negligible insofar as understanding it is necessary for following the plot.		length of the setting for other words; and 3) its syncopation with the accompaniment.
The second line of this speech, which is spoken by the Nurse and addressed to the Wife, contrasts to the first one in its significance; it is important to plot development because it prepares for the appearance of the Youth: Die Luft ist rein und kostbar die Zeit! Wie ruf ich den, der nun herein soll? (D III 181.)	Barak exits and the Nurse runs over to the Wife, who removes the scarf from her head to reveal an elaborate coiffure in which strands of pearls are woven. The Empress, holding a mirror, kneels before her.	Strauss does not appear to have considered this verse line important, for he did nothing to make it prominent or to make it easily comprehended other than to indicate a pianissimo dynamic level for the orchestra. An important counter-melody in the orchestra may, moreover, make comprehension difficult.
When the Wife does not answer the question, the Nurse rephrases it: O du meine Herrin seit diesem Tage, gib mir doch Antwort! Wie sind deine Bräuche? Soll diese laufen? Oder ruf ich ihn? Mit einem sehnsüchtigen Ruf? Oder einem fröhlichen? (D III 181.) The fourth and fifth lines of this speech stand out from the other lines 1) because of their importance to plot development and 2) because they are stylistically differentiated by a comparative brevity and simplicity.		As with the preceding question (Wie ruf ich den, der nun herein soll?"), Strauss did nothing to emphasize the significant lines of this speech (verse lines four and five). Again, orchestral counterpoint is likely to impede comprehension. The composer's interest in this speech was apparently programmatic in nature, as evidenced by his treatment of the word "fröhlichen" both with orchestral trills on a high B and also with a fuller orchestral sound than he had previously employed.
According to the stage direction ("scharf"), the Wife responds sharply to the Nurse's question: Auf wen geht die Rede? (D III 181.) This line is important to character delineation, for it shows if not the Wife's loyalty to Barak, at least her lack of romantic attachment to another.		Strauss set this line to the chromatic Erotic Love Motive, thereby giving it significance, especially in comparison to the previous settings of the Nurse's lines which were set to melodic material which is essentially non-recurring. This is the first use of this motive in the vocal line.
The Nurse answers the Wife's question with: Auf den, der thronet in deinem Herzen, und fur den du dich schmückest! (D III 182.) These lines, because they do not exhibit the stylistic characteristics of monosyllabicity and		Strauss gave the first line of the Nurse's answer ("Auf den, der thronet in deinem Herzen") emphasis by setting it to the Heart Motive; this is the first time this motive has been used to set a verse line.

135

Text	Visual Effects	Music
simplicity with which Hofmannsthal designated significant lines, appear to have been intended by the poet for a lyrical setting.		Strauss related the Wife's answer ("Im leeren Herzen wohnet keiner") to the preceding verse line of the Nurse ("Auf den, der thronet in deinem Herzen") by employing the Heart Motive to set both lines. The response of the Wife differs from the Nurse's question, however, by being given in a minor key. As is true for most other lines in this scene, comprehension is likely to depend upon the diction of the singer and the balance between the singer and the orchestra. Strauss did not give the remaining lines any special treatment.
The first line of this speech is significant because it expresses the Wife's lack of commitment to Barak. The second and third verse lines, which express her vanity, may be best expressed by means of her gestures before the mirror; comprehension is, therefore, not necessary. Frau ruhig: Im leeren Herzen wohnet keiner, und geschmückt hab ich mich für den Spiegel. (D III 182.)		Strauss set the opening words of the first verse to the Heart Motive, the motive which he used for setting both the Wife's line "Im leeren Herzen wohnet keiner" and also the Nurse's line "Für den, der thronet in deinem Herzen." The orchestra plays Barak's Desire for Children Motive against the vocal line. This motive moves into the vocal line for the second verse line. Strauss thereby suggested that the Wife's unconscious thoughts are loyal to Barak.
In response to repeated enticements by the Nurse the Wife states: Ich weiss von keinem Manne ausser ihm, der aus dem Hause ging. (D III 182.)	The Wife stands up.	
The Wife's change of body position emphasizes the verse lines, but it also betrays nervousness on her part. The ambiguity of the gesture expresses the Wife's ambivalence toward Barak.		
The Nurse continued to entice the Wife until the Wife betrays a secret romantic interest by blushing. The words are unimportant.	The Wife shows confusion.	Strauss indicated the Wife's confusion by slightly quickening the tempo for her lines. The original tempo returns with the Nurse's verse lines.
The Nurse triumphantly offers to bring the Wife's sweetheart to her: Wir bringen ihn dir, zu dem du jetzt eben mit süssem Erröten dein Denken geschickt! (D III 183.)		The orchestra plays the Hypocrisy Motive against the Nurse's first line; the dynamic marking is forte for the accompaniment. For the second and third lines the orchestra doubles the Erotic Love Motive of the vocal line. Comprehension will probably depend upon the singer's diction and upon the balance between the singer and the orchestra. If either of these factors is not done well, the audience is likely to become bored for lack of knowing what is happening.
The first verse line is significant because it prepares for the magical conjuring forth of the Youth.		
The Wife regains some of her composure, stating her lack of real involvement with any lover: Lachen muss ich über dich! - - - - - - - 3 - - - - - - - 4 Wenn ich dir sage: 5 ich weiss kaum die Gasse.	The Wife laughs at the Nurse.	Strauss set the fourth and fifth lines to variations of the Hypocrisy Motive and the Deception Motive; the orchestra doubles the vocal line. The sixth line is separated from the fifth by a measure's rest--the longest rest since Barak's exit. This separation of two verse lines which belong together from the point of view both of syntax and also of meaning is undoubtedly

TABLE OF ANALYSIS (continued)

Text	Visual Effects	Music

wo ich ihn traf,
nicht das Viertel der Stadt,
noch seinen Namen!
    (D III 183.)
 	
It is important that the audience realize that the Wife has not previously been untrue to Barak. This will be clear if the audience understands the fifth and sixth lines.
 	
Hofmannsthal structured the Nurse's command to the Wife so that rhyme and meter create a short four-line poem:
Nun schliess deine Augen
und ruf ihn dir!
Und schlägst du sie auf,
steht er vor dir!
    (D III 183.)
 	
The Wife sinks into a daydream about the Youth:
Frau: Nur, dass ich auf einer Brücke ging
unter vielen Menschen,
als einer mir entgegenkam,
ein Knabe fast,
der meiner nicht achtete--
    (D III 183.)
 	
The words are not as significant as her retreat from the reality of being Barak's wife into a fantasy world.
 	
The Nurse prepares to conjure forth the Youth:
Du Besen, leih mir die Gestalt!
Und Kessel du, leih mir deine Stimme!
    (D III 184.)
 	
These lines, whose ultimate purpose is to conjure forth the Youth, need not be understood if the pantomime and music effectively convey the impression that a spell is being cast. The audience will probably be able to deduce from the previous conversations that the spell has to do with the Youth.
 	
The Empress reacts negatively to the Nurse's attempt to produce a lover for the Wife:
Weh! Muss dies geschehen
vor meinen Augen?
    (D III 184.)
 	
This is the first of three speeches in this scene
	
	The Nurse furtively picks up a piece of straw from the floor.
	
	The Empress directs her speech to the Nurse.
		detrimental to comprehension. Nor did Strauss follow Hofmannsthal's intent as indicated by the third line, a line without words which apparently indicates the Wife's mirth.
		
		Strauss set these lines so that lines one and three employ the Deception Motive; lines two and four also employ similar melodic material. The relationship of the verse lines is thereby emphasized.
		
		Strauss expressed the Wife's daydreaming by inserting a full measure's rest into the first verse line. This appears to represent the Wife's groping after thoughts which lie deeply buried within her.
		
		The contrast between the preceding smoothly flowing melody of the Wife and the broken melodic lines and heavily marked rhythm of the Nurse is very great. The meter also changes from the preceding moderate 3/4 beat to a very fast 2/4 for these lines. The marked difference which occurs between this passage and the preceding and following ones definitely convey the impression that something extraordinary is happening.
		
		Strauss set these lines of the Empress in a moderately high range; the orchestra doubles the vocal line, where the first statement of the Sorrow Motive occurs. (See musical example #39.) The rhythm reverts to a three beat meter from the immediately preceding two beat meter of the Nurse's conjuring song, but the faster

6

TABLE OF ANALYSIS (continued)

Text	Visual Effects	Music
by the Empress. Since it consists primarily of an emotional outburst, it need not be comprehended, provided that the emotional meaning is conveyed.		tempo is retained. The more rapid tempo, the moderately high range, and the shift in meter--perhaps symbolizing the Empress' unwillingness to submit to the Nurse's means of obtaining a shadow--all give emotional intensity to her lines.
The Nurse tells the Empress that what she does is for her gain: Zu gutem Handel und dir zu Gewinn. (D III 184.)		Strauss did not utilize any device, such as an omission of accompaniment or a doubling of the vocal line, to give the lines pre-eminence. This seems to be in keeping with Hofmannsthal's intent.
The Empress does not react to being informed of her complicity in the actions now being performed. Because these lines demonstrate the Empress' inability at this time to accept any responsibility for others, they are not totally negligible. Understanding them, however, does not appear to be essential for following the plot.	The Nurse goes to the Wife with the straw hidden behind her back.	
The Nurse instructs the Wife to close her eyes: Geschlossen dein Aug und geöffnet dein Herz, du Liebliche, du! (D III 184.)		Strauss set the lines to the Deception Motive with the accompaniment paralleling the vocal line. These two qualities give the verses a good chance to be comprehended, even though this may be unnecessary for following the plot.
These verse lines are unimportant because the gestures on the stage will convey the meaning.		
The Empress reacts negatively once more, whispering to herself: Sind so die Menschen? So feil ihr Herz? (D III 184.)	The Nurse throws the straw over the Wife. There is a flash and the light remains changed thereafter. (The change in the lighting which is indicated here will probably be a darkening because the demonic aspects of the Nurse correspond to darkness in the traditional relationship of good-light and evil-darkness of Middle Eastern mythology.)	These lines were set by Strauss to the Heart Motive in a minor key. The orchestra doubles the vocal line and also adds contrapuntal melodies which may make comprehension difficult.
The Empress' negative feelings toward the conjuration must be comprehended by the audience. If the words are not understood, then gesture must carry this meaning.		
The Nurse answers the Empress' questions with a variation on those lines from Act I wherein she expressed contempt for mankind:		The orchestra plays the Nurse Motive and the Sorrow Motive while the Nurse sings her verse lines. This counterpoint, the use of percussion in the orchestra,

TABLE OF ANALYSIS (continued)

Text	Visual Effects	Music
Kielkröpfe und Molche sind zu schauen so lustig als sie! (D III 184.) These lines serve more to characterize the Nurse than to facilitate the action. Comprehension is unnecessary.		the cross-rhythms in the vocal and orchestral lines, and the rapidity of the setting of the verse lines effectively portray the Nurse's vehement feelings toward men.
The Wife daydreams aloud about the Youth: --der meiner nicht achtete mit hochmütigem Blick-- - - - - - - - - - - und des ich gedachte heimlich, zuweilen, um Träumens willen! (D III 184-85.) The specific words are not as significant as the act of her retreat into a dream world.	The Wife sings with her eyes closed, a tangible indication of her tendency to daydream.	The Wife's lines are set in a triple (3/4) meter. This change offers a distinct contrast to the complex rhythms of the immediately preceding setting of the Nurse's lines, as does also the change in instrumentation, especially the cessation of the percussion. The Erotic Love Motive occurs both in the orchestra and also in the vocal line; the Flattery Motive occurs only in the orchestra. The Youth Motive appears for the first time in the vocal line, setting the words "mit hochmütigem Blick." The dreamy aspect of the lines is conveyed by the frequent alternation in the vocal setting between a triple meter and a duple meter.
The Nurse commands the Youth to appear: Es ist an der Zeit, herbei, mein Gebieter! (D III 185.) These lines summoning the Youth need not be understood, provided their invocative nature is conveyed, because the appearance of the Youth on the stage will demonstrate their meaning.	The Nurse claps her hands to summon the Youth. He immediately stands before them, supported by two small dark figures who instantly disappear. The Youth seems nearly lifeless.	To set these lines Strauss repeated the music which set the Nurse's lines "Du, Besen, leih mir die Gestalt! / Und Kessel du, leih mir deine Stimme!" Because both speeches are basically incantations, this relationship is appropriate. As with the previous passage the verse lines will probably not be comprehended, but the effect of the casting of a spell is conveyed. An orchestral interlude of four measures, wherein the Youth Motive and the Erotic Love Motive provide the melodic material, emphasizes the appearance of the Youth.
Upon perceiving the Youth the Wife cries out: Er und der Gleiche! Und doch nicht! (D III 185.) These lines indicate that the Youth is similar but not identical to the young man who is the subject of the Wife's daydreams. He is, therefore, not the real person of whom she has been dreaming, but a chimera. The meaning of these lines will probably be conveyed by the actions of the Youth on stage and by the singing of his lines from the orchestra pit.	The Wife opens her eyes and looks at the Youth. According to a letter of Strauss to Hofmannsthal (Briefwechsel, 27. V. 1915), for these directions stand in neither the Steiner edition nor in the score, the part of the Youth is to be taken by a dancer who stands with his back to the audience while his vocal lines are sung from the orchestra pit. Strauss made these suggestions to alleviate Hofmannsthal's distress when	Strauss set the Wife's first verse line to the Youth Motive and doubled it in the orchestra; it will probably be comprehended. The second line is likely to be covered by the dissonance which occurs in the accompaniment at this point.

TABLE OF ANALYSIS (continued)

Text	Visual Effects	Music
	the poet discovered that the Youth's verse lines were set to music which was similar to that of the Wife rather than to that of the Falcon. Hofmannsthal was eager that the genesis of the Youth through the magical powers of the Nurse not be mistaken.	The apparent insignificance of the words offered Strauss the opportunity for a lyrical passage; this he wrote. He introduced new melodic material in the first three verse lines, using a duple meter (2/4) for the vocal line while retaining the triple meter (3/4) for the accompaniment. (See musical example #40, the Youth Awakening Motive.) The composer employed the Erotic Love Motive and the Deception Motive in the vocal line for the remaining verses, returning to the 3/4 meter in the vocal line. The accompaniment is marked by the use of the Youth Motive and the high string tremolo which has persisted since its initial appearance during the arrival of the Youth.
The Nurse continues her attempt to estrange the Wife from Barak by seeking to involve the Wife in a romantic affair with the Youth: Um ihretwillen bist du hier, du Vielersehnter! Wie ist dir um jede Stunde, da du diesen nicht gekannt hast? (D III 185.) The gestures on stage will probably convey the meaning.	The Nurse runs to the Youth, who gradually comes to life, to speak to him. She next rushes to the Wife to speak to her. (The stage directions do not indicate that the Nurse is to point toward the Youth and toward the Youth as she talks to the Wife, but this gesture seems implicit in the speeches.)	Strauss made no special provision to ensure that these words would be understood. On the contrary, he designated that the accompaniment was to play forte in a triple meter; against this the vocal line must hold its own while being set in a duple meter. Although there is some doubling of the vocal line in the orchestra, the difference in meter tends to nullify the help this offers.
The Wife indicates her unwillingness to cooperate with the Nurse: Ich will hinweg und mich verbergen! (D III 185.) These lines emphasize both the Wife's independence from the Nurse and also her attachment to Barak. They are significant for a complete characterization of the Wife.	The Wife holds out her hands toward the Youth in a gesture of rejection; he hangs his head in apparent sorrow.	This pantomime is accompanied by a short orchestral interlude in which the Youth Motive and the Erotic Love Motive are most in evidence.
The Nurse's efforts to break the tie linking Barak and the Wife take the form of urging the Wife and the Youth to take advantage of their being together. Amme: Sei schnell, mein Gebieter! Und kühn, du Herrin! Unsagbar fliehend ist solches Glück! Stimmen: Sei schnell, mein Gebieter! Und kühn, du Herrin! Unsagbar fliehend	The Nurse stands between the two and tries once more to bring them together; she then attempts to leave the room, pulling the Empress after her.	In keeping with Hofmannsthal's apparent intent, Strauss did not try to emphasize the words, although at various times and for brief moments the orchestra doubles the vocal line an octave higher. Rather than utilize the final line of the Voices as it is given at the left, Strauss chose to set it as it occurs in the Nurse's speech. He apparently did this because he desired to repeat exactly for the verse line of the Voices the melodic line as he had written it for the Nurse. This would have been awkward for the

TABLE OF ANALYSIS (continued)

Text	Visual Effects	Music
ist das Glück! (D III 185.) The actions on the stage will convey the meaning of the words.		word "das". Musically, the first section of Act III ends with the cadence which closes the verse lines of the unseen chorus.
The Empress hears Barak's approach: Ach! Wehe! Dass sie sich treffen müssen, der Dieb und der, dem has Haus gehört, der mit dem Herzen und der ohne Herz! (D III 186.) This is essentially an emotional outburst of dismay at the prospect that Barak and the Youth should meet. Nevertheless, the speech delineates so clearly the Empress' sympathy for Barak that a setting which would allow comprehension seesm desirable.		The initial "Ach! Wehe!" of this speech is given emotional intensity by means of the high pitch (high C on "We-") of the setting. The remainder of the text is set to the Dissension Motive and to new melodic material. The angularity and rapidity of the vocal line, the high dynamic level of the accompaniment, and the dissimilarity between most of the vocal line and the accompaniment will make comprehension difficult, perhaps impossible. Although the plot can be followed without comprehension of these verses, the gradual development of the Empress from one who states "Ich will den Schatten Küssen, den sie wirft" to one who cries out "Dir, Barak, bin ich mich schludig" is lost. Musically, these lines of the Empress, the immediately following lines of the Nurse, and thereafter the orchestral interlude preceding Barak's arrival constitute a transition to the last part of Act III, to Barak's Feast. The dominant triple meter of the first part of the act is abandoned for a rapid duple meter which relaxes to a slower beat when Barak appears. There is also a transition to the key of D major, which remains the key center for the remainder of the scene.
Hofmannsthal prepares for Barak's entrance by having the Nurse announce his arrival before its occurrence: Voneinander! Ihr ist gegeben, zu hören, was fern ist, sie meldet: der Färber kehrt nach Hause! (D III 186.) The flurry of activity on the stage will probably demonstrate the meaning of these lines.	The Nurse rushes from the rear to the front of the stage where the Wife and the Youth are standing. As she throws her cloak over the Youth, the room darkens momentarily, during which time the Youth disappears. The Nurse picks up a straw from the floor which she hides in a recess in the wall. Barak arrives, carrying a huge copper dish. He is preceded by the Three Brothers and followed by the Beggar Children.	A gradual escalation of dramatic intensity begins with the Nurse's second verse line and culminates with Barak's arrival. The pitch level of the Nurse's vocal line ascends step by step until it reaches a high point on the first syllable of the word "Färber". At this point the escalation is taken up by the orchestra; a gradually ascending pitch and a crescendo provide the means whereby this is accomplished. Barak's Work Motive offers the primary melodic and harmonic material for both the accompaniment to the Nurse's lines and also for the following orchestral interlude.
Barak addresses the Wife: Was ist nun deine Rede, du Prinzessin,	The Wife turns her back on Barak, leaving his question unanswered for the present.	In keeping with Hofmannsthal's apparent intent, no special attempt was made by Strauss to make the words comprehensible. The vocal line consists primarily of new material:

TABLE OF ANALYSIS (continued)

Text	Visual Effects	Music
vor dieser Mahlzeit, du Wählerische? (D III 187.) The actions on the stage will probably demonstrate that Barak is asking for the Wife's approval of his purchases. The words need not, therefore, be understood.		one motive, Barak's Desire for Children Motive, is employed. That Barak should address the Wife utilizing this motive is particularly appropriate, since he views her principally as the mother of his children. The choice of this motive probably was not made for this reason, however, since it occurs as the most frequently used motive throughout the entire feast.
The Three Brothers relate the experience of purchasing the food and wine for the feast: Brüder: O Tag des Glücks, o Abend der Gnade! Das war ein Einkauf! Schlag ab, du Schlächter, ab vom Kalbe und ab vom Hammel! Und her mit dem Hahn! Du Bratenbrater, heraus mit dem Spiess! Heran, du Bäcker, mit dem Gebackenen, und du, Verdächtiger, her mit dem Wein! Wenn wir einkaufen, das ist ein Einkauf! O Tag des Glücks, o Abend der Gnade! Die Bettelkinder: O Tag des Glücks, o Abend der Gnade! (D III 187.) The structure of the Brothers' verse lines follows an ABCBA form: line one is part A; line two is part B; lines three to eight is part C; line nine is part B again; line ten is part A again. Comprehension is not necessary; these verse lines serve to express the excitement and happiness of the Brothers and the Children over the purchases and the impending feast.	The Three Brothers stand to the right of the stage in a row.	Strauss did not give the music the exact form of the structure of the verse; he did, however, employ a rondo form insofar as the first two and the last two lines of the Brothers were given settings which are predominantly harmonic while the remaining central lines are contrapuntally set. Strauss had the Brothers and the Children repeat the words "O Tag des Glücks!" at the close of the chorus; this repetition rounds off the first part of the feast with a strong cadential formula.
The Wife responds to Barak's question with a long tirade wherein she criticizes him for interrupting her dream: Wahrlich, es ist angelegt aufs Zertreten des Zarten, und es siegt das Plumpe, und dem, der Brot will, wird ein Stein gegeben! Und wer von der Schüssel der Träume kostete, zu dem treten Tiere und halten ihm den Wegwurf hin vom Tisch des Glücklichen, und er hat nichts wohin er sich flüchte, als in seine Tränen! Das ist meine Rede, du glückseliger Barak! (D III 187-88.)	The Wife will not look directly at Barak as she speaks. When she finishes, she bursts into tears.	The Wife's lines are accompanied by Barak's Work Motive, the Renunciation of Motherhood Motive, the Erotic Love Motive, the Youth Motive, the Irritability Motive, the Beating Motive, and Barak's Desire for Children Motive. Strauss thereby presented the Wife as confused by many conflicting desires. The vocal line is angular and not beautiful; at the rapid speed with which it must be sung, comprehension will probably not occur. The high emotional pitch will, however, be conveyed.

142

TABLE OF ANALYSIS (continued)

Text	Visual Effects	Music
Understanding the specific meaning values of the words is not essential, although it is necessary that the audience comprehend the Wife's negative reaction to the feast. This will probably be accomplished both by the ferocity with which she attacks the Dyer and also by her tears.		Strauss took pains to ensure that Barak's first line would be comprehended by accompanying it with chords only and by eliminating obtrusive contrapuntal lines. The vocal line employs Barak's Desire for Children Motive; this factor also facilitates comprehension since the audience is not forced to assimilate new melodic material at the same time as it must understand the words.
Barak tells the Brothers to eat and enjoy themselves, in effect saying that they should not let the Wife's bad mood ruin the feast. He then repeats the verse lines of forgiveness from Act III:	Barak puts the large dish he has been holding on the floor, pauses for a minute, and then addresses the Brothers.	The accompaniment becomes more complex after the first verse line, primarily doubling the vocal line until the forgiveness lines from Act III begin. At this point the importance of the orchestra increases, for it plays the Blessedness Motive in counterpoint to Barak's vocal line.
Esset, ihr Brüder, und lasset euch wohl sein! Ihre Zunge ist spitz, und ihr Sinn ist launisch, aber nicht schlimm— und ihre Reden sind gesegnet mit dem Segen der Widderufflichkeit um ihres reinen Herzens willen und ihrer Jugend. (D III 188.)		The effect is that of a duet between the Dyer and the orchestra. It is possible that the audience will comprehend some of the words, especially since the orchestral part does not contain new melodic material. The verse lines, however, have been set anew.
In the first verse line the Dyer takes upon himself the role of father-provider to the Three Brothers. This quality has been previously demonstrated, so comprehension of the words is not essential to following the plot. The audience will have, however, a better understanding of Barak's character if his patient forgiveness of the Wife—yet again—is comprehended.		
	The Brothers lounge around the food, surrounded by the Beggar Children. As neighbors, cripples, and dogs gather, Barak feeds the Children. He beckons to the Empress.	This orchestral interlude consists of a long and sustained melody, very simple in its harmonic structure. Because the same melody is repeated for the following text wherein Barak offers a delicacy to the Empress and seeks to send something special to the Wife, it may appropriately be called Barak's Generosity Motive. (See musical example #41.)
Barak offers food to the Empress and also to the Wife: Komm her, du still gehende Muhme, das ist für dich! Und geh hin zu der Frau: ob sie nicht will vom Zuckerwerk oder vom Eingemachten mit Zimmet. (D III 188–89.)	Barak gives the Empress a delicacy. The Empress starts to walk over to the Wife.	The first two verse lines are set to a melodic line which is of secondary importance to the accompaniment. The next two lines are essentially unaccompanied, Strauss taking this means of assuring that the actions on stage which follow these verse lines will be understood. The final line is again accompanied and may be covered. The second line of this speech reads as follows in the score: "da ist für dich!" The vocal line suggests
The pantomime on stage will convey the meaning of the first two lines, possibly also of the last three. The final line of the speech serves as a variation of the fourth line and hence is of lesser importance.		that Strauss may have chosen this variation in order to soften the total effect.

143

TABLE OF ANALYSIS (continued)

Text	Visual Effects	Music

These lines serve primarily as a vehicle to express the anger of the Wife:
 	
  Meinen Pantoffel in dein Gesicht,
  du Schleichende!
  Bitternis will ich tragen im Mund
  und nicht sie verzuckern!
  Was brauch ich Gewürze,
  Der Gram verbrennt mich!
  Um der grausamen Tücke willen
  und des erbärmlichen Geschickes!
    (D III 189.)
 	
The words need not be comprehended in order for the plot to be followed. The anger of the Wife will be readily perceived from her gestures and the manner in which the lines are sung. The listener familiar with the text will observe that the Nurse's influence is behind this outburst of anger, for the last two lines of the Wife's speech are a rephrasing of the Nurse's previous line: "O des blinden Geschicks und der Tücke des Zufalls!"   (D III 170.)
 	
Hofmannsthal intended these lines of the Wife to be sung in ensemble with the lines of the Three Brothers and of Barak given below. This may be deduced from the stage direction given with Barak's lines: "zugleich mit ihr und ihnen."
 	
The lines intended for ensemble with the Wife's lines above are:
 	
  Die Brüder: Wer achtet ein Weib
    und Geschrei eines Weibes?
    Aber der Langmütige,
    der bist du von je!
    Und der Grossmütige
    vom Mutterleib!
    Und der Wohltätige!
    Und der Freigebige!
    Das bist du!
    O unser aller Vater!
  Barak: Hier ist vom Guten,
    lasset euch wohl sein,
    meine Brüder,
    und freuet euch,
    dass ihr lebt!
    Es ist euch gegönnt,
    und ihr seid mir
    anstatt der Kinder!
  Die fremden Kinder: O du Färber unter den Färbern
	The Wife flies into a rage and throws her shoe at the Empress.
	
	Barak steps forward to sing his lines. (This direction is given in the piano score but not in the Steiner edition.)
		Strauss used these lines as a vehicle for emotional expression. For both the vocal line and the accompaniment the tempo is rapid with many notes of fairly short duration. Dissonances abound and seem particularly harsh following the consonances of the Generosity Motive. Motives utilized in the accompaniment are the Youth Motive, the Anger Motive, the Irritability Motive, and Barak's Desire for Children Motive. (See musical example #42 for the Anger Motive.) There is no occurrence of a motive in the vocal line, with the possible exception of the setting for the verse line "Bitternis will ich tragen im Mund." The melodic line utilized here—without exposition—occurs in Act II scene iii as a full-blown motive. (See musical example #43 for the Bitterness Motive.)
		
		Strauss structured the ensemble in a manner different from that intended by Hofmannsthal. 1) He has the Wife sing her lines alone. 2) Immediately after she has finished singing, the Three Brothers begin their lines and are joined by Barak after the Brothers' fourth line. 3) After the Brothers have sung their ninth line, the Wife enters and sings her lines again, omitting the first two ("Meinen Pantoffel in dein Gesicht, / du Schleichende!") 4) The final line of the Brothers ("O unser aller Vater!") is omitted. 5) The Brothers return to the lines which they sang at the beginning of the feast, preceding them with "Das war ein Einkauf! O Abend der Gnade!" They ("O Tag des Glücks, o Abend der Gnade!" etc.) are repeated exactly as they were initially used, even being set to music which in all essential respects is the same. 6) The Wife enters, singing lines from her initial response to the feast. Upon her entrance the exact repetition of the music ceases. The lines which she now sings are:
		
		  Es siegt das Plumpe,
		  und dem, der Brot will,
		  wird ein Stein gegeben;

144

TABLE OF ANALYSIS (continued)

Text	Visual Effects	Music
und unser aller Vater! (D III 189-90.)		und er hat nichts, wohin er sich flüchte, als in seine Tränen! (D III 187-88.) 7) As Barak sings his final lines ("Es ist euch gegönnt, / und ihr seid mir / anstatt der Kinder!"), the Brothers and the Beggar Children close the ensemble with repetitions of "O Tag des Glücks, o Abend der Gnade!" and a final "O Tag des Glücks!" The repetition of the words and music from the opening ensemble of the feast gives the overall scene from the entrance of Barak to the close of Act I scene ii a musical structure of ABA.
The lines of the Brothers (beginning "Wer achtet ein Weib") are constructed with reference to the Wife in the first two lines and with reference to Barak in the remaining ones. The total structure reveals itself as A (lines 1-2) B (lines 3-10).		Strauss followed the AB form of the verse lines of the Brothers by setting the first two lines monophonically; the remaining lines, excluding "O unser aller Vater!", are set polyphonically. Strauss omitted this line, setting it only for the Beggar Children as distant to the final ensemble.
	The stage directions given in the Steiner edition require that the Brothers, half-drunk, should bow and kiss the ground in front of Barak. This direction is omitted in the piano score, consistent with the omission of the line "O unser aller Vater!"	The omission of the line "O unser aller Vater!" for the Brothers represents a significant shift from Hofmannsthal's obvious intent that the close of this scene should focus on Barak as the communal father. The musical form which Strauss desired to employ did not allow inclusion of this idea.
Barak's lines in the ensemble are of the utmost simplicity. Although most of the time when Hofmannsthal wrote in this style he was signifying the importance of the meaning of the lines, this cannot be the case here since these lines were designed to be sung in ensemble. In this particular instance the simplicity may be interpreted as indicative of Barak's uncomplicated character.		Strauss utilized Barak's lines as a cantus firmus for much of the final ensemble. Musically, this occasions a slower tempo for these lines than for those of the Brothers, an effect which appears to be entirely in keeping with Hofmannsthal's intention of stressing Barak's simplicity in this speech. An orchestral interlude which is based on Barak's Joy Motive and Barak's Desire for Children Motive closes the scene and provides the transition to Act II scene ii by means of the Generosity Motive.
	Act II Scene ii	
	The curtain opens to reveal the solitary Imperial Falconer House bathed in moonlight. The Emperor	The orchestra provides a gradual transition from Barak's feast to the Falconer House, the location of the Emperor's major scene. The motives associated with the feast scene die away and the Falcon Cry Motive

TABLE OF ANALYSIS (continued)

Text	Visual Effects	Music
	arrives on horseback, dismounts, and hides himself in the trees to observe the house. The house is dark and silent; its door is closed.	and the Falcon Motive provide an introductory passage to the Emperor as Lover Motive and the Love Themes #1 and #2. The key which is most in evidence throughout the scene is G minor.
Hofmannsthal wrote the monologue of the Emperor in a primarily lyrical vein in which the meaning of most of the lines is conveyed by pantomime or gesture on the stage. In a letter to Strauss dated June 3, 1913, the poet characterized this scene and the Empress' parallel scene (Act II scene iv) as "lyrische Ausströmungen (als Ruhepunkte in der beständig fortschreitenden, irdischen Handlung IIa, IIc, IIe)."		Strauss interpreted Hofmannsthal's characterization of this scene ("lyrische Ausströmung") in such a way that he wrote the most extended melodious section which occurs in the entire opera. The principal musical ideas are the Emperor as Lover Motive, which is expanded to the length of a theme in the orchestra before the Emperor sings one word, and the two Love Themes. The greater length of these musical ideas provides greater thematic continuity than has previously occurred. The abundance of rich, flowing melodic lines makes this scene a primarily musical one; in this sense Strauss seems to have captured Hofmannsthal's intent exactly.
		Musically, the scene may have been written in rondo form. At least, Heinz Röttger, in analyzing the music of this scene, detects a rondo form which is preceded by an introduction and followed by a coda.[1] To discover this form one must identify or relate the Emperor as Lover Motive with the Stone Motive and the Love Theme with the Emperor as Hunter Motive because they serve to replace one another in certain of the reprises. Moreover, some of these motives occur in the subordinate as well as in the principal sections.
		This form is not incipient in the text; by far the greater number of verse lines are set in the secondary sections of the music rather than in the main sections. Twenty-eight lines occur in the secondary sections; fifteen and parts of four others occur in the primary section. The musical form is, therefore, external to the form of the text.
All of the text for this scene was written for the Emperor. The first thirteen lines of the monologue establish the location; this is the Falconer House where the Empress is supposed to be staying: Falke, Falke, du wiedergefundener— wo führst du mich hin, kluger Vogel?		The cuts which were made in Act 1 scene 1 of the original libretto necessitate comprehension of a minimal number of words. (See the discussion at the left.) These words are not given any special musical treatment to ensure comprehension. The vocal line does, however, carry the principle melodic idea; the orchestra doubles

[1] Das Formproblem bei Richard Strauss: gezeigt an der Oper "Die Frau ohne Schatten" mit Einschluss von "Guntram" und "Intermezzo", Neue Deutsche Forschungen: Abteilung Musikwissenschaft, Bd. 5 (Berlin: Junker und Dünnhaupt, 1937). See the discussion "Zweiter Aufzug, dritte Periode."

Text	Visual Effects	Music
"Das Falknerhaus, einsam im Walde,-- soll die drei Tage mir Wohnung sein-- niemand um mich als die Amme allein,-- ferne den Menschen, verborgen der Welt"-- So schrieb meine Frau--sie gabs dem Boten, künstlich ihr Haarband umflocht den Brief. Nun führst du mich über Berg und Fluss hierher den Weg, Seltsamer du-- Soll ich mich bergen hier im Schatten als ihr Jäger immerdar? Hast du darum mich hergeführt? (D III 190.) The audience needs to understand the words quoted from the Empress' letter wherein she claims that she will be living in the Falconer House: "Das Falknerhaus . . . / soll die drei Tage mir Wohnung sein . . ." If these lines are not understood, the anger which the Emperor expresses upon discovering her absence becomes unmotivated. In the line which immediately follows the reading of the letter the Emperor identifies the letter writer as the Empress: "So schrieb meine Frau . . ." The order in which this significant information is conveyed--the reading of the text preceding identification of the writer--is not consistent with the high standards of clarity which Hofmannsthal has previously established. Perhaps this seeming lack of clarity does not represent a momentary lowering of standards, however, but merely reflects cuts which were made in Act I scene i. As this scene was originally written, it contained reference to and perhaps portrayal of the banishment of the Empress to the Falconer House by the Emperor and also a short scene portraying the writing and sending of this letter to the Emperor. (Briefwechsel, Strauss to Hofmannsthal, 20. IV. 1914.) Had these cuts not been made, this scene would have carried no verse lines of significance as far as comprehension of the plot is concerned. The plot would instead have been entirely carried by the stage action. Indeed, this view of the scene--that significant actions carry the plot rather than significant verse lines--is substantiated by an analysis of the style of the scene. The verse lines are demonstrably longer than was the case for Act I scene I; the criteria for lines carrying significant information--simplicity, monosyllabicity, and brevity--are almost totally lacking.	The lines which the Emperor sings as a quotation from the Empress' letter will undoubtedly be read from an appropriate scroll or leaflet, even though no stage directions specify this action.	the vocal line as well as providing a chordal underlay. The words may or may not be comprehended, depending upon the singer's enunciation, stage location, and the balance between the orchestra and the singer. The consistent lyrical vein in which Strauss composed most of the scene is, however, at one with the style of the text. This unity of style is probably more important than audience comprehension of the words.

147

TABLE OF ANALYSIS (continued)

Text	Visual Effects	Music
In lines twelve to eighteen the Emperor realizes that the house is empty: Schläft sie? Mich dünkt, das Haus ist leer! Falke, mein Falke, was ist mir das? Wo ist deine Herrin zu nächtiger Zeit? Falke, mir ist: zur unrechten Stunde hast du mich hierher geführt. (D III 190-191.)		The central importance of the Empress to this scene is maintained by Strauss in his disposition of the music. There are 161 measures from the introduction to the end of verse line twenty-two and 154 measures thereafter to the end of the coda.
Lines nineteen to twenty-two prepare for the entrance of the Empress and the Nurse: Still, mein Falke, und horch mit mir! Es kommt gegangen, es kommt geschwebt-- ist das die Beute, die du mir schlägst? Stille-- (D III 191.) Occupying a position of central importance in the scene, which contains forty-four verses, is the return of the Empress, which occurs here after line twenty-two.	The Empress and the Nurse appear on stage and walk noiselessly to the Falconer House. Lights go on inside the house.	The principle melodic idea is located in the vocal line for nearly all verse lines of the first half of the scene. This ratio drops in the lines immediately following the appearance of the Empress; hereafter the orchestra is given much greater importance, particularly in its repetition of the Anger Motive. At no time does this motive occur in the vocal line, for it is not a cantabile line suited for singing. As the entire scene becomes more dramatic, the vocal line looses in cantabile expressiveness. This is not to say that the vocal line is subordinated to the orchestra; the Emperor as Hunter.Motive occurs frequently in the vocal line and the voice is given dominance at several different cadences.
Lines twenty-three to twenty-eight contain the Emperor's decision to kill the Empress: O weh, Falke, o weh! Wo kommt sie her! Wehe, o weh! Menschendunst hängt an ihr, Menschenatem folgt ihr nach, wehe, dass sie mir lügen kann-- wehe, dass sie nun sterben muss! (D III 191.)		
In lines twenty-nine to thirty-seven the Emperor contemplates one weapon after another and rejects them all as unsuitable to kill the Empress: Pfeil, mein Pfeil, du musst sie töten, die meine weisse Gazelle war! Weh! da du sie ritztest, ward sie ein Weib!-- Schwert, mein Schwert, du musst auf sie!	As the Emperor mentions the weapons with which he might kill the Empress, he handles each in turn.	Strauss achieved intensification in the weapon sequence by gradually raising the pitch of the vocal line. At "Pfeil, mein Pfeil" the principal note is Eb, at "Schwert, mein Schwert" the principal note is F, at "meine Hände" the note is G. The final line "Meine Hände vermögen es nicht" is unaccompanied, giving added emphasis to the meaning of the words.

Text	Visual Effects	Music
Weh, ihren Gürtel hast du gelöst-- du bist nicht, der sie töten darf! --Und meine nackten Hände! Weh! Meine Hände vermögen es nicht! Wehe, o weh! (D III 191-92.) Hofmannsthal seems to have designed the weapon sequence as a means of affording intensification through delay of the ultimate action. Lines thirty-eight to forty-four contain the decision to depart: Auf, mein Pferd, und du, Falke, voran! und führ mich hinweg von diesem Ort, wohin dein tückisches Herz dich heisst, führ mich ins öde Felsgeklüft, wo kein Mensch und kein Tier meine Klagen hört! Wehe, o weh! (D III 192.) The importance of this scene lies in its depiction both of the deteriorating relationship between Barak and the Wife and also of the Empress' growing concern for Barak. It is constructed so that conversations between Barak and the Wife provide an opening and closing frame around the appearance of the Youth. The Wife berates Barak for being slow to go to market. Comprehension of the lines is not imperative for understanding the plot; it is only important that the audience see her tendency to nag and to be unpleasant to Barak. Barak replies: Schon geh ich. Es ist heiss. Ich habe schwer geschafft seit diesem Morgen, und nicht viel vor mich gebracht.	The Emperor exits. Act II Scene iv The third scene of Act II, set again in the Dyer's hut, depicts events occurring on the second day of the pact. Attention is focused both at the beginning and also at the end of the scene upon the Empress' service to Barak. As the scene opens Barak is working; the Wife and the Nurse exchange impatient glances. As Barak speaks to the Wife, he turns away from his work to face her.	The cantabile style and themes of the beginning of the scene return, this time in Eb minor, for the departure section of the aria. The melodic ideas occur in the vocal line with doubling in the orchestra. Following the exit of the Emperor and the Falcon the orchestra continues briefly with a fortississimo reading of the Love Themes and then gradually subsides in preparation for the third scene of this act. The scene opens in F# minor with a single orchestral statement of the Wife's Bitterness Motive. The key center for the first part of the scene is F minor. Characterization of the Wife's dissatisfaction by means of an irregular setting of the verse lines takes precedence over a setting designed to assure comprehension. The orchestral accompaniment expresses her irritation by means of rapid note values. The Work Motive, doubled by the orchestra, occurs in the vocal line as she sings the final verse line ("und ist der Markt vorbei, / so kommen sie auch noch zurecht"). (D III 192.) Barak's lines are given an entirely different kind of setting than are the immediately preceding lines of the Wife. The rhythm is relaxed and the accompaniment is primarily chordal with the movement from one chord to another being very slow. A leisurely

149

TABLE OF ANALYSIS (continued)

Text	Visual Effects	Music
Gib mir zu trinken, Frau? (D III 192.) Short sentences in conversational style here frame a longer sentence in a lyrical style.		paced and mournful Market Song occurs in the orchestra. The first sentence ("Schon geh ich") is unaccompanied; the final line ("Gib mir zu trinken, Frau?") is doubled by the orchestra.
The Wife's refusal to serve Barak comes in the form of the curt assertion that maids are present: "Sind Mägde da." Simplicity and brevity signify the importance of this line. This is also true of Barak's pathetic reply: "Gibst du mir nicht?"	The Wife does not respond to Barak's attempt to communicate with her; she refuses to face him or to speak directly to him.	Strauss left the Wife's line unaccompanied and set Barak's reply over a sustained chord in the accompaniment, thereby assuring comprehension.
	The Nurse gives the drink, which she has, unbidden, drugged with a sleeping potion, to the Empress, who is then instructed by the outstretched arm of the Wife to take it to Barak. He drinks.	The Descent Motive dominates the musical interlude during which the Empress performs this service.
Barak's growing sleepiness is indicated verbally in a verse line of brevity and simplicity: Mich schläfert. Es ist heiss. (D III 193.)		Strauss set the words of the first sentence to a dominant to tonic drop in F# major. This is the third occurrence in this scene of a falling fifth interval in the vocal line of Barak. It was also used to set: 1) "Es gibt derer"; 2) "Schon geh ich." The first sentence ("Mich schläfert") is unaccompanied; the second is accompanied by a sustained chord.
The Wife makes fun of Barak in a longer speech consisting of five lines. The meaning is not as significant as her expression of contempt for her husband, of which the verse lines are only one outward indication.		The characterization of the Wife is carried here primarily by the orchestra which plays the Irritability Motive, the Bitterness Motive, and Barak's Work Motive. The Wife's vocal lines contain neither significant thematic material nor motives.
Barak replies to the Wife's expression of contempt without anger: Mich schläfert sehr. Ich muss hier liegen, Frau. Zu Abend-dann--trag ich-die Ware zu Markt. (D III 193.) The simplicity and brevity of the first verse line seem to indicate that the lines carry meanings which are significant for following the plot. In this case, however, the concomitant stage action should make the plot clear.	Barak goes to sleep on a sack of herbs.	Barak's sleepiness is conveyed in the orchestral accompaniment where broken fragments of the Market Song are sounded. The vocal line itself conveys the drowsiness by means of rests which occur in the middle of lines. This is especially evident in the use of the Market Song for setting the last verse line; the Song is broken off at three different points before the statement reaches its end. The ritardando which occurs here gives additional emphasis to the drowsiness which is overcoming him.

Text	Visual Effects	Music
Once again the Wife expresses her contempt for Barak. She finishes the Market Song, which Barak had left unfinished, mocking him as she sings: Und sparst den Esel, der sie dir schleppt! Sparst den Esel, der dir sie schleppt! (D III 193.)		Strauss followed Hofmannsthal's cue by using fragments from the Market Song to set these verse lines. The folk-song quality of its original appearance is distorted by the rapidity of the tempo and the dissonance of the accompaniment where the melody is set in parallel ninths.
The Nurse tells the Wife to be quiet, for Barak sleeps because she has given him a sleeping potion: Herrin, halt inne mit Schreien und Zürnen! Ich hab ihm einen Schlaftrunk eingeschüttet! (D III 193.)	The Nurse runs to the Wife in order to silence her.	Strauss set the Nurse's second verse line to a step-wise ascending and descending vocal line; this is unusual in his setting of the Nurse's verse lines and appears to represent an attempt to make the line comprehensible. The vocal line is also unaccompanied.
It is important that the audience understand that the Nurse has given Barak a sleeping potion without the knowledge of the Wife.		
The Wife's previous scorn for Barak gives way to concern for him: Wer hiess dich das tun? Barak! Barak! (D III 193-94.)		The first verse line is unaccompanied, reflecting Strauss's apparent desire to assure comprehension. The second line is accompanied by the Irritability Motive in a version which is exceedingly tamed down by the harmony which is employed.
Simplicity and brevity indicate the significance of the speech.		
In an exchange between the Nurse and the Wife the Nurse assures the Wife that Barak is well and alludes to the hours of happiness which await her, the mistress: Die Amme: Er schläft bis an den Morgen. Ihm ist wohl. Viel schöne Stunden, Herrin, sind vor dir. Die Frau: Wer hat dich gelehrt, welche Stunde mir schön heisst? Ich will ausgehen? Du bleib dahinten. Ich will nicht in deinen Händen sein, und dass du ausspähest all mein Verborgenes, du alte weiss und schwarz gefleckte Schlange! (D III 194.)	The Wife runs over to Barak and looks at him. The Nurse pulls her away.	The Wife's assertion of independence is written into the setting of the first verse line by means of the emphasis given each word and the concurrent relaxation of the tempo which this forces. The last half of the line ("welche Stunde mir schön heisst") is also unaccompanied. The motives for the setting include the Youth Motive, the Irritability Motive, and the Nurse Motive. None of these occur in the vocal line.
Of primary importance here is the Wife's refusal to follow the Nurse's suggestion. The meaning is not otherwise significant.		
The Nurse persists in her attempt to draw the Wife into erotic play with the Youth:		Strauss modulated to V of E major and then established E major, his erotic key, as the key center for the

TABLE OF ANALYSIS (continued)

Text	Visual Effects	Music
Willst du den in der Ferne suchen, Herrin, der deiner harret und deines Winkes? Gewähre! Ich breit ihm vor deine Füsse— und sprich es aus: er darf heran! (D III 194.) This speech refers to the Youth in every line; the increasing simplicity of vocabulary and syntax give to the speech a growing intensity, culminating in the last half of the final line. The simplicity of vocabulary and near monosyllabicity of the final line attest to its significance. The Wife replies to the Nurse's request that she be allowed to "call" the Youth with the following lines: Spräch ich es aus und spräche einerlei Rede mit dir, es wäre einerlei Rede nicht. Der darf wohl heran, der, den ich meine— doch eben von dir darf nichts heran: darum auch er nicht. Von ihm darf heran, was du nie wahrnimmst: was nie an deiner Hand sich mir naht. – – – – – – – – – Von wo der Strand nie betreten wurde, beträte ihn einer von dort her, dem wehrte keine Mauer und kein Riegel. (D III 194–95.) Lines four to ten, which contain the Wife's refusal to be compromised by the Nurse, were written in conversational style. Comprehension of these verses assures that the complexity of the Wife's personality is observed. Hofmannsthal prefaced the last six lines of this speech with the direction "Träumerisch, sehnsüchtig." The tendency of the Wife to escape from reality by dreaming is an important aspect of the Wife's personality and must be comprehended by the audience if Hofmannsthal's vision is not to be distorted. The Nurse's reaction to the obvious softening of the Wife's resistance to meeting the Youth is to conjure the Youth: "Ich ruf ihn!" The activity on stage will probably convey the meaning of the verse.	The Nurse prepares to conjure the Youth.	following section of this scene. The second verse line is largely unaccompanied; the use of a dropping sixth interval is much in evidence. (The interval of the sixth is dominant in the Nurse's attempts to persuade the Wife to enter into the pact in Act I scene ii.) The final line is not unaccompanied as the text appears to require. Strauss did, however, give it emphasis by using the highest pitch of the speech for the word er of "er darf heran!" None of the significant lines (lines four to ten) is set with the ultimate means which Strauss employed to assure comprehension; none is unaccompanied. The sixth line utilizes the Youth Motive, however, and the fourth and fifth lines are set with stress marks. The principle melody for this speech is given to the orchestra; occasionally the vocal line joins the orchestra and participates in the main theme. Lines seven to ten are accompanied by an intermingling of variations on the Erotic Motive and Barak's Desire for Children Motive. Perhaps in setting these lines, which speak of the Youth, in this manner Strauss was indicating that the Wife's secret desire was to establish an erotic relationship with Barak and not with the Youth of whom she speaks. Strauss interpreted the last six lines of this speech, the "dreamy" lines, in this fashion: 1) the accompaniment is highly pitched with no note below middle C# employed until the cadence on the final line; 2) the vocal line tends to be more melodious than has been customary for the settings of the Wife's lines; 3) the tempo increases in speed; 4) the key center is F# major and minor, Strauss's dream key. The third means listed here, the increase in tempo, appears to be contradictory to Hofmannsthal's desires since a faster tempo usually conveys additional excitement and activity rather than a dreamy retreat from life. Strauss set the Nurse's verse line to the Youth Motive, but the vocal line is covered by the fortissimo dynamic level of the orchestra and by a contrapuntal line in the orchestra which constitutes the first appearance of the Magic Motive. (See musical example #44.)

152

TABLE OF ANALYSIS (continued)

Text	Visual Effects	Music
The Wife reacts negatively to the appearance of the Youth, avoiding interaction with him by denigrating the Nurse: Schlange, was hab ich mit dir zu schaffen! und solchen, die du bringest! (D III 195.) These lines need not be comprehended, provided that the emotional tone of anger and rejection is conveyed.	The room darkens momentarily, then brightens with a sudden flash of light. The Youth appears, led by the Nurse.	Strauss gave these lines a rapid setting which is more declamatory than lyrical in style. The accompaniment consists of a highly pitched motivic figure centering on C. The lightness of the accompaniment may allow comprehension.
Surprisingly, the Youth also dislikes his sudden appearance before the Wife, lamenting the power which forces such an unprepared visit: Wer tut mir das, dass ich jäh muss stehen vor meiner Herrin! Der Macht ist zu viel! Zu jäh die Gewalt! (D III 195.) The audience need not comprehend these lines in order to follow the plot.	The score is supplied with a note, not given in the Steiner edition, that the Youth is to be portrayed by a dancer with his back to the audience while the vocal lines are to be sung from the prompt box. This means of presenting the Youth originated with Hofmannsthal, as can be proved by his letter to Strauss of 14. V. 1915. (Briefwechsel.)	Tremolos in the strings relate this speech to the Pavilion scene of Act I scene 11.
The Wife criticizes the Nurse once again and then demands her scarves so that she may go for a walk. The meaning of the lines is not as significant as her continued rejection of the Youth, which will be clear from her gestures on the stage.	The Wife refuses to look at the Youth when she shows anger with the Nurse. As she claims that she had been planning to go for a walk, however, she glances coquettishly at him. She then prepares to go.	Strauss began a new section with these lines, using A major as the key center. A rhythmic variation on Barak's Desire for Children Motive provides the principal melodic material. The motive does not occur in the Wife's vocal line; instead the Anger Motive sets her lines.
The Nurse asserts that the Wife actually desires nothing other than the meeting with the Youth. The words are not significant as far as following the plot is concerned, for their meaning will be conveyed by the gestures on stage.	The Nurse grasps the feet and legs of the Wife, preventing her exit.	The Nurse's lines are set to a variation of the Desire for Children Motive, exemplifying Strauss's musical use of motives. These lines and the immediately preceding ones by the Wife represent something of a dead spot because no essential information is contained in them and lyricism does not predominate in the music. The gestures alone must maintain the interest of the audience.
	The Nurse blows into the fire, an action symbolizing her role as pander.	

153

TABLE OF ANALYSIS (continued)

Text	Visual Effects	Music

The following lines of the Nurse, of the Youth, and of the Wife do not require comprehension by the audience and are, therefore, ideally suited for an ensemble:
 	
Amme: Wer teilhaftig ist der Wonne,
    der fürchtet auch den Tod nicht,
    denn er hat gekostet von der Ewigkeit,
    aber wie er dahin gelangt ist,
    das ist ihm vergessen!
Jüngling: Bin ich dir ferne, so ists deine Nähe,
    die mich zerbricht,
    bin ich vor dir, so wirst du unnahbar,
    und deine Ferne ists, die mich tötet!
Frau: Ich habe geträumt, dass ich zu dir fliege
    mit unablässigen Küssen
    wie eine Taube, die ihr Junges füttert—
    und mein Traum hat dich getötet!
        (D III 196-97.)
 	
Although an ensemble would appear to be the ideal setting for these lines, this is not specifically indicated in the Steiner edition.
		Strauss wrote an ensemble for these lines, employing the Heart Motive, the Youth Motive, and the Anger Motive. String tremolos and a high register characterize the accompaniment.

	As the Youth completes his lines, he falls over backwards as though he were unconscious. The Wife bends over him and removes his hands from his face, whereupon he looks at her and reaches out for her. She retreats with a cry, just as the Nurse, pulling the Empress after her, is leaving.	A short orchestral interlude accompanies the activity on stage. Motives employed are those of the previous ensemble.
		Strauss set the Wife's outcry on a high C, giving tremendous dramatic impact to her confrontation with the Youth. The final musical section of Act II scene iii begins with the measure of her outcry; the key center is F major. Choice of this key to complete the scene represents a rounding off of the scene because it opened in F major / F# minor. (Intervening key centers were E major and A major.) Immediately following the Wife's cry of alarm the Barak's Desire for Children Motive, restored to its original rhythm, occurs.
The stage direction which precedes the following speech is prefaced with "jäh verwandelt.": Weh mir, wohin? Verrätterinnen! Hierher! Zu mir! Sind die Toten lebendig, so sind wohl die Schlafenden tot!		Strauss indicated the transformation which the Wife undergoes primarily by means of a key change (A major to F major) and an increase in tempo. The accompaniment is also altered from sustained chords and a melodic line paralleling the vocal line to rapid sixteenth notes and rests. The final line cf this speech in the Steiner edition is "Ich will! wach auf!

TABLE OF ANALYSIS (continued)

Text	Visual Effects	Music
Wach auf, mein Mann! Ein Mann ist im Haus! Ich will! wach auf! zu mir! (D III 197.) The sudden transformation of the Wife which occurs here is one from that of day-dreamer ("Ich habe geträumt . . .") and retreat from reality to an engagement with life through awakening Barak. The change in length of verse line reflects the Wife's transformation; the lines in this speech average slightly more than five syllables per line while the verse lines in the dream speech average nearly ten syllables per line. Moreover, half of the verse lines of this speech are broken in the middle, creating the effect of even greater activity. Only one of the eight lines has a sense-meaning carried into the immediately following line while the dream speech consists only of one sentence. For perhaps the first time in her life the Wife wills to engage herself with another ("Ich will!"). The meaning of this speech will be conveyed by the Wife's stage actions and by the change in setting required by the short verse lines.		zu mir!" Strauss altered this to: "Ich will! wach auf, wach auf, wach auf! zu mir!" These broken lines give an impression of great haste and urgency, emphasizing Hofmannsthal's original intention.
The Steiner edition gives the following reading of Barak's first lines upon being awakened and of the Nurse's reaction to the Wife's awakening of her husband: Amme: Gott schütz uns vor einer jungen Närrin! Sei du getrost! Schnell dreht sich der Wind, und wir rufen dich wieder! Barak: Was schlief ich so schwer? Wer rüttelt mich auf? (D III 197.)	The Nurse throws her coat over the Youth as Barak awakens and sits up.	Strauss altered the order of Barak's and the Nurse's lines so that they read: Amme: Gott schütz uns vor einer jungen Närrin! Sei du getrost! Barak: Was schlief ich so schwer? Amme: Schnell dreht sich der Wind, und wir rufen dich wieder! Barak: Wer rüttelt mich auf? This change does not appear to destroy the sense of the verses, but the relationship of Barak's lines to each other, where the second line intensifies the first, is destroyed. The Nurse's proverb ("Schnell dreht sich . . . .") is set with a programmatic accompaniment suggestive of a wind blowing. Barak's lines are slow and unaccompanied, thereby accruing weight and solemnity.
The Wife reproaches Barak for sleeping and threatens to leave him if it happens again: Du sollst nicht schlafen am hellen Tag! Sollst wahren dein Haus vor Dieben und Räubern und meiner achten! Geschieht mir dergleichen von dir noch einmal,		Strauss set the Wife's lines to the motive which has dominated this scene, the Desire for Children Motive. It occurs both in the vocal line and also in the orchestra where it is used contrapuntally. Although the first five verse lines are set with the orchestra doubling the voice, the additional contrapuntal lines will probably prevent comprehension. This is also true of the rest of the speech where the vocal line does not

155

TABLE OF ANALYSIS (continued)

Text	Visual Effects	Music
so ist meines Bleibens hier nicht länger! Verstehst du mich! (D III 197-98.) In the fourth line the Wife demands of Barak that he respect her. In the light of Barak's blindness to the mystery and beauty of her personality, this appears as a plea to be loved for all that she is and not just because she is a female who could become the mother of his children. Were the audience to understand these lines, they would gain an insight into the Wife's character and into her relationship to Barak. The shortness of the verse lines continues the style which she had used previously for awakening Barak and represents a continuation of her efforts to communicate with him.		have the advantage of orchestral doubling.
Barak does not sense the Wife's urgent desire for recognition of her individuality; instead he is possessed by the thought that robbers are in the house: Sind Räuber hier? Den Hammer dort! Ihr Brüder her! Zum Bruder her! (D III 198.)	Barak stands up and looks around wildly. The Dyer picks up a hammer and looks around for robbers.	Strauss continued to emphasize Barak's verse lines, setting them here so that they are largely unaccompanied. Fragments of the Market Song sound from the orchestra.
When Barak does not respond to her attempt to communicate, the Wife reverts to her previous scornful treatment of him: Lass du dein Schreien und tölpisch Gehaben! Unter der Arbeit schlägst du mir hin, kommst mir von Sinnen, redest fremd. Hast du die Sucht, oder schierts dich so wenig, mich zu erschrecken täppisch und roh! (D III 198.) The verse lines are once again long; this demonstrates Hofmannsthal's use of a change in style to communicate changes in emotional states.	The Wife takes the hammer away from her husband.	This speech of the Wife was accorded greater significance by Strauss than her preceding one, "Du sollst nicht schlafen . . ." The emphasis may be misplaced, for these verse lines are probably not as important as the previous ones.
The following three lines spoken by the Nurse exhibit a different aspect of her personality, a tendency toward sexual perversion: Wie sie ihm sich hernimmt und sattelt und aufzäumt, die Prächtige die! (D III 198.) These verse lines are insignificant as far as plot development is concerned; the actions of the Nurse	These lines are not directed to anyone; the Nurse in isolation speaks for herself.	Strauss set these lines to the Youth Motive. In congruence with their lack of significance as far as plot development is concerned, he made no attempt to ensure comprehension.

TABLE OF ANALYSIS (continued)

Text	Visual Effects	Music
on stage, especially in the last act, will demonstrate this grotesque facet of her personality better than words.		As is customary for Barak's verse lines, these are set at a slow tempo with a minimum of movement in both the accompaniment and the vocal line. This type of setting facilitates audience comprehension. Strauss interpreted the Wife's verse lines as an emotional outburst, setting them to angular melodic lines containing wide leaps and utilizing hardly any step-wise movement.
Barak answers the Wife, showing at last recognition of her concern for him, but the opportunity for a closing of the spiritual gap which exists between them has passed and the Wife responds scornfully:		

Barak: War dir bange um mich,
    du Gute!
  Bin ja wieder bei dir!
  Frau: Wieder bei mir! Das ist ja recht viel!
  Er ist wieder bei mir! Ei, grosse Freude!
  Wieder bei mir!
    (D III 198-99.)		

The Wife's rejection of Barak's attempt to draw closer to her demonstrates the precariousness of their relationship. Comprehension of Barak's lines will help the audience to follow these changes more easily. The Wife's verse lines, however, serve more as a vehicle to express her scorn for Barak than as a means to convey information; comprehension of her lines is not necessary.		
The lines of Barak and the Wife plus the preceding three lines of the Nurse are customarily cut for performances. The latent Lesbianism, the irrelevance to the main plot, and a lack of lyrical interest in the music of the Nurse's part have apparently caused the cutting of her lines. As omission of only her lines would have occasioned an awkward musical entrance for Barak, his lines and the Wife's reply are usually dropped, too.	Barak gathers his scattered work tools together, then stares off into space.	Barak's lines are given continuity by the use in the orchestra of a motive from the song "Kinder waren sie einmal" from Act I scene ii. Although this motive has previously been used, it receives here its most extensive use and can be fittingly termed Barak's Animal Motive. (See musical example #45.) Strauss interpreted the second verse line as an intensification of the first, using a rise in pitch both in the vocal line and also in the orchestra to accomplish this purpose. The greater movement in the orchestra than is customary for the accompaniment of Barak's vocal line will probably prevent comprehension of the important fourth line, although circumstances of performance may ultimately determine this.
Barak comments on his falling to sleep:		

Es widerfährt mir, was ich nicht kenne,
  und ist eine Gewalt über mir im Dunklen--
  Mein bester Mörser ist mir zersprungen--
  Versteh ich mein Handwerk nicht mehr?
    (D III 199.)		

The first two lines, in which Barak expresses an awareness of an external power over his life, are the opening statement of the concern which dominates the final scene of this act. Audience comprehension would be helpful, but it does not appear to be essential. The meaning of the third line will probably be conveyed visually on the stage. The final line must be understood if the Wife's reply to Barak is to make sense.		

157

TABLE OF ANALYSIS (continued)

Text	Visual Effects	Music
The Wife answers Barak's question ("Versteh ich mein Handwerk nicht mehr?") by stating that he certainly does not understand one craft or else he would not speak at this moment about himself and his work: Ein Handwerk verstehst du sicher nicht, wie dus von Anfang nicht verstanden, sonst sprächest du jetzt nicht von dir und diesem Mörser. Geschah dir das, was dir eben geschah, dein Herz müsste schwellen vor Zartheit, und es müsste dir bangen, die Hand zu heben und deinen Fuss vor dich zu setzen, um des Köstlichen willen, das du zerstören könntest. Aber es geht ein Maulesel am Abgrund hin, und es ficht ihn nicht an die Tiefe und das Geheimnis! (D III 199.) The first line is important for an understanding of the plot because here the Wife verbalizes Barak's failure in his relationship to her. Comprehension of this line is necessary if a complete picture of the mutual failures of this marriage is to be perceived. Hofmannsthal wrote the speech with three clearly defined sections. The first section consists of a torrent of criticism directed at Barak and ends with the short line "und diesem Mörser." The brevity of the line, five syllables compared to the previous eight and nine, indicates a relaxation of tempo. In the second section, lines five to ten above, the Wife reflects upon her wishes for Barak's behavior. The section is constructed so that the entire passage reaches a climax in the last two lines. The preceding verse lines delay the arrival of this climax and thereby gradually build tension. This section exhibits the Wife's tendency to dream and to search outside of her life for the beauty which she is unable to perceive within it. In the third section, lines eleven to fourteen above, the Wife expresses her perception of Barak's behavior, which contrasts so greatly with her vision of what it might be.	The Wife looks fixedly at Barak.	Strauss set the significant first line of the speech to the Denial of Motherhood Motive and left it unaccompanied. These two factors, the use of a motive in the vocal line and the omission of any accompaniment, would in most cases assure comprehension. This is not necessarily true here because of the nature of this particular motive, which is very difficult to sing. The second line, although not set to a motive, is also unaccompanied, giving it importance but making it secondary to the first line. In accordance with the structure of the text, the final line of this section is set poco ritardando. The second section of her speech, the dream passage, is provided with a stage direction that does not occur in the Steiner edition: "sehr verhalten und nicht laut." Strauss thereby required the music to be performed in an appropriately dreamy manner. Musically, the voice, doubled an octave lower in the orchestra, carries the primary line. The orchestra becomes more of a partner than a subordinate during the next few lines with statements of Barak's Desire for Children Motive, his Animal Motive, and a variation of the Shadow Motive. The effect of a dream is created throughout most of the first two lines by means of a string tremolo. This is subsequently dropped and the Barak Animal Motive assumes ever greater importance as a disturbing counterpoint to the vocal line. Strauss placed the climax of the second section on the first syllable of the word "Köstlichen", giving it an entire measure on a high $G^{\#}$. The preceding melodic lines gradually build up to this note; the following ones subside. The third section differs greatly from both the second and the first because its primary characteristic is neither dominance of the words over the music as in section one nor sustained melody of a quiet nature as in section two. Instead it is an emotional expression of anger. The orchestra employs the Work Motive, the Desire for Children Motive, the Keikobad Motive, and parallels the voice in its use of the Secret Motive from Act I scene ii for the setting of the word "Geheimnis". Were this a primary motive (the Secret Motive), Strauss might be criticized for using this motive to set the word "Geheimnis" here. Although the same word is involved in both passages, the meaning is entirely different. In Act I scene ii the underlying reference is to the pact; here the reference is to the sense of mystery surrounding an individual's being. A stage direction is given for the last two verse lines which is not included in the Steiner edition: "langsam und

TABLE OF ANALYSIS (continued)

Text	Visual Effects	Music
Barak's total lack of comprehension of his failure in his relationship to the Wife is demonstrated by his reply to her speech: Ich höre und weiss nicht, was eines redet, und habe vergossen den Leim, da ich hinfiel— und mir ist bange um mein Handwerk, und dass ich nicht werde nähren können, die meinen Händen anvertraut sind. (D III 199-200.) Barak's character will not be fully understood if this speech, with the exception of the second line which is negligible, is not comprehended.	Barak speaks to the maid (the Empress), who is helping him pick up his tools.	düster." The underlying Keikobad Motive which occurs here imparts a sense of gloom and foreboding, suggesting that Strauss is responsible for the addition. For the first time in the opera Barak's lines are set against complex contrapuntal lines in the orchestra. The simplicity which up to this point has characterized the accompaniment of his vocal line is replaced by an accompaniment which carries comparatively greater tension and leads toward the dramatic finale at the end of this act. The Sorrow Motive and the Animal Motive, including its characteristic contrapuntal form as it was developed in the immediately preceding lines of the Wife, are used in the orchestra. Although the orchestra's increased significance causes a relative diminishing of importance of the vocal line for the first three verse lines, the vocal line once again attains dominance over the orchestra in the last two lines, where the Desire for Children Motive occurs in the vocal line. Another stage direction not occurring in the Steiner edition precedes Barak's lines here: "etwas schwer-mütig." No conflict is apparent with Hofmannsthal's intent.
The Wife resents Barak's narrowness of vision which prevents him from seeing the mystery which her being represents. She threatens to leave him: Um Nahrung für mich gräme dich nicht! Und wenn du mich siehst meine Tücher nehmen, vielleicht zu fahren auf dem Flusse, oder was immer die Lust mich wird heissen— kann sein, dann komme ich eines Abends nicht wieder heim zu dir.— Denn es ist nicht von heute, dass du meine Stimme hörest und fassest sie nicht in deinem Sinn, und ist dir ferne, die du nahe glaubst, und wähnest, du hättest sie im Gehäuse wie einen gefangenen Vogel der dein ist, um wenig Münze gekauft auf dem Markt: die doch anderswo, anders daheim. (D III 200.) There are two lines here which need audience	The Wife takes her scarves and prepares to go out for a walk.	For the first time in the opera Strauss gave the Wife an extended lyrical passage which dominates over the orchestra. A new motive, the Lack of Commitment Motive, which receives its first complete statement in the voice is partly responsible for this change. An increasingly frequent repetition of this new motive—in the orchestra, however—parallels the intensification in the verse lines here. (See musical example #46.) The significant line "kann sein, dann komme ich eines Abends" is set to a new motive, the Freedom Motive. (See musical example #47.) The second important line, "nicht wieder heim zu dir," is largely unaccompanied. With the exception of the last three lines Strauss set the second half of the speech with greater emphasis given to the orchestra than had occurred in the first half of the speech. The frequent repetition of the Bitterness Motive and the Lack of Commitment Motive in the orchestra causes this change. As the orchestra assumes this greater importance, the essentially instrumental nature of the Lack of Commitment Motive becomes increasingly clear; the vocal line is simplified and the characteristic triplet opening figure is reduced to one note. Strauss did not choose to reduce tension in the second

159

TABLE OF ANALYSIS (continued)

Text	Visual Effects	Music
comprehension if the plot is to be followed: "kann sein, dann komme ich eines Abends / nicht wieder heim zu dir.--" The remaining verse lines constitute an expression of her sense of freedom from any commitment to Barak, in essence a rephrasing of the two key lines given immediately above. Because these remaining lines contain the same idea as was previously given, Hofmannsthal implies that the music is to attain some measure of dominance here. The lines preceding the key ones ("kann sein, dann komme . . .") serve to delay them, causing intensification from the beginning of the speech to that point. The drop in the average number of syllables per line at the end of the speech suggests a ritardando and a lessening of tension. The lessening of tension is also supported by the structure of these lines wherein the sense of the lines is completed as they occur. No intensification through delay occurs.		half of the speech as was suggested by the structure of the verse lines. Instead he piled climax on climax throughout the last four lines, beginning with an orchestral crescendo and ending with a high B in the vocal line on the word Markt.
	The Wife gestures to the Nurse to accompany her, to the Empress to remain, and leaves. Barak, perplexed and gloomy, stares into space. Nearby the Empress is on her knees gathering his tools together. With a start Barak becomes aware that he is not alone.	Strauss continued the high intensity level of the Wife's solo for thirty-one measures, allowing the Wife more than sufficient time to put on her scarves and make a dramatic exit. Use is made of the Bitterness Motive, the Lack of Commitment Motive, and the Freedom Motive. The interlude gradually subsides during the next eight measures, ending with a sudden, loud chord which occurs simultaneously with Barak's discovery that he is not alone.
On becoming aware that he is not alone, Barak asks simply, "wer da?" (D III 200.)	The Empress looks up at Barak.	These two words assume dominance over the accompaniment which consists of a soft chord, played in a low-pitched tremolo.
One of the most significant of the Empress' lines occurs in answer to Barak's question: "Ich, mein Gebieter, deine Dienerin!" (D III 201.) The Empress expresses verbally her willingness to serve Barak. The entire scene serves as one gigantic preparation for this line and the corresponding pantomime. In this manner the role of the Empress grows in relative significance. The focus on the Empress which occurs here also serves to prepare for the following scene which is entirely dominated by the Empress.		A short orchestral interlude of nine measures follows Barak's words, during which time the pitch gradually rises and a crescendo takes place; this leads to the Empress' line and gives it emphasis. The transition to B minor, the key center for the next scene, begins at this point. Strauss set the verse line in the middle soprano range and paced it slowly, giving each syllable emphasis. The orchestra plays the Empress Motive and the Suffering Motive at a low dynamic level.

160

Text	Visual Effects	Music
	Act II Scene iv	

This scene is the pendant to the second scene of this act, as Hofmannsthal indicated in his letter to Strauss of June 3, 1913. (Briefwechsel.) Both were designed to present lyrical moments of repose between the movement toward catastrophe occurring in scenes i, iii, and v of this act. As in scene ii, the relationship between the Emperor and the Empress is explored, but while scene ii presented the relationship from the Emperor's point of view, the opposite viewpoint is brought to the surface here.

The number of verses in the three sections of this scene is unequal; the first section contains five verse lines for the Empress, the second none by the Empress but six by voices emanating from the interior of the cavern and two by the Falcon. The third section contains twenty-five verse lines for the Empress.

The Empress sings the lines of the first section of the scene in her sleep:

Sieh--Amme--sieh
des Mannes Aug, wie es sich quält!
Vor solchen Blicken liegen Cherubim
auf ihrem Angesicht!
Dir--Barak--bin ich mich schuldig!
(D III 201.)

Visual Effects column:

The scene has a tripartite construction visually. The first section occurs in the Empress' bedroom in the Falconer House. The Empress sleeps uneasily and sings in her sleep. In contrast to her, the Nurse sleeps well.

Music column:

Musically, this scene begins with the Empress' final word, "Dienerin", of the preceding scene. At that point the key center, B minor, for the scene is firmly established. A long orchestral interlude enables the scene change to occur and creates a background of uneasiness throughout the Empress' dreams. The Blessedness Motive is primarily responsible for this uneasiness because of its frequent appearance in its more tense form; the final interval drops a major or minor seventh rather than its more usual major sixth. Strauss also used the Stone Motive, the Emperor Motive, the Empress Motive, both Love Themes, and at one point the Nurse Motive. The Keikobad Motive, the Traitor Motive, and the Desire for Children Motive also occur briefly. The only new material is the Servant Motive, which does not, however, play a significant role. (See musical example #48.) The Blessedness Motive assumes ever greater importance throughout the interlude, finally establishing itself as the principal melodic material for the first section of this scene.

Strauss used the Blessedness Motive to set those words of the Empress which refer to Barak's eyes: "des Mannes Aug," and "Vor solchen Blicken." The translation into music of Hofmannsthal's stage direction "Traumhaft, feierlich," which precedes the third verse line ("Vor solchen Blicken liegen Cherubim"), is accomplished by giving this line and the immediately following one a high tessitura, including a high A♭ and a high B♭, and

161

TABLE OF ANALYSIS (continued)

Text	Visual Effects	Music
The significant line here is the final one. As the preceding ones both prepare for and also delay this one, a gradual increase in tension is achieved. This line must be comprehended if the Judgment Scene (Act III scene iii), where the Empress is forced to choose between the welfare of Barak and the life of the Emperor, is to make any sense.		a slow tempo. A nearly identical melodic and harmonic structure also underlies both lines in the accompaniment. An orchestral interlude separates the first four verse lines from the important fifth verse line. During this time Barak's Desire for Children Motive is transformed into the Judgment Motive and movement toward a climax begins, achieving fulfillment in the vocal line of the fifth verse. (See musical example #49 for the Judgment Motive.)
	The second visual section of this scene portrays the Empress' nightmare. She dreams of an ancient cavern containing graves hewn out of the rock. A bronze door leads into the interior of the mountain, while a simple opening at the opposite end leads out into the daylight. The Emperor appears at the opening of the cavern and enters; he takes a lantern from the wall and becomes aware of the bronze door.	An orchestral interlude provides both the transition to the second section of this scene and also a portrayal of this second section in a programmatic interpretation of the Emperor's actions on stage. The key center shifts to C major, although reaching that key only upon the entrance of the chorus, approximately half-way through the section, A new motive also appears, the Cavern Motive, and occurs frequently, as do the Keikobad Motive, the Judgment Motive, the Emperor as Hunter Motive, the Emperor as Lover Motive, the Stone Motive, and the Love Theme #1. (See musical example #50 for the Cavern Motive.)

An unseen chorus speaks to the Emperor from the interior of the mountain: Lockend
 	
Zum Lebenswasser!
        Drohend
Zur Schwelle des Todes!
        Lockend
Nahe!
Wage!
 	
Wehe!   Drohend
Zage!
         (D III 202.)
 	
The text of the chorus need not be understood in order for the plot to be followed. Of primary importance is the contrast between "lockend" and "drohend", which Hofmannsthal indicated for the different lines of the speech.
		The contrast between "lockend" and "drohend," which Hofmannsthal directed for the lines of the chorus, was accomplished by Strauss both by juxtaposing major and minor modes and also by coloristically contrasting rushing harp and strings, apparently portraying water (Lebenswasser), and blaring brass, apparently portraying the horns of the Last Judgment.

The Falcon also speaks to the Emperor: Die Frau wirft keinen Schatten, der Kaiser muss versteinen! (D III 202.) The word for word repetition of these verse lines from the first act indicates their prophetic nature.		The Falcon's lines are set to the characteristic Falcon Cry Motive. The rhythm is identical to the initial occurrence in Act I, but the accompaniment has been changed to give the prophecy a more threatening undertone. The similarity to the other settings of the prophecy probably will allow comprehension.

TABLE OF ANALYSIS (continued)

Text	Visual Effects	Music
Understanding these lines will help to clarify the action on stage for the audience. In the third section of Act II scene iv the Empress expresses awareness that she has transgressed against both Barak and the Emperor. The entire speech is elevated in style with most of the verse lines exhibiting the characteristics of simplicity and brevity: Wehe, mein Mann! Welchen Weg! Wohin? Durch meine Schuld! Die Tür fiel zu, als wärs ein Grab. Er will heraus und kann nicht mehr. Ihm stockt der Fuss, sein Leib erstarrt. Die Stimme erstickt. Sein Auge nur schreit um Hilfe! Weh, Amme, kannst du schlafen!-- Da und dort alles ist meine Schuld-- Ihm keine Hilfe, dem andern Verderben-- Barak, wehe! Was ich berühre, töte ich! Weh mir! würde ich lieber selber zu Stein! (D III 202-03.) The text divides logically into two sections which are roughly parallel in construction. The first section opens with the emotional outburst "Wehe, mein Mann!" The second opens with the emotional outburst "Weh, Amme, kannst du schlafen?" The fourth lines of both sections speak of the Empress' guilt (Schuld). The first section concludes with a description of the Emperor's turning to stone. The second section ends with the Empress' stating that she would prefer to turn to stone herself. The description of	The Emperor exits through the bronze door. The lanterns in the Empress' bedroom beam more brightly once again. The Empress, finally awake, sits up suddenly in her bed. (This return to the location of the first section of the scene gives the scene an ABA visual form.)	As the Emperor exits, the orchestra plays a mournful sounding Emperor as Lover Motive and a fragment of the Love Theme #1, both in a minor key. The second section closes with a return to the Judgment Motive and the Keikobad Motive; this interlude also provides a transition to the third section of the scene. The opening key center for the scene, B minor, is reinstated for the third and final section of the scene, giving the scene an ABA key relationship. (Heinz Röttger in his analysis professes to have discovered a rondo form for this scene; this is, however, only generally true. See his discussion of Act II, period VIII.) A new motive, the Guilt Motive, occurs both in the vocal line and also in the orchestra during the first verse line. (See musical example #51.) The verse line "Die Stimme erstickt" is given a programmatic representation in the orchestra by means of several incomplete reiterations of the Emperor as Lover Motive; the same thing is accomplished in the vocal line by means of the insertion of a measure and a half of silence into the middle of the vocal line. This verse line, "Die Stimme erstickt," and the preceding ones are brought into relationship to each other because motives relating specifically to the Emperor, the Stone Motive and the Emperor as Lover Motive, provide the primary melodic material. The final verse lines of the first part of the speech ("Sein Auge nur / schreit um Hilfe!") contain the climax of this first half of the speech in the high B of the vocal setting; it is held for two and a half measures and occurs on the first syllable of Hilfe. A short orchestral interlude of seven measures separates the end of the first section of the text from the beginning of the second section. The emotional outburst which begins the second section of the text ("Weh, Amme, kannst du schlafen?") is set to the Blessedness Motive, attaining a high Bb on the word schlafen and providing thereby great dramatic interest. This motive is also unaccompanied, although apparently not to facilitate comprehension, for the very high pitch makes comprehension unlikely, but rather to heighten the drama at this point. A sixteen measure orchestral interlude follows this climax, during which time the Blessedness Motive and both Love Themes occur. The Empress enters again with the significant lines "Da und dort / alles ist / meine Schuld--" on a variation of the Guilt Motive.

TABLE OF ANALYSIS (continued)

Text	Visual Effects	Music

Text column:

the Emperor's turning to stone in the first section builds steadily toward the last two lines: "Sein Auge nur / schreit um Hilfe!" Intensification is achieved by the change from sentences comprising two verse lines ("Die Tür fiel zu / als wärs ein Grab") to an essentially one verse line sentence: "Ihm stockt der Fuss." The meaning of these lines, wherein the progressive petrification of the Emperor is described, also imparts intensity to each succeeding line.

An analysis of the second section also reveals an ever-growing intensification as the speech proceeds. The Empress first regards her actions as bringing "no help to him [the Emperor] and destruction to the other [Barak]." She next regards these actions with the despairing fear that "what I touch I kill!" Finally she states that in preference to having the Emperor turn to stone, she would rather turn to stone herself: "Würde ich lieber / selber zu Stein!" These last intensifications are separated by emotional outbursts which heighten the drama even more.

The audience must comprehend the Empress' awareness of guilt in order for the Temple Scene, Act III scene iii, to become plausible; understanding the following verse lines appears necessary:

        Da und dort
    alles ist
    meine Schuld—

    · · · · · · :
    würde ich lieber
    selber zu Stein!

Hofmannsthal wrote this scene with a parallelism in the structure; the form is A A' (with a "coda"). Both sections begin with lines by Barak ("Es dunkelt" and "Hat sie solch"), followed by lines of the Three Brothers ("Es ist etwas" and "Sie wirft") and lines of the Nurse ("Es sind Übermächte" and "Auf und hin"). An ensemble for all persons on stage occurs next; the Wife's solos close each section ("Es gibt" and "Barak, ich hab es"). The "coda" consists of the Nurse's repetition of:

Visual Effects column:

The curtain closes.

Act II Scene v

Music column:

The verse lines of the middle part of the second section ("Da und dort" to "dem andern Verderben") are doubled in the orchestra with the exception of the final one which is unaccompanied. Here Strauss achieved the climax of the aria, writing a high Db, the highest vocal note in the entire opera, for the second syllable of the word Verderben. The Blessedness Motive provides the melodic material for this vocal line.

A ten measure orchestral interlude, which employs the Blessedness Motive, the Sorrow Motive, and the Love Theme #1 at a fortissimo dynamic level, follows this dramatic vocal line. The voice then re-enters ("Barak, wehe!") with a variation of the Guilt Motive, which provides the principal melodic material until the final verse line. This line, like the final two lines of the first section, is set to the Emperor as Lover Motive. Strauss, in writing this climax of the aria for the word Verderben, did not follow the structure of the verses.

The vocal setting of those verse lines which are important to the plot development tends to allow comprehension because of the frequent use of motives, the Guilt Motive, and the inversion of the Emperor as Lover Motive. The high tessitura may obscure some of the syllables, however, if the singer is not exceedingly careful with her diction. Although the form of the verse lines for this third section of scene iv suggests a strophic form, the section is through-composed with the Guilt Motive, the Blessedness Motive, and the Emperor as Lover Motive providing unity between the sections and verses.

An orchestral interlude closes the scene, just as one had opened it. The Love Themes, the Judgment Motive, the Blessedness Motive and the Shadow Motive provide the principal melodic material. The Keikobad Motive then leads directly into the final scene of this act.

Text	Visual Effects	Music
"Übermächte sind im Spiel! / Her zu mir!"	The curtain rises on the interior of Barak's hut. The room becomes increasingly dark throughout the scene. Barak sits on the floor, attempting to work.	The orchestral interlude which closes the previous scene provides a transition to this scene, moving gradually from the Love Theme #1 to the Keikobad Motive. Nine measures occur following the opening of the curtain and introduce Barak's lines. Considerable uneasiness pervades the music which is set in a low register. The meter, which wavers between duple and triple, is characteristic both for the opening orchestral measures and also for the solos and the ensembles which follow.
Barak comments on the growing darkness at midday: Es dunkelt, dass ich nicht sehe zur Arbeit mitten am Tage. (D III 203.) Hofmannsthal provides here the significant information that the growing darkness is an unnatural occurrence.		The accompaniment for Barak's lines consists of a continuation of the chords from the preceding interlude. The vocal line is simple, providing an excellent chance that the lines will be comprehended. On the word Tage the key of Bb minor first appears: this is the key center for this scene. The second act thus closes in the sub-dominant of F minor, the key which occurs most frequently in the opera.
The Three Brothers express a sense of helpless foreboding at the unnatural occurrences: Es ist etwas, und wir wissen nicht, was es ist, o mein Bruder! Die Sonne geht aus mitten am Tage, und der Fluss bleibt stehen und will nicht mehr fliessen o mein Bruder! Es widerfährt uns, und wir wissen nicht, was uns widerfährt! (D III 203-04.) The meaning of the Brothers' lines is not important, but the anxiety and sense of impending doom are.	The Three Brothers enter, displaying anxiety. As they open the door, it is apparent that it is dark outside.	Strauss set only the first two lines of the Three Brothers' speech, reserving the remainder for the ensemble. The Beating Motive occurs in their vocal line, while a new motive, the Fear Motive, makes its first appearance in the orchestra. (See musical example #52.) The low register of the accompaniment maintains the sense of doom which has pervaded the scene from its beginning.
The Nurse identifies the power which has caused the darkness: Es sind Übermächte im Spiel, o meine Herrin, und ein Etwas bedroht uns, aber wir werden anrufen gewaltige Namen, und dir wird werden, worauf du deinen Sinn gesetzt hast! (D III 204.) The first line of this speech must be comprehended, if the intervention of the Superior Powers at the end of the act is not to become nonsensical.	The Nurse stands at the side of the stage and speaks to the Empress.	Strauss utilized the Keikobad Motive for the word Übermächte; the use of the motive and the low dynamic level and chordal nature of the accompaniment will facilitate comprehension of this verse line. The remainder of the speech, considering the wide leaps which Strauss employed, will probably not be understood.

165

TABLE OF ANALYSIS (continued)

Text	Visual Effects	Music
Comprehension of the words of the ensemble is not important. Hofmannsthal did request of Strauss, however, that the composer do everything in his power to impart significance to the Empress' lines in the second act. (Briefwechsel, 25. VII. 1914.)	The Wife is sitting on the earthen floor of the hut as she sings. The Empress and the Nurse are together at one side of the stage while Barak and the Three Brothers form a group at the other side.	Strauss fulfilled Hofmannsthal's request that the importance of the Empress be stressed in Act II by setting her lines highest in pitch in the ensemble. Motives employed for the ensemble are the Irritability Motive, the Independence Motive, the Fear Motive, the Judgment Motive, the Empress Motive, the Emperor as Lover Motive, and the Dissension Motive.
Hofmannsthal structured both sections of this scene so that the ensembles lead directly into the Wife's monologues.	The Wife suddenly stands up and looks maliciously at Barak; then she paces back and forth without looking at him.	Strauss built the ensemble to a climax at its very end; at this time the Wife suddenly stands up and immediately begins her solo.

The Wife's long monologue falls into two major sections. The first section has a tripartite (A B A') construction consisting of 1) a strident, tongue-lashing aimed at Barak which is fifteen lines in length; 2) a lyrical section wherein the Wife asserts that she has been unfaithful to Barak which is six lines in length; and 3) a renewal of the criticism of Barak, twelve lines in length. The difference in style between sections A and B is particularly noticeable in the contrast between the relative regularity in the number of accents and syllables of the lyrical section (B) and the great variation in the number of accents and syllables of the criticism sections (A). The second major section of this speech by the Wife contains the incantation by which the Wife rids herself of her shadow and simultaneously her children. The entire monologue is extremely garrulous, reflecting the Wife's inner turmoil. (See the discussion of the Wife in Chapter III for insights into her manner of speaking.)
Part A of the first major section consists of these verses:

Es gibt derer, die bleiben immer gelassen,
und geschähe, was will, es wird keiner jemals
ihr Gesicht verändert sehen.
Tagaus, tagein
gehen sie wie das Vieh
von Lager zu Frass,
von Frass zu Lager
und wissen nicht, was geschehen ist,
und nicht, wie es gemeint war.
Darüber müssen sie verachtet werden
und verlacht
wer zu ihnen gehört
und ist in die Hand eines solchen gegeben.

The orchestra introduces the Wife's monologue with a statement of the Dissension Motive. The Wife's opening verse line is set to the Bitterness Motive with doubling in the accompaniment; the beginning of the second line is unaccompanied. This setting may allow these lines to be comprehended, a boon considering both the thoughts expressed here and also the length of the monologue. The verse lines "Tagaus, tagein / gehen sie wie das Vieh" are given a programmatic interpretation which obscures the words. Strauss thus conveyed the Wife's criticism of Barak by means of the first two lines of his setting rather than by means of the symbol (Vieh), which the verse suggests. Verse lines nine to twelve of Part A are largely unaccompanied, although they do not appear to be

Text	Visual Effects	Music

Text column:

Aber ich bin nicht in deiner Hand,
hörst du mich, Barak?
    (D III 205-06.)

There are four important lines in this part A of the first major section, as reflected by the change in the style of the verse lines:

    Tagaus, tagein
    gehen sie wie das Vieh
    Von Lager zu Frass,
    von Frass zu Lager . . .

The Wife's contempt for Barak is expressed here in the symbol of the animal which is too dull to apprehend the needs of another. This failure on Barak's part must be understood by the audience, if the responsibility for their unsuccessful marriage is not to be unfairly ascribed to her alone.

The relatively lyrical part B of the first section of the monologue consists of these lines:

    Und wenn du ausgegangen warst
    und trugest dir selber die Ware zu Markt,
    so habe ich meinen Freund empfangen,
    einen Fremdling unter den Fremdlingen,
    und wenn ich dich weckte aus deinem Schlaf,
    so kam ich aus seiner Umarmung!
    (D III 206.)

The significant lines in this part of the monologue are "Und wenn du ausgegangen warst . . . so habe ich meinen Freund empfangen . . ." The audience must understand that the Wife claims to have been unfaithful. If they do not comprehend, the retraction at the end of the scene will make no sense.

In part A' Hofmannsthal returned to the style of the verse lines which he had employed for the beginning of the Wife's speech:

    Hörst du mich, Barak?
    Schweige doch diese,
    damit du mich verstehen kannst!
    Ich will nicht, dass du ein Gelächter sein müsset
    unter den Deinen,
    sondern du sollst w i s s e n !
    Dies alles tat ich hier im Hause
    drei Tage lang:
    aber die Freude war mir vergällt,
    denn ich musste dich denken,
    wo ich dich hätte vergessen wollen,
    und dein Gesicht kam hin,
    wo es nichts zu suchen hatte!

Music column:

especially significant. (Comprehension of these lines will certainly help maintain the interest of the audience, however, a result not to be denigrated at this late point in the second act.)
The Irritability Motive and a fragment of the Bitterness Motive provide the primary melodic material for this first part of the solo. A new motive, the Stupidity Motive, also occurs here. (See musical example #53.)
The Wife's tirade opens in A minor, touches upon C minor, and then settles in F major for the lines "Aber ich bin nicht in deiner Hand. / hörst du mich, Barak?" The style of the music becomes noticeably more lyrical at this point, Strauss apparently anticipating the relatively lyrical verse lines which follow. The principle melodic material, the Bitterness Motive, remains, however, the same.
The lyrical verses comprising Part B of the monologue's first section also constitute a new section in the music. The Independence Motive occurs both in the vocal line and also in the orchestra; the Youth Motive is restricted to the orchestra. The section reaches a climax in the last verse line, "so kam ich aus seiner Umarmung;" where a high B♭ and a marked cadence in F major occur.
The first significant verse line ("Und wenn du . . .") is obscured by the accompaniment and probably will not be comprehended. The second is doubled by the orchestra and probably will be.

The Irritability Motive and the Stupidity Motive recur once again after an absence during the preceding lyrical section. The Youth Motive and the Independence Motive occur shortly thereafter in the orchestra, imposing a structure thus far upon the verse lines of A B a b; the small case letters represent a much shorter version of the capital letters. The short version b also closes with a marked cadence, as did Part B, but the cadence is raised one-half step to F♯ minor. This indecisiveness of key, where a wavering occurs between F minor and F♯ minor, apparently represents the Wife's inner conflict and indecision. (Musically, there is no doubt as to the key; the indecision is the Wife's.) The lyrical vein of part b is however, continued, with the Youth Motive and the Independence Motive providing melodic material. These motives are then joined by

167

TABLE OF ANALYSIS (continued)

Text	Visual Effects	Music
Aber es ist mir zugekommen, wie ich dir entgehe und dich ausreisse aus mir, und jetzt weiss ich den Weg! (D III 206.) The stylistic similarity to the opening lines of the monologue in the irregular length of the verse line is obvious. There are two significant statements in this section of the speech. In the first the Wife claims disloyalty to Barak: "Dies alles tat ich hier im Hause / drei Tage lang . . ." In the second the Wife claims to know a way to be rid of the Dyer: "Aber es ist mir zugekommen, / wie ich dir entgehe . . . ." The text of the second section of the Wife's monologue falls into two parts. The first part is the incantation itself (lines one to four); the second part consists of commentary on the incantation (lines five to twelve): Abtu ich von meinem Leibe die Kinder, die nicht gebornen, und mein Schoss wird dir nicht fruchtbar und keinem andern, sondern ich habe mich gegeben den Winden und der Nachtluft und bin hier daheim und woandern, und des zum Zeichen habe ich meinen Schatten verhandelt: und es sind die Käufer willig, und der Kaufpreis ist herrlich und ohnegleichen! (D III 206-07.) The first four lines must be comprehended if the audience is to follow the plot. Of no less importance are the two lines "und des zum Zeichen / habe ich meinen Schatten verhandelt." The final tense moments of this scene, where the Wife retracts these statements, becomes nonsensical if the audience does not understand that here the Wife is renouncing her shadow, her children, and her humanity. With Barak's response to the Wife's monologue the second half of the scene begins. (For details see the analysis at the beginning of this scene, p. 192.) Barak reacts initially to the Wife's renunciation of her children with the thought that she has gone mad: Das Weib ist irre,	Barak stands up suddenly, knocking the Three Brothers over with the vehemence of his movement.	the Sorrow Motive and the Judgment Motive, enlarging the musical structure to A B a b b'. The musical form is not yet complete, however, for Strauss returned to the Dissension Motive, the opening motive of the Wife's solo. This provides the first half of the monologue with a frame and the following musical form results: A B a b b' a. The verse lines "Dies alles tat ich hier im Hause / drei Tage lang" are given no special emphasis. This may cause the audience to have trouble in following the plot; the Wife's retraction of her claim to have deceived Barak will make no sense if the claim of deception has not been comprehended. The statement of her intention to be rid of Barak ("Aber es ist mir zugekommen . . .") is unaccompanied and probably will be comprehended. The first section of the Wife's monologue cadences in F minor, the minor dominant of B^b minor, which is the key center for this scene: the key of the incantation, the second section of the monologue, wavers between F minor, the key associated with Barak, and F# minor, the key of the shadowless Empress' aria in Act I scene i. Strauss set the incantation on a single pitch (F) and accompanied it with a string tremolo for the first two verse lines, doubling in the orchestra for the third verse line, and a cadential formula for the fourth verse line. The verses will probably be comprehended. The Children Motive and the Renunciation of Motherhood Motive provide brief orchestral interludes between the lines. Following the first four lines the key moves up one-half step to F# minor and the Bitterness Motive occurs in the orchestra. The line "habe ich meinen Schatten verhandelt" is unaccompanied and set to the Shadow Motive in F minor again. The Wife's final verse lines take her into Strauss' erotic key, E major. Simultaneously with her cadence in E major a B^b major chord occurs as a string tremolo, the dissonance heightening the drama on stage. The tremolo at the end of the Wife's solo serves as a background to Barak's lines, which are spoken, not sung.

TABLE OF ANALYSIS (continued)

Text	Visual Effects	Music
zündet ein Feuer an, damit ich ihr Gesicht sehe! (D III 206.) This is primarily an emotional response to the Wife's monologue; the words need not be comprehended.	The fire flares up.	The Shadow Motive provides a programmatic interpretation of the rising flames.
The Three Brothers cry out in horror: Sie wirft keinen Schatten. Es ist, wie sie redet! Sie hat ihn verkauft und abgehalten die Ungeborenen von ihrem Leibe! Der Schatten ist abgefallen von ihr, und sie ist ohne, die Verfluchte! (D III 207.) The first line must be comprehended, for the lack of the Wife's shadow cannot be visually presented. The remaining lines are negligible.		Strauss had the Three Brothers speak the important first verse line; the remaining lines are set contrapuntally in ensemble. The principal melodic material is provided by the Activity Motive in the orchestra and the Beating Motive in the voice.
The Nurse instructs the Empress to take possession of the shadow: Auf und hin, nimm den Schatten. Reiss ihn an dich! Sie hat es gesprochen mit wissendem Mund, so ist es getan! Und nicht der Sterne Gericht macht diesen Handel zunicht! (D III 207-08.) Hofmannsthal gave the first three lines brevity and simplicity; they are significant because here the Nurse tempts the Empress.		Strauss set the first three verse lines of the Nurse for her alone with orchestral accompaniment. Thereafter she sings in ensemble with the Three Brothers who continue their verse lines after having remained temporarily silent for the Nurse. The Shadow Motive, the Nurse Motive, and the Beating Motive provide the principal musical materials here.
Barak's reaction is one of rage: Hat sie solch eine Hurenstirn und sieht lieblich darein und schämt sich nicht? Heran, ihr Brüder, einen Sack herbei und hinein von den Steinen, dass ich dies Weib ertränke im Fluss mit meinen Händen! (D III 208.) These lines are significant only as a vehicle to express Barak's anger. The audience must, however, understand		Strauss silenced the Nurse and the Three Brothers for Barak. The Activity Motive and a string tremolo, as with the spoken verse lines "Das Weib ist irre . . .," accompany him. The composer indicated that the lines "dass ich dies Weib / ertränke im Fluss" were to be emphasized ("sehr stark"). The verse lines will probably be covered by the orchestra, but the intent to kill should be apparent both from his actions and also from the high emotional intensity of the music. Simultaneously with Barak's last line ("mit meinen Händen"), the Empress answers the Nurse, saying that she does not want

169

TABLE OF ANALYSIS (continued)

Text	Visual Effects	Music

his murderous designs upon the Wife; these will probably be apparent from the actions on the stage.
 	
The ensemble, toward which the preceding lines have been moving, becomes full-blown at the end of Barak's verses above. The following verses appear in the ensemble:
 	
Brüder: Kein Blut auf deine Hände, mein
    Bruder!
Auf und jage sie aus dem Hause,
einer Hündin Geschick über sie
in Gosse und Graben!
Barak: Mein Aug ist verdunkelt,
helft mir, ihr Brüder!
Herbei einen Sack
und Steinen hinein,
dass ich sie ertränke
mit meinen Händen!
Brüder: Kein Blut auf deine Hände, mein
    Bruder!
Halte dich rein, o unser Vater!
Barak: Helft ihr mir nicht,
tret ich euch nieder!
Ich hab es verhängt
in meiner Seele
und will es vollziehen
mit meinen Händen!
Amme: Wer schreit nach Blut
und hat kein Schwert,
dem wird von uns
die Hand bewehrt!
Und fliesst nur schnell
das dunkle Blut,
wir haben den Schatten,
und uns ist gut!
Kaiserin: Ich will nicht den Schatten:
auf ihm ist Blut,
ich fass ihn nicht an.
Meine Hände reck ich
in die Luft,
rein zu bleiben
von Menschenblut!
Sternennamen
ruf ich an
gegen mich,
diese zu retten,
geschehe was will!
   (D III 208-10.)
	Barak starts to walk toward the Wife, while at the same time the Three Brothers attempt to detain him. He struggles to free himself. The Empress has been held back by the Nurse, but she finally breaks free, raising her hands into the air as she sings her lines.	the shadow. This actually is the beginning of the final ensemble. The key of B♭ minor, toward which the ensemble has been moving, is definitely established here.
		
		A new motive, the No Blood Motive, occurs both in the orchestra and in the vocal lines of the ensemble. (See musical example #54.) Other motives employed in the ensemble are the Dissension Motive, the Anger Motive, the Desire for Children Motive, the Beating Motive, the Sorrow Motive, and the Keikobad Motive.

Text	Visual Effects	Music
Hofmannsthal requested of Strauss that he allow the voice of the Empress to dominate this ensemble: "Im grossen Septett muss es Ihrer Meisterschaft überlassen bleiben, der Stimme der Kaiserin einen Klang zu geben, der beherrschend über dem Ganzen schwebt und worin sich alles Frühere zusammenfasst und die hohe Bedeutung dieser Figur für den dritten Akt vorauskündet." (Briefwechsel, 25. VII. 1914.)	Barak lifts his hand to swear that he will kill the Wife; as he does so, a sword appears in it. It is clear from the text of the ensemble that the Nurse is responsible for the sudden appearance of the sword. Because the words are lost in the ensemble, some gestures of conjuration seem necessary if the audience is not wrongly to assume that the Empress has done this. The Wife, pale but transfigured, approaches Barak and the raised sword.	Strauss accomplished Hofmannsthal's desire by having the Empress initiate the ensemble, by giving her a high Bb in the first verse line to sing, and by setting her lines above the others in pitch. In the brief six measure interlude which separates the end of the ensemble and the beginning of the Wife's solo the Sword Motive heralds the appearance of the sword on stage. (See musical example #55.)
Hofmannsthal desired the Wife to dominate ("stellenweise dominierend," D III 210) the ensemble at this point. The change in style of her verse lines, from a capriciousness in length of line and a tendence toward loquaciousness to a short line of four to five syllables in length with a fairly regular beat, symbolizes her emotional change from an ambivalence toward Barak to a commitment to him: Barak, ich hab es nicht getan! Noch nicht getan! Höre mich, Barak! Verräter ward mein Mund an mir, zuvor die Seele die Tat getan! Muss ich sterben muss ich sterben vor deinem Angesicht, um was nicht geschah, o du, den zuvor ich niemals sah, mächtiger Barak, strenger Richter,		Strauss suspended the ensemble for the Wife's verse lines. He gave the vocal line dominance over the accompaniment by means of its high tessitura, the ebb and flow of the accompaniment, and the dramatic cadence in Gb major in the vocal line which occurs at the end of the second verse line. A new motive, the Denial Motive, occurs both in the vocal line and also in the orchestra. A second new motive, the Transformation Motive, occurs only in the orchestra. (See musical examples #56 and #57.) The important verse lines which close the speech (from "Muss ich sterben" to the end of the monologue) are given settings which are either primarily unaccompanied or else doubled by the orchestra, aiding audience comprehension. Strauss paralleled the climax which is reached in the final two verse lines with a musical climax which is reached at the same place. The solo cadences in Ab minor.

171

TABLE OF ANALYSIS (continued)

Text	Visual Effects	Music
hoher Gatte-- Barak, so töte mich, schnell! (D III 210.) The first two verse lines and the last two verse lines must be comprehended if the plot is to make sense. A powerful climax is inherent in the structure of the last part of the speech; the concluding clause ("Barak, so töte mich / schnell!") is separated from the opening clause ("Muss ich sterben / vor deinem Angesicht") by seven lines. Within these seven lines an intensification is achieved by a piling up of vocatives: o du . . . . mächtiger Barak, strenger Richter, hoher Gatte-- Barak . . .	The Wife lies on the floor in front of Barak, who lifts the sword to kill her. The Three Brothers prevent him from striking. The room is lighted only by the sword, for the fire has died down.	In setting the verse lines of the Three Brothers Strauss returned to the motives which he employed for the ensemble immediately preceding the Wife's solo: the No Blood Motive, the Keikobad Motive, and the Sword Motive. The Wife's cantilene is, therefore, framed.
The Three Brothers try to prevent Barak from killing the Wife: Sie werden dich behängen mit Ketten und dich schlagen mit der Schärfe des Schwertes, erbarme dich unser, o unser Vater! (D III 211.) The lines are unimportant, for the actions on stage will convey the meaning.	As Barak lifts the sword, it suddenly disappears. A dull rumbling makes the room tremble, the earth opens, and the river flows in through the split wall. The Three Brothers flee out the door, Barak and the Wife sink separately into the ground, and the Nurse saves herself and the Empress by climbing onto the wall. Complete darkness reigns.	An orchestral interlude employing the Sword Motive and the Denial Motive at the fortissimo dynamic level follows the Three Brothers' ensemble.
The Nurse identifies the power which has taken command: Übermächte sind im Spiel! Her zu mir! (D III 211.) Comprehension of the first line will aid the audience		The Nurse's lines are sung over a soft, low-pitched tremolo on a Bb minor chord. The key center for the scene thus returns. Comprehension of the Nurse's lines is likely.

TABLE OF ANALYSIS (continued)

Text	Visual Effects	Music
as they follow the plot.		Following the Nurse's lines the Judgment Motive resounds in the orchestra. A rapid tempo and a fortississimo dynamic level characterize the dramatic closing of the act.

Act III Scene 1

Text	Visual Effects	Music
The Strauss-Hofmannsthal correspondence reveals that Strauss found the text for Act III scene 1 too brief. On both April 15 and May 27, 1915, he requested more text, but received no answer, for Hofmannsthal was in Poland on government business at this time. As a consequence, Strauss proceeded to invent and to repeat lines to fulfill his own wishes. On June 8, 1915, he wrote to Hofmannsthal that he had composed the first scene of the third act and that he had completed the text himself. Strauss also requested that the poet either approve or rewrite the verse which he had put together. Hofmannsthal, having since returned from Poland, replied on June 22, 1915: "Die erste Szene haben Sie ja einstweilen ausgeführt, ich lasse das einstweilen auf sich beruhen; muss ich den von Ihnen zusammengestellten Text teilweise übermalen, so kann das später geschehen, wahrscheinlich werde ich ja das meiste davon gutheissen können." There is no further discussion of this scene in the correspondence. Whether Hofmannsthal ever found the time to approve Strauss's text or to rewrite it is uncertain. There is considerable divergence, however, between the text as it is printed in the Steiner edition and the text as it was set by Strauss. The Steiner edition prints these verses as the opening lines for the scene: Schweiget doch, ihr Stimmen! Ich hab es nicht getan!! (D III 212.) Strauss set these lines: Schweigt doch, schweigt doch, schweigt doch, ihr Stimmen! Schweigt doch. Ich hab es nicht getan! Stylistically, the verses as printed in the Steiner edition are softer both because of the placement of an unaccented syllable between the syllables "schweig-" and "doch" and also because the voiced "g" in "schweiget" is softer than the consonant cluster "kt" at the end of "schweigt." The final verse line is an exact repetition of one in the Wife's Denial Speech at the end of Act II.	The curtain opens to reveal an underground chamber which is divided into two rooms by a heavy wall. Barak occupies one cell, sitting upon a stone and brooding. The Wife cries in the other, her hair in disarray. They are unaware of each other, nor do they hear each other. The Wife starts suddenly as she hears the voices of the children in the instruments of the orchestra.	Before the curtain rises, the orchestra plays a short introduction of twenty-one measures; fourteen additional measures follow before the Wife begins to sing. The introduction is characterized by a cello solo in a low register and by a pianississimo pedal point on a low B. The Irritability Motive and the Blessedness Motive provide the principal melodic material for the cello solo. After the curtain opens, the entire musical setting for the chorus of the Unborn Children in Act I is repeated in the instruments of the orchestra. Strauss desired to use a setting for the line "Schweigt doch!" from the Children's Song of Act I scene ii. This setting already contained a sixteenth note upbeat ($\flat$/♩♩); this structure would have been so altered by the additional sixteenth required for setting "Schweiget doch!" ($\flat$/♫) that he found changing the text a preferable solution. Obviously, a true repetition of the Children's Song seemed more important to Strauss than the use of the softer verse line. The verse line taken from the Denial Speech ("Ich hab es nicht getan!") is given a vocal setting similar to the setting with which it first appeared in Act II scene v. The verse line ends with a marked cadence in F minor, the key center for the Wife's solo; it is first established at this point.

TABLE OF ANALYSIS (continued)

Text	Visual Effects	Music
After the Wife reacts to the voices of the Unborn Children as they are programmatically portrayed in the orchestra, she laments her separation from Barak. The lament falls into two sections, the first part constituting an expression of longing for her husband: Barak, mein Mann, o dass du mich hörtest, dass du mir glaubtest vor meinem Tode! (D III 212.) The words, apart from the name Barak, are not significant, provided that the Wife's longing is conveyed. The second section of the monologue is printed in the Steiner edition as follows: Dich wollt ich verlassen, o du, den zuvor niemals ich sah! Dich wollt ich vergessen und meinte zu fliehen dein Angesicht: dein Angesicht, es kam zu mir--- o dass du mich hörtest, o dass du mir glaubtest.-- Dich wollt ich vergessen--- da musste ich dich denken: und wo ich ging verbotene Wege, dein Angesicht . . . es kam zu mir und suchte mich, zuvor die Seele die Tat getan! Ein fremder Mann, ich zog ihn her, er war mir nah--- aber nicht völlig---		An orchestral interlude follows the Wife's opening lines. Strauss had requested more verse lines for this particular point in the opera, but did not receive them. (Briefwechsel, 28. V. 1915.) Consequently, he composed the section for orchestra rather than voice. This interlude parallels the opening orchestral statement in its use of a pedal point and in its employment of the Irritability Motive and the Blessedness Motive. One new motive makes its first appearance here: the Vision Motive. (See musical example #58.) A fourth motive of the interlude is a variation of the Denial Motive from Act II scene v. Strauss moved the singing melodic lines from the cello solo of the interlude into the Wife's vocal line, giving her solo a feeling of great organic unity with the preceding musical materials. These four verse lines are integrated into the second section of the solo, the composer not differentiating between the two sections of the speech. Strauss structured the music as the verse lines were structured or, if Strauss wrote the text, perhaps he structured the verse lines as he had structured the music. Tension increases during the first two sentences, and a climax occurs during the third sentence. Thereafter, the music subsides. The vocal line is given dominance over the orchestra to a much greater degree than has been previously customary for the Wife's solos. This appears to be the direct result of the extensive employment in the vocal line of the Vision Motive, the Denial Motive, the Countenance Motive (a new motive; see musical example #59), the Sorrow Motive, and the Desire for Children Motive. So extensive is the use of motives in the vocal line that only two verse lines in the entire first three sentences lack one. (There is, in fact, a motive employed here, but it is a fragment of the Bitterness Motive which is so simplified in character that it has lost its function as an identifiable motive.) The vocal line of the fourth sentence, during which the dramatic intensity subsides, is considerably lacking in motives by these standards. Here the Heart Motive occurs in the orchestra but not in the vocal line.

TABLE OF ANALYSIS (continued)

Text	Visual Effects	Music
Barak, Barak, dich weckt ich doch, weisst du es nicht? (D III 212-13.) In this section of the speech the Wife reminisces about the events which occurred in Act II. The first sentence consists of three verse lines, the second of six verse lines, the third of eight (possibly nine) and the fourth of seven. The increasing length of the sentences implies ever less emphasis on comprehension by the audience. The significant factor is that the Wife now sings of her newly found respect for Barak. The speech reaches a climax in the third sentence, the longest sentence, and then recedes slightly in the fourth, as reflected by the greater independence of the verse lines therein ("Ich zog ihn her"; "er war mir nah'; "dich weckt ich doch"). There is a distinct possibility that Hofmannsthal wrote the parallel verses given below: und wo ich ging verbotene Wege, und meinte zu fliehen dein Angesicht . . . . These are the verses which Strauss composed. Perhaps Steiner, in omitting the third line above, has erred. The third sentence would then consist of nine verse lines. There is considerable doubt as to how much of this part of the monologue was written by Hofmannsthal and how much by Strauss. The many repeated verse lines suggest that Strauss's part in it was great. Even so, the text as set by Strauss varies from this one in containing even more repetitions; the text in the piano score contains twenty-nine lines while the Steiner edition contains twenty-four. The score contains one clause which is completely ommitted in the Steiner edition and which can probably be ascribed to Strauss: [dein Angesicht] das ich Unselige für immer verlor. (B&H Act III #13.) Barak's verse lines constitute a counterpart to the Wife's lines just above: Mir anvertraut, dass ich sie hege,		For the direct address to Barak which occurs three verse lines before the end of the monologue, Strauss quoted his earlier setting of the Wife's calling to Barak in the midst of the sleeping potion scene (Act II scene iii). The aria cadences in F major. Strauss seized upon the rhythmic regularity of the verse lines to create a motive for Barak's aria which is more rhythmic than melodic; that is, the rhythm ♩ ♪ ♩ (long, short, long, which is taken

175

Text	Visual Effects	Music
dass ich sie trage auf diesen Händen und ihrer achte und ihrer schone um ihres jungen Herzens willen! (D III 213.) The length of this speech, seven verse lines, may roughly indicate just how much padding went into the Wife's aria to give it a total of thirty verses. Barak's lines are very simply constructed: 1) each verse line is meaningful in and of itself; 2) lines five to seven form a parallel relationship to lines two to four; 3) the verses, with the exception of the first and the last ones, have an identical rhythm. Comprehension of only a few of the verses should make it clear to the audience that Barak sings of his pro-tective love for the Wife. The Steiner edition indicates that the Wife is to join Barak during part of his solo with the following verses: Dienend, liebend dir mich bücken: dich zu sehen! atmen, leben! Kinder, Guter, dir zu geben!-- (D III 213.) Strauss found these four lines to be an insufficient vehicle for the duet which he planned; he, therefore, requested more verses (Briefwechsel, 15. IV. 1915). As Hofmannsthal was in Poland, Strauss finally provided himself with the text lines he desired, writing to Hofmannsthal on June 8, 1915: "Ich habe nun die erste Szene des III. Aktes musikalisch fertig. Es ist eine sehr gut aufgebaute und schön sich steigernde Szene geworden, für die ich mir mühsam den Text zusammengruppiert habe, wie Sie aus der Beilage ersehen." (Briefwechsel.) For the duet Strauss had Barak repeat all of the verse lines of his solo plus the following lines, giving him a total of twelve lines: dass ich sie hege, dass ich sie trage und ihrer achte, ihrer schone, die mir anvertraut! (B&H Act III #23-#25.) Strauss set the following lines for the Wife's part of the duet:		directly from the rhythm of the word "anvertraut" occurs at the end of every verse line although with different melodic intervals. (See musical example #60 for the Protection Motive.) A rising movement in the melody dominates the first four lines, pausing momentarily upon the word Händen; thereafter the rising movement begins once again, this time falling during the seventh and final line for a cadence. The key center for the aria is Db major. The vocal line is dominant over the orchestra, which provides a fairly simple accompaniment of arpeggios and repeated chords. This pre-eminence of the vocal line will probably allow sufficient verses to be comprehended, preventing confusion among the audience. Strauss composed the duet from musical materials occurring in Barak's solo. The Wife's melodic line is constructed in contrary motion to Barak's, falling when his rises and rising when his falls. The embodiment of the traditional male quality in Barak's rising, dominating line and of the traditional female quality in the line which, falling, adapts itself to the dominating line is obvious.

TABLE OF ANALYSIS (continued)

Text	Visual Effects	Music
Dir angetraut, dein zu pflegen, dienend, liebend dir mich bücken: dich zu sehen, atmen, leben, Kinder, Guter, dir zu geben, Kinder dir zu geben. (B&H Act III #21-#25.) The Wife's verses for the duet are thus enlarged by three over the number given in the Steiner edition. Because the verses for the duet only repeat the ideas expressed by each in their solos, comprehension is not necessary. After the conclusion of the duet, Barak continues his solo, this time expressing regret that he should have threatened to kill the Wife: Mir anvertraut-- und taumelt zur Erde in Todesangst vor meiner Hand! Weh mir! Dass ich sie einmal noch sähe und zu ihr spräche: Fürchte dich nicht. (D III 213-14.) The regularly increasing length of the lines (from four to six to eight to ten syllables) indicates a growing lyrical intensity which points to: "und zu ihr spräche / Fürchte dich nicht!" The brevity and simplicity indicate Hofmannsthal's apparent desire that these lines be comprehended. (For a more detailed discussion of these lines see the section on Barak in Chapter III.) A voice calls to Barak: Auf, geh nach oben, Mann, der Weg ist frei! (D III 214.) Understanding the words will contribute to an understanding of the plot, even though the actions on the stage will convey the meaning.	A ray of light falls into Barak's cell, revealing steps hewn out of the stone which lead upward. Barak stands up and begins to climb the steps.	Strauss partially followed the structure given by Hofmannsthal; he gradually increased emotional tension throughout the first three verses of the speech. An increase in tempo, more rapidly changing harmonies in the accompaniment, and the appearance of the Sword Motive all contribute to this effect. A climax is reached with the emotional outburst "Weh mir", after which Strauss inserted a short orchestral interlude which subsides from this peak. The key center is Db major, the composer's ceremonial key. The two lines which immediately follow the emotional outburst prepare for the verse "Fürchte dich nicht!" This line was given tremendous impact by the composer both by means of a sudden key shift to D major and also by means of the omission of all accompaniment. The verse is repeated with orchestral accompaniment one octave higher. Within the solo the following motives occur: the Desire for Children Motive, the Vision Motive, the Judgment Motive, and the Joy Motive. Strauss preceded the vocal line with a short brass fanfare; this, of course, prepares for and emphasizes the vocal line. Both verses are set to a new motive, the Release from Prison Motive. (See musical example #61.) The accompaniment is chordal; the vocal line, written for an alto voice, is distinctly predominant. Both the relationship between the accompaniment and the vocal line and also the deliberate tempo at which the lines proceed will ensure audience comprehension. Strauss emphasized Barak's release from his prison cell and prepared for the immediately following Wife's solo with a short orchestral interlude. The interlude 1)

TABLE OF ANALYSIS (continued)

Text	Visual Effects	Music
The Wife resumes her expression of love for Barak: Barak, mein Mann! Strenger Richter, hoher Gatte! Schwängest du auch dein Schwert über mir, in seinem Blitzen sterbend noch sähe ich dich! (D III 214.) The first three lines are an exact repetition of lines which occurred in the Denial Speech at the end of Act II. The lines which Strauss actually set include all of these plus one more which precedes the rest of the speech: "Komm zu mir!" The structure of the music at this point suggests that Strauss inserted this line. (See the discussion in the right-hand column.) Structurally, the speech intensifies as it proceeds. This occurs both by means of the piling up of vocatives at the beginning of the verses and also by means of the dependence of the fourth to the seventh lines upon the last line ("Schwängest du auch" to "sterbend noch"). As long as the audience understands that the Wife sings of Barak with love, the words are unimportant.	The light in Barak's cell goes out; a ray of light falls into the Wife's cell.	sweeps upward in pitch; 2) replaces the leisurely tempo of the alto solo with a rapid pace; 3) contains the Vision Motive dovetailed with the Guilt Motive in a manner characteristic of the Wife's solo. Strauss apparently inserted the verse line "Komm zu mir!" in order to develop a parallel structure of Vision and Guilt Motives. This is the pattern which he employed: Vision Motive) Guilt Motive) Orchestral interlude Vision Motive) Guilt Motive: "Komm zu mir!" Vision Motive: Orchestral interlude Guilt Motive: "Barak, mein Mann!" The Guilt Motive occurred in the Denial Aria (Act III scene v), as did the Sword Motive, which frequently occurs in the orchestra during the remainder of the solo. Strauss thus referred musically back to the Denial Aria, much as Hofmannsthal referred to it by quoting lines from it. Strauss associated the verse line "Komm zu mir" with the verse "Barak, mein Mann" by means of the motivic structure of the music. He then related the lines "Strenger Richter" and "hoher Gatte!" to each other by means of a melodic similarity of their settings. These lines and the remaining ones tend to move steadily toward a climax in the last line, which reaches a peak on a high Bb pitch in the vocal line. The final line is emphasized not only by this high pitch but also because of Strauss's use of the Freedom Motive in the vocal line here. Even though the orchestra doubles the vocal line, the words are unlikely to be comprehended, for the high pitch obscures them; the subject of the verse lines, the Wife's love for Barak, will, however, probably be conveyed by the emotional intensity of the music. The vocal solo cadences in F major, thus relating it to the Wife's opening aria which was centered in F minor.
In the Steiner edition the verse lines of the Voice which offers the Wife release from prison are slightly varied from those which were spoken to Barak: Frau, geh nach oben, denn der Weg ist frei. (D III 214.)		Strauss retained essentially the same vocal melody which he had previously used for these verse lines. In order to do this he altered the second line slightly, omitting the word "denn" and making the verse identical to the second verse line spoken to Barak by the Voice.

Text	Visual Effects	Music
	The Wife climbs the steps illuminated in her cell. The underground chamber disappears from view as clouds cover the scene on stage.	The accompaniment is changed, however, with the omission of the preceding fanfare and the adoption of an inverted pedal point in place of the previous chords. An orchestral interlude in D major, the key of Barak's opening lament, accompanies the scene change. Motives employed are the Blessedness Motive, the Joy Motive, the Desire for Children Motive, and the Judgment Motive. Parts of the vocal melody from Barak's first lament are repeated here, suggesting the following musical structure: A: Barak's first lament and the duet; D♭ major B: Barak's second lament; D♭ major, F major, D major Voice ("Geb nach oben"); C major Wife's second lament; F major Voice ("Geb nach oben"); F major A: Orchestral interlude; D♭ major The form is not clearly defined, however, because some motives which occur in the final section A, the Blessedness Motive, the Joy Motive, and the Desire for Children Motive, are not present in the initial section. The Joy Motive and the Desire for Children Motive, which Strauss employed for the final orchestral interlude, also occur in section B.
	Act III Scene ii The clouds drift away, revealing a cliff similar to the one which appeared during the Empress' dream (II iv). Opposite the cliff is a dark river; stone steps lead from the water to a temple-like entrance in the cliff, which is open. On the top step the Messenger waits with other Spirits. A boat without a tiller arrives wherein the Empress sleeps, the Nurse holding her protectively. The boat stops at the steps. The Messenger and the Spirits, upon perceiving the boat, enter the mountain through	The orchestral interlude continues after heavy emphasis on the D♭ major chord. Bitonality momentarily occurs following this chord as the Empress' Motive sounds in F-sharp minor while the Love Themes #1 and #2 occur in A-flat minor. The key of A minor, Strauss's key designating fulfillment of fate, soon establishes itself as the key center for the remainder of the interlude. Motives occurring include the Empress Motive, the Blessedness Motive, the Emperor as Lover Motive, and the Love Themes #1 and #2. Halfway through this part of the interlude the tempo slackens and the meter changes from 3/2 to 4/4. Strauss also employed different melodic material at this point, utilizing the Keikobad Motive, the Cavern Motive, and the Bronze Door Motive, a new motive, (See musical example #62.) Interwoven within the orchestral interlude are the cries of the Messenger and of the Spirits. The interlude cadences in C major, the key center for the first part of the conversation between the Empress and the Nurse.
The Spirits comment that "they" are coming, whereupon the Messenger instructs the Spirits to leave. This incident does not further the action, nor is it an act indispensable for the comprehension of the plot. Instead it prepares for the arrival of the Empress and		

179

TABLE OF ANALYSIS (continued)

Text	Visual Effects	Music
the Nurse and makes visible the "Superior Powers" which intervened at the end of Act II.	the bronze door, which closes behind them. The Empress awakens and observes the landscape. The Nurse attempts to prevent her from getting out of the boat, at the same time trying to push the boat free of the landing. The landscape becomes more brightly lighted. The Empress attempts once again to disembark.	This orchestral interlude, which provides the bridge from the prison scene to the landscape scene of the fourth act, supplies a pendant to the transition in the first act from the palace to Barak's hovel. The two interludes contain the longest sections of purely orchestral music in the opera.
The Nurse reacts to the Empress' attempt to get out of the boat with physical movement and with a speech: Fort von hier! Hilf mir vom Fels lösen den Kahn! Übermächte spielen mit uns! Zum gräulichsten Ort eigenwillig strebt das Gemächte aus bösem Holz! Wär ich nicht gewitzigt, was würde aus dir! (D III 215-16.) The actions of the Nurse should make it clear both that she desires to leave the place where they have stopped and also that she desires to leave because she is afraid. Comprehension of the words is, therefore, unnecessary.	The Nurse pushes the Empress down into the boat.	Comprehension of the first three lines, although unnecessary, may occur because Strauss left them unaccompanied and used a motive to set them. In addition to employing the Nurse Motive for the vocal line, Strauss also utilized the Keikobad Motive and the Judgment Motive in the orchestra. The Nurse's fear and tension are reflected in the dotted rhythms of the accompaniment. The Nurse's lines are also set at a faster tempo than the preceding orchestral interlude with a meter change from the previous 4/4 to 3/4.
The Empress, exhibiting none of the Nurse's anxiety, perceives that the boat desires to stay at this place where it has arrived: Der Kahn will bleiben-- siehst du denn nicht? Die Treppe, schau! (D III 216.)		A soft alternation of chords accompanies the Empress' vocal line, perhaps enabling her words to be understood and certainly reflecting her calmness.
The physical actions of the Nurse on stage will make known the content of these lines: So lass den Kahn! Nun fort von hier! Ich weiss den Weg, Mondberge sieben sind gelagert, dies ist der höchste: ein böses Bereich!	The Nurse abandons her attempt to make the boat leave.	Strauss returned here to two of the motives which he used to set the Nurse's first speech of this act: the Nurse Motive and the Judgment Motive. An increase in tempo once again reflects the Nurse's impatience. The musical setting of the description of the Mondberge is similar in its avoidance of step-wise movement to the setting of the Messenger's reference to it in Act I scene i.

TABLE OF ANALYSIS (continued)

Text	Visual Effects	Music
Geschürzt dein Kleid und hurtig die Füsse: ich führ dich hinunter, ich finde hinaus! (D III 216.) The Empress, maintaining a steadfast interest in her surroundings, refuses to be panicked by the Nurse: Hier ist ein Tor! Einmal vordem sah ich dies Tor! (D III 216.) Hofmannsthal structured the preceding conversation so that twice an eleven-line speech of the Empress is answered by a three-line speech of the Nurse, the wordy anxiety of the Nurse contrasting with the calm self-assurance of the Empress.	The Empress steps out of the boat and onto the stairs.	The lack between the Empress and the Nurse of a common reaction to their common experience is made musically apparent by the contrast between the settings of their verse lines. The vocal line and the accompaniment of the Empress reflect calmness and perhaps a quiet self-confidence; the Nurse's vocal line and accompaniment reflect nervousness and tension. As was the case with her first response ("Der Kahn will bleiben . . ."), the Empress tends to ignore the Nurse. This reaction is exhibited in the meter change from 3/4 to 3/2 and in the composer's choice of a different motive, the Cavern Motive, to set the Empress' words. The verses of the Empress can be comprehended, but not those of the Nurse. The difference in tempo and in characterization are responsible.
Hofmannsthal structured the aria so that it falls into two principle parts: [Posaunenruf] Hörst du den Ton? Der lädt zu Gericht! Mein Vater, Ja? Keikobad? Sag? Lang sah ich ihn nicht, doch weiss ich wohl: er liebt es zu thronen wie Salomo und aufzulösen, was dunkel ist, Hoch ist sein Stuhl und abgründig sein Sinn-- doch ich bin sein Kind: ich fürchte mich nicht. [Posaunenruf] Mein Herr und Gebieter! Sie halten Gericht über ihn um meinetwillen! Was ihn bindet, blindet mich. Was er leidet, will ich leiden, ich bin in ihm,	The Nurse goes to the side of the stage, anxiously searching for an exit.	The Keikobad Motive resounds off-stage, giving the cue for the Empress' first aria in Act III; it opens in A-flat minor, the key of the initial appearance of the Keikobad Motive at the opening of the opera. The tessitura of the first half of the aria lies considerably lower than the tessitura of either her Act I scene i aria or of her Act II scene iv aria. This apparently represents Strauss' realization of the following suggestion made by Hofmannsthal: ". . .erst im dritten Akt wird die Stimme der Kaiserin ihren vollen menschlichen Klang annehmen--die tierhaft geisterhaften Elemente werden dann in einem höheren Medium zu einer neuen Wesenheit verschmolzen erscheinen." (Briefwechsel, Hofmannsthal to Strauss, 28. XII. 1913.) Strauss accepted Hofmannsthal structural division of the aria and gave the two sections different keys; the first section occurs in A-flat minor, Keikobad's key, while the second section occurs in E-flat minor and E-flat major, keys associated with the Emperor. He also differentiated between the sections by means of the motives which he employed for each, using the Keikobad Motive, the Messenger Motive, the Empress Motive, and the Traitor Motive for the first section and the Emperor Motive, the Sorrow Motive, the Descent to Earth Motive, and the Anger Motive for the second section. The Judgment Motive and the Bronze Door Motive

TABLE OF ANALYSIS (continued)

Text	Visual Effects	Music

er ist in mir!
Wir sind eins.
ich will zu ihm.
       (D III 217-18.)
 	
With the first two lines ("Hörst du den Ton? Der lädt zu Gericht!") regarded as prefatory to the entire aria the two sections are nearly equal in length, the first part comprising twelve verses and the second part eleven. In fact, the sections would be equal in length, were the verse "Was er leidet, will ich leiden" considered two verses, which the lines both preceding them and also following them suggest.
 	
The two sections are parallel in construction, although the first is concerned with Keikobad and the second with the Emperor. Both begin with a statement of the Empress' relationship to either Keikobad or the Emperor:
 	
  Part I: Mein Vater, Ja?
        Keikobad? Sag?
  Part II: Mein Herr und Gebieter!
This is followed by comments upon either the Emperor or Keikobad:
 	
  Part I: Lang sah ich ihn nicht
        . . . .
  Part II: Sie halten Gericht
        . . . .
 	
Both sections close with the Empress' statement of her relationship to either Keikobad or the Emperor:
  Part I: doch ich bin sein Kind
        ich fürchte mich nicht.
  Part II: Wir sind eins.
        ich will zu ihm.
 	
There is some question as to the accuracy of the Steiner edition printing of the verse line "Mein Herr und Gebieter!" The score gives the line as "Mein Herr und Geliebter!" (B&H Act III #60.) Because the Empress refers to Barak with the name Gebieter ("ich, mein Gebieter, deine Dienerin!" D III 201), the probable correct choice would be "Geliebter".
 	
The Nurse pleads once more with the Empress to leave:
Fort mit uns!
ich schaffe dir den Schatten!
So ist es gesetzt
und so geschworen!
Du bleibst die gleiche,
Töchterchen, liebes,
		occur in both, serving as unifying elements. The aria ends with a stylistic similarity to the Mozartian heroic aria, Strauss thereby paying homage to one of his favorite predecessors. The theme employed here will henceforth be referred to as the Marriage Theme. (See musical example #63.) The vocal line dominates the musical structure, primarily because of the many motives which occur in it.
		
		The music, paralleling the structure of the verse lines, falls into two parts because of the different motives which occur within them. There is, however, no framework in the music which corresponds to the verse line "Fort mit uns." The first part contains the Shadow Motive; the second part contains the Love Theme #2, the Beating Motive, and the Judgment Motive. The Nurse

TABLE OF ANALYSIS (continued)

Text	Visual Effects	Music

und durch deinen Leib
gleitet das Licht--
allein des Weibes
trauriger Schatten,
dir verfallen,
haftet der Ferse!
Ihresgleichen
scheinst du dann
und bist es nicht:
doch du erfüllst,
was bedungen war!
So hab deinen Liebsten
und herze ihn!
Ich helf dir ihn finden,
ich will es tragen,
dass ich ihn sehe
in deinen Armen
auf Jahr und Tag
und bleibe die Hündin
in seinem Hause!
Wehe mir!
Nur fort von hier!
Fort von der Schwelle:
sie zu betreten
ist mehr als Tod!
    (D III 218-19.)
 	
This speech, like the immediately preceding one of the Empress, falls into two parts, the second section beginning with "So hab deinen Liebsten." There is additionally a framework provided by the following opening and closing verse lines:
 	
    Fort mit uns!
 	
  . . . . .
    Nur fort von hier!
    Fort von der Schwelle:
    sie zu betreten
    ist mehr als Tod!
 	
In the first part of the speech (from "Ich schaff dir den Schatten!" to "was bedungen war!") the Nurse speaks of acquiring the shadow for the Empress. The lines contain an apparent logical inconsistency, the line "ich schaff dir den Schatten" implying that the shadow is yet to be acquired and the lines "allein des Weibes / trauriger Schatten, / dir ver-fallen, / haftet der Ferse!" implying that the shadow has been acquired. The letter of Hofmannsthal to Strauss dated April, 1915, makes the poet's intent clear: ". . . am Schluss von Akt II schwebt der Schatten in der Luft, die eine hat ihn verwirkt, die andere hat ihn
		Motive occurs in both parts as a binding element. Of a total of thirty verse lines (excepting the one verse line which is set to a cadential formula) motives occur within only four verse lines of the first part and within only seven of the second part, only slightly more than one-third of the verses.
		By comparison, the immediately preceding aria of the Empress with a total of twenty-three lines (two excepted because they are set to cadential formulas) has eight set to motives with six more related rhythmically or melodically to each other in the Mozartian heroic aria style. This constitutes more than half of the verse lines.
		The verse lines of the Nurse will probably not be comprehended with the exception of the final line "ist mehr als Tod," which is partially unaccompanied and partially set to a cadential formula. The key center for the solo is E-flat major; the tempo, reflecting the Nurse's frenetic activity on stage, is a fast 6/8.

TABLE OF ANALYSIS (continued)

Text	Visual Effects	Music

nicht rechtsgültig erworben--dieser schwebende Handel und seine Schlichtung durch ein salomonisches Urteil höherer Mächte, als deren Wortführer die "Ungeborenen" figurieren, bildet ja das Zentrum des dritten Aktes . . . ." (Briefwechsel.) The second part of the speech (from "So hab deinen Liebsten" to "Wehe mir!") depicts the happiness of the Empress and the Emperor once the shadow has been acquired.
 	
If the Nurse is to become for the audience something other than a shadowy background figure, some of these lines must be comprehended. Her inflexibility and lack of growth since the first act are demonstrated in this speech by the consistency with which she continues her attempts to acquire the shadow by magical means. Comprehension of the lines, although unnecessary for following the plot, would give depth to the audience's understanding of the Nurse.
 	
The Empress becomes aware of the Nurse's anxiety and realizes that the Nurse knows what this place is to which they have come. She begins to question her:
  So kennst du die Schwelle?
    So wiesst du, wohin
    dies Tor sich öffnet?
  Antworte mir!
  Amme: Zum Wasser des Lebens.
    Kaiserin: Antworte mir!
    Zur Schwelle des Todes!
  So scholl der Ruf,
  Steh mir Rede!
  Du weisst das Geheime
  und kennst die Bewandtnis.
  .Antworte mir!
      (D III 219.)
 	
The verse line "Antworte mir!" occurs like a refrain throughout the exchange. The verse which speaks of the dangerous nature of that which lies beyond the entrance ("Zur Schwelle des Todes!") needs to be comprehended; the Empress' courage and the Nurse's fear are thereby put into perspective.
 	
The Empress directs two more questions to the Nurse; receiving no answer she abandons her attempt to communicate with her and considers how to save the Emperor:
  Schweigst du tückisch?
  Willst du mit Fleiss
		Although the E-flat key signature of the Nurse's preceding solo remains, the key center for this exchange between the Empress and the Nurse shifts first to G minor and then to C minor, the composer's key for heroic rebellion. The refrain verse "Antworte mir!" is set at each appearance to the same motive, the Answer Motive. (See musical example #64 for this new motive.) Strauss also employed the Judgment Motive, the Secret Motive, the Cavern Motive, and the Anger Motive. The significant line "Zur Schwelle des Todes!" is unaccompanied, but it spans two octaves (from high C to middle C) on the word Todes and will probably not be comprehended for this reason.
		
		Strauss inserted a pause between the last question directed to the Nurse and the Empress' statement. "Hell ist in mir!" In order to distinguish further between the Empress' resolve to aid the Emperor and the preceding dialogue, the composer modulated to

TABLE OF ANALYSIS (continued)

Text	Visual Effects	Music
den Sinn mir verdunkeln? Hell ist in mir! Hell ist vor mir! Ich muss zu ihm! Wasser des Lebens, ich muss es erspüren, ihn besprengen-- Wasser des Lebens-- ist es das Blut aus diesen Adern? Fliesse es hin, dass ich ihn wecke! (D III 219-20.) The Empress indicates in this passage her willingness to give her life in order to save the Emperor. The line "Ich muss zu ihm" is important because it demonstrates her great resolve in the face of danger; the remaining lines are unimportant as far as plot development is concerned because they repeat the meaning conveyed earlier, that the Empress desires to save the Emperor.	The Empress turns and begins to climb the steps. The Nurse throws herself in the way, clutching at the Empress' clothes in a desperate attempt to stop her.	a new key, D major, which becomes the key center of the opera until after the Empress' exit. For the first three lines after the questions (from "Hell ist in mir!" to "Ich muss zu ihm") Strauss gave the words and their vocal setting dominance over the orchestra. The brightness and clarity with which the Empress sees her course before her (Hell ist in mir!) is programmatically portrayed both by a high string tremolo and also the generally high pitch of the accompaniment. The remaining lines are unimportant from the point of view of conveying information. Neither the lyrical musical element nor the purely dramatic element comes to the fore in the remaining lines of the speech. Perhaps this explains why both the rest of the speech and the following one by the Nurse are traditionally omitted.
The Nurse continues in her attempts to dissuade the Empress from entering the bronze door; she makes it clear that there actually is a spring in the mountain and that this spring is dangerous to spirits like the Empress and herself: Hab Erbarmen! Du verfängst dich: tausend Netze, Gaukelspiel, gräulicher Trug! Wasser des Lebens, gräuliches Blendwerk-- müsst ich darüber mein Blut hingeben-- halte ich ab von deiner Seele und deinem Herzen! Ein Wasser springt wirklich im Berge. Leuchtend steigt es, goldene Säule,		When a speech such as this one occurs, which has for its primary purpose a retarding of the action, the lyrical and musical elements must dominate. Otherwise, the lack of both dramatic interest and also musical intensity will result in a section lacking in enough intensity to prevent boredom. Unfortunately, the musical structures at this point seem incapable of sustaining interest. There is a noticeable lack of new melodic material; instead, a recombination of the Emperor as Hunter Motive, the Sorrow Motive, the Judgment Motive, the Descent to Earth Motive, the Anger Motive and the Traitor Motive occurs. Only three of twenty-eight verse lines are set to motives; the motivic interest obviously lies in the orchestra.

TABLE OF ANALYSIS (continued)

Text	Visual Effects	Music
aus dem Grund: Wasser des Lebens! Wer daran die Lippen legte-- einer der unsern, von Geistern stammend--, mehr als Tod, gräulich unsagbar teuflisches Unheil schlürft er in sich rettungslos. (D III 220-21.) This speech is significant only in the devotion which the Nurse here exhibits toward the Empress, a quality which will probably be conveyed by gestures on the stage. Generally speaking, the primary function of the speech is to delay the Empress' ultimate exit. In her attempt to stop the Empress the Nurse frantically mentions the punishment which awaits the Empress for having married the Emperor: Hörst du mich nicht? Fürchterlich ist Keikobad! Was weisst du von ihm! Du bist sein Kind und hast dich gegeben in Menschenhand und dein Herz vergeudet an einen von den Verwesenden! Fürchterlich straft er dich, wenn du fällst in seine Hand. Denn er kennt kein Greuel über diesem, dass eines spiele mit den Verhassten und sich mische mit den Verfluchten! Weh über sie, die dich gebar, und Menschensehnsucht dir flösste ins Blut! Weh über dich! (D III 221.) Structurally, the speech has an introductory single line ("Hörst du mich nicht?") followed by two longer sections, each beginning with the word "Fürchterlich".		The key shifts to D minor, as Strauss attempts to differentiate this speech from the immediately preceding one. Newly recurring motives, the Keikobad Motive, the Dissension Motive, and the No Blood Motive, also serve this purpose. Six of twenty-one verse lines contain a motive or a part of one; the vocal line thus carries a potentially greater source of interest than occurred with the immediately preceding speech, where the ratio is three of twenty-eight.

TABLE OF ANALYSIS (continued)

Text	Visual Effects	Music
The first section has eight verse lines; the second has nine. These are followed by a short four-verse line segment which is primarily an emotional outburst ("Weh über sie" to "dir flösste ins Blut"). The speech ends with the single opening verse line "Weh über dich!" which balances the preceding one, serves to retard the action and to build up the scene which the audience senses to be coming between the Empress and Keikobad.	The Empress has reached the top step.	Strauss made structural divisions in the music which correspond closely to the structural divisions in the text. The first five verse lines comprise the first structural unit. The vocal line dominates, as the orchestra doubles the vocal line or provides a high string tremolo. During the next two verse lines the vocal line also dominates, but the cantabile style of the first five lines is replaced by a more declamatory style. Thereafter, the cantabile style returns, with the Freedom Motive and the Youth Motive providing the melodic material. At the verse line "Mit welchem Preis" the key center, D major, of this section of the opera returns. New motives also occur here, giving the aria great musical interest. (See the Price Motive, musical example #65, and the Phoenix Motive, musical example #66.) The final verse line ("du taugst nicht zu mir!") is unaccompanied, giving maximum exposure to the vocal line as the Empress decisively rejects the Nurse.

The Empress replies to the entreaties of the Nurse:

Aus unsern Taten
steigt ein Gericht!
Aus unserm Herzen
ruft die Posaune,
die uns lädt.--
Amme, auf immer
scheid ich mich von dir.
Was Menschen bedürfen,
du weisst es zu wenig,
worauf ihrer Herzen
Geheimnis zielet,
dir ist es verborgen.
Mit welchem Preis
sie alles zahlen,
aus schwerer Schuld
sich wieder erneuen,
dem Phönix gleich,
aus ewigem Tode
zu ewigem Leben
sich immer erhöhen--
kaum ahnen sies selber--
dir kommt es nicht nah.
Ich gehöre zu ihnen,
du taugst nicht zu mir!
(D III 222.)

The speech falls into two parts, with the first part (from "Aus unsern Taten" to "die uns lädt") constituting the Empress' acceptance of a judgment upon her deeds. The second part (from "Amme, auf immer" to "du taugst nicht zu mir") consists both of the Empress' rejection of the Nurse as a companion and also of her hymn in praise of mankind. The lines rejecting the Nurse ("Amme, auf immer / scheid ich mich von dir"; "Ich gehöre zu ihnen, / du taugst nicht zu mir!") provide a frame for the remaining lines. The length of sentences

TABLE OF ANALYSIS (continued)

Text	Visual Effects	Music
in these remaining lines (five verse lines for the first sentence and ten verse lines for the second) suggests that here the content is not important and that the music is to dominate. The Empress' rejection of the Nurse and acceptance of humanity for herself ("Ich gehöre zu ihnen, / du taugst nicht zu mir!"), on the other hand, represents a decisive step on the part of the Empress and needs to be comprehended.	When the Empress sings the verse lines rejecting the Nurse, she holds her hand up and out in a gesture signifying her intent.	The orchestral interlude which accompanies the Empress' entrance into the mountain is comprised of the Love Theme #1, the Empress Motive, the Emperor as Lover Motive, and the Judgment Motive.

With the exit of the Empress the "big scene," as Strauss termed it, for the Nurse arrives. (Briefwechsel, Strauss to Hofmannsthal, IV. 1915.) The Nurse begins with a speech of nineteen verse lines which is interspersed with the outcries of Barak and the Wife:
 	
Amme: Was Menschen bedürfen?
    Betrug ist die Speise,
    nach der sie gieren.
    Betrüger sie selber!
    Fluch über sie!
Das ewige Trachten,
    vorwärts ins Leere,
    der angstvermischte
    gierige Wahnsinn—
    hinübergeträufelt
    in meines Kindes
    kristallene Seele!
    Fluch über sie!
Baraks Stimme: Ah!
Der Frau Stimme: Ah!
Barak: Dass ich dich fände!
Frau: O mein Geliebter!
Barak: Fürchte nichts!
Sieh, o sieh!
Frau: Finde mich,
    töte mich!
	The Empress approaches the door which silently opens for her. After she enters, the door closes. The Nurse follows the Empress up the stairs, but does not have the courage to enter the door.	The Nurse's first solo of her "big scene" is noticeably intensified by the many outcries from Barak and the Wife, but the basic form remains the same as Hofmannsthal designed it. The first section of the aria (from "Was Menschen bedürfen!" to the first "Pluch über sie!") is set in the key of F minor; the second section is set primarily in E minor but ends in D minor. The third section, which is precipitated by a relatively long section of outcries from Barak and the Wife, occurs primarily in D minor.
		
		The music for the solo seems to have been conceived more as a scherzo for orchestra than as a vocal solo, for the principal melodic materials, the new Agitation Motive and the Traitor Motive from Act I, never occur in the vocal line. (See musical example #65 for the Agitation Motive.) Other motives which Strauss employed include the Shadow Motive, the Desire for Children Motive, the Nurse Motive, the Beating Motive, a phrase of the Protection Theme, the Dissension Motive, the Judgment Motive, the Children Motive, the Blessedness Motive, the Vision Motive, the Guilt Motive, and the Anger Motive.
		
		The third section of the solo (beginning with "Menschen! Menschen!") builds up to a climax for the final curse "Tod über sie!" by means of a gradual rise in pitch up to the last line and by a relatively more rapid setting of the last four lines.

TABLE OF ANALYSIS (continued)

Text	Visual Effects	Music
Beide: Weh, weh, o weh! Amme: Menschen! Menschen! Wie ich sie hasse! Wimmelnd wie Aale, schreiend wie Adler, schändend die Erde! Tod über sie! (D III 223-24.) The Nurse's speech falls into three parts, the points of division being marked by the curses "Fluch über sie!" and "Tod über sie!" The first section comprises five verse lines, including the curse, and is directly related to the immediately preceding speech of the Empress; the second section contains eight verse lines and is a reflective comment on the detrimental effect of people on the Empress. The third section, which is separated above from the preceding two by the outcries of Barak and the Wife, contains six verse lines and is an expression of the Nurse's hatred of men. The vehemence of this hatred is expressed in the relative independence of the verse lines from each other, which give a cumulative effect of great emotional intensity. Barak and the Wife address the Nurse in separate interviews: Barak: Ich suche meine Frau, die vor mir flieht! Hast du sie nicht gesehn-- O meine Muhme? Amme: Dort hinüber! Dort hinauf! Sie verflucht dich in den Tod! Strafe sie-- räche dich-- schnell! Barak: Zu ihr! Zu ihr! Frau: O du--o du--wo ist mein Mann? O du-- ich will zu ihm! Amme: Dort hinüber! Dich zu töten, mit seinen Händen. Rette dich, flieh! Frau: Barak! Hier! Schwinge dein Schwert. Töte mich schnell!	Barak, in search of the Wife, enters from the right. Upon recognizing the Nurse, he shows fear of her. The Nurse sends him off to the upper left, whereupon the Wife enters from the lower left. The Nurse sends her off to the right.	Strauss related the two conversations to each other by using essentially the same motives for each one: the Traitor Motive, the Judgment Motive, the Beating Motive, and the Sword Motive. Additionally the Agitation Motive occurs during Barak's interview with the Nurse and the Guilt Motive and the Freedom Motive occur during the Wife's interview. The key centers of the two exchanges are differentiated, however, Barak's being set in A minor and the Wife's being set in C minor and A-flat minor.

189

TABLE OF ANALYSIS (continued)

Text	Visual Effects	Music
(D III 224-25.) Each exchange, the Nurse with Barak and the Nurse with the Wife, spans exactly eleven verse lines. These interviews provide no new information, but they do emphasize the new sense of commitment which Barak and the Wife feel for each other, even when the Nurse falsely portrays the opposite partner as eager to destroy the other.		
Following the exit of the Wife, the Nurse resumes her monologue: Wehe, mein Kind, ausgeliefert, Gaukelspiel vor ihren Augen, Fallen und Stricke vor ihrem Fuss! Sie ist hinein! Sie trinkt! Das goldne, flüssige Unheil springt auf die Lippen, wühlt sich hinab! Ihr Gesicht gräulich zuckt, ein menschlicher Schrei ringt sich aus der wunden Kehle! Ihr zu Hilfe! Müsste ich sterben! Keikobad! (D III 225-26.) Like her opening monologue, this one has nineteen verse lines. The Nurse's speeches and the exchanges between the Nurse and Barak, the Nurse and the Wife thus form a symmetrical structure: nineteen verse lines of monologue by the Nurse (interspersed with outcries of Barak and the Wife), eleven verse lines as an exchange between Barak and the Nurse, eleven verse lines as an exchange between the Wife and the Nurse, nineteen verse lines of monologue by the Nurse. In the monologue given immediately above the Nurse's concern for the Empress becomes paramount as she depicts for herself the events taking place within the mountain. These lines, provided they are understood, heighten suspense for the next scene, the Temple Scene.	The stage continues to darken.	Strauss made a noticeable effort to enable the Nurse's words to be comprehended. A low string tremolo provides the principal accompaniment for the first six lines; the seventh line ("Sie ist hinein!") is unaccompanied and set to the familiar Judgment Motive. The eighth line ("Sie trinkt!" and the fourteenth line ("ein menschlicher Schrei") are set above low string tremolos while the remaining lines, with the exception of the last three, are either doubled in the orchestra or accompanied by a chord. Comprehension of the next to the last lines ("Ihr zu Hilfe! / Müsste ich sterben!") is sacrificed to the climax which is being created for the benefit of the final line "Keikobad" with its echo effect. The composer did not create a symmetrical musical structure, as the poet did of the speeches at this point.

TABLE OF ANALYSIS (continued)

Text	Visual Effects	Music
Hofmannsthal constructed the remainder of the scene so that dialogues between the Nurse and the Messenger, punctuated with outcries from Barak and the Wife, frame an ensemble which includes all four of these figures. The first dialogue consists of these lines: Bote: Den Namen des Herrn? Hündin, zu wem hebst du die Stimme? Fort mit dir von der Schwelle! Pack dich, für immer! Amme: Mir anvertraut-- du selber, Bote! drei Tage lang! ich hab sie gehütet, ich rang mit ihr-- sie stiess mich von sich-- sie kennt mich nicht mehr-- Keikobad! Er muss mich hören! Bote: Sie ist vor ihm! Wer bedarf deiner? Niemand. Such dir den Weg! Amme: Keikobad! Deine Dienerin schreit zu dir-- Strafe sie, aber verwirf sie nicht ungehört! Mir übergeben, ich steh dir Rede! Keikobad! Bote: Wer bist du, dass du ihn rufest? Was weisst du von seinem Willen, und wie er verhängt hat ihr die Prüfung? Wenn er dich hiess des Kindes hüten, wer heisst dich raten, ob er nicht wollte, dass sie dir entliefe? Und trotzdem dich	The Messenger comes out of the bronze door.	Strauss set the Messenger's lines almost entirely without accompaniment, only interposing orchestral phrases between the verse lines. The verses are also given a simple melodic and harmonic setting so that comprehension is almost assured. The Nurse's verse lines are given a far more passionate setting than are the Messenger's, focusing attention upon her frenzied emotional state. Motives employed include the Messenger Motive, the Judgment Motive, the Nurse Motive, the Dissension Motive, the Keikobad Motive; the key center is C minor. The intensification in the Nurse's verse lines ("ich hab sie gehütet" to "sie kennt mich micht mehr") is paralleled by a similar intensification in the melodic setting. The first note of each succeeding verse line rises one-half step in pitch; similarly ascending chords punctuate the rests in the vocal line. Strauss began to build toward the ensemble which forms the central section of the scene with the last two speeces of the Nurse and the Messenger ("Keikobad! / Deine Dienerin"; "Wer bist du?"). A modulation to D-flat major occurs here and the voices of the Dyer pair are first used at this point. Strauss used the Agitation Motive, the Traitor Motive, and the Protection Theme in the orchestra as binding elements for the ensemble. Above these melodies the vocal lines of the Nurse, the Messenger, Barak, and the Wife occur, sometimes parallelling the primary orchestral melody, sometimes not. The principle musical interest lies in the orchestra.

TABLE OF ANALYSIS (continued)

Text	Visual Effects	Music

verwirft auf ewig:
dass du nicht vermochtest,
ihrer zu hüten!
(D III 226-28.)
 	
The last two speeches here (Amme: "Keikobad!";
Bote: "Wer bist du") seem to have been conceived
as a duet, for these lines essentially repeat what
has already been said.
The meaning of these lines will be conveyed by the
actions of the Nurse and the Messenger on the stage.
Comprehension is not necessary.
 	
The following verse lines were obviously written as an
ensemble passage, although no direction indicating this
is given in the Steiner edition:
  Barak: Mir anvertraut,
  dass ich dich hege,
  und dich trage
  auf diesen Händen.
  Amme: Schlage er mich
  mit seinem Zorn!
  Ich will zu ihr!
  Bote: Mit seinem Zorn
  schlägt er dich,
  dass du ihr Antlitz
  nicht wiedersiehst!
  (D III 229.)
 	
The following lines of the Wife, which were omitted from
the Steiner edition, occur in the score, where they and
the immediately preceding eleven lines are set as a
quartet:
  Frau: O, dass ich dich fände,
  dich zu erquicken,
  dienend, liebend dir mich bücken!
  Kinder, Guter, dir zu geben!
  (B&H Act III #123-#125.)
 	
The passage thus builds from solo lines by the Nurse and
the Messenger with frequent outbursts from Barak and the
Wife to a full-blown quartet. The words are not important;
the significance of the ensemble lies in the turmoil
which it embodies: "Die ganze Szene [Act III scene ii]
nun voll innerer Unruhe, der Katastrophe zutreibend.
In circa 14 Tagen hoffe ich mich nach Erledigung anderer
Geschäfte mit ganzer Kraft der Hauptszene im Tempel
zuzuwenden, welche durch die vorliegende Szene
entschieden besser vorbereitet."
(Briefwechsel, Hofmannsthal to Strauss, 7. VII. 1915.)
	The fog becomes denser and
	the storm more violent.
	The Steiner edition indicates
	that Barak and the Wife are
	not to be visible; the score
	indicates that they are to
	appear occasionally.
		Strauss gave the principal melody of the ensemble to
		Barak, who sings the Protection Theme, and secondly
		to the Wife, who sings the countermelody to the
		Protection Theme.

TABLE OF ANALYSIS (continued)

Text	Visual Effects	Music
The scene closes with this dialogue between the Messenger and the Nurse: Amme: Weh, mein Kind! Mir verloren! Fluch und Verderben über die Menschen— fressendes Feuer in ihr Gebein! Bote: Unter den Menschen umherzuirren, ist dein Los! Die du hassest, mit ihnen zu hausen, ihrem Atem dich zu vermischen immer aufs neu! 1 Amme: Die ich hasse, mit ihnen zu hausen, ihrem Atem mich zu vermischen immer aufs neu! Bote: Auf, du Kahn, trage dies Weib Mondberge hinab den Menschen zu! Amme: Fressendes Feuer in ihr Gebein! Bote: Verzehre dich! Dir widerfährt nach dem Gesetze! 　　　　　(D III 230-31.) Although the actions on stage will help to convey the meaning, the Messenger's speech banishing the Nurse ("Auf, du Kahn"), provided that it is understood, will help the audience to follow the plot.	The Messenger grasps the Nurse and pushes her down the steps and into the boat. The Nurse collapses in the boat, which immediately departs for the world of people. The Messenger disappears. Thunder and lightning, which have been steadily increasing in intensity during the scene, accompany the Nurse's departure. Darkness covers the stage, with the exception of occasional flashes of lightning.	Strauss included the Nurse's first speech (from "Weh, mein Kind" to "in ihr Gebein") in the quartet itself. The first three lines of the Messenger ("Unter den Menschen / umherzuirren, / ist dein Los!") are set as a solo, then a duet between the Messenger and the Nurse occurs with the lines of the Messenger echoing the lines of the Messenger in this manner: Messenger: Die du hassest, Nurse: Die ich hasse, Messenger: mit ihnen zu hausen, Nurse: mit ihnen zu hausen, [etc.] The Messenger Motive appears as a setting for the first three lines of the exchange ("Unter den Menschen . . ."). Because this motive was the primary motive for the initial dialogue between the Nurse and the Messenger, this imparts an A B A form to the music. Solo passages for the Messenger's last two speeches and the intervening speech of the Nurse close this scene. The ensemble passage (from the Nurse's "Keikobad! deine Dienerin / schreit zu dir" to the end of the Nurse's speech "Die ich hasse, / mit ihnen zu hausen") is invariably omitted in performance. The ensemble does not appear to be successful when half of it is not present on the stage. The dominance of the orchestral part over the vocal line, moreover, would tend to make the ensemble musically uninteresting were it staged. Strauss set the important lines wherein the Messenger banishes the Nurse from the world of spirits without accompaniment; the audience should be able to comprehend them. The composer dropped the final syllable of "Gesetze" in order to fit the line into a cadence. The Nurse's curse was set by Strauss with the last syllable on a high B-flat, effectively conveying the emotional intensity which she feels. The orchestral interlude offers a programmatic portrayal of the storm which is occurring on the stage. The Keikobad Motive, the Dissension Motive, the Judgment Motive, and the Sword Motive all participate. The voices of the Wife and Barak become fainter and fainter, indicating that the distance between them and the stage is becoming greater. The storm in the orchestra begins to subside.

Text	Visual Effects	Music
	Act III scene iii	
	The stage becomes lighted once more, revealing the interior of a temple-like room. A center niche is concealed by a curtain.	Relative quiet and repose become the mood of the orchestra during the second part of the interlude. Motives employed include the Bronze Door Motive and the Cavern Motive. The key center for the entire interlude is D minor.
The following verse lines are sung by spirits who greet the Empress: Erster: Hab Ehrfurcht! Zweiter: Mut! Dritter: Erfülle dein Geschick! (D III 231.) These three commands both summarize and also anticipate the Empress' character development. (Details of the Empress' change of character are given in Chapter III.) The lack of continuity with any other activity or speech in the opera will make comprehension difficult if not impossible; this would be true even if the lines were spoken and not sung. Comprehension is not, however, essential for following the plot.	The Empress appears and is greeted by Spirits carrying torches. (Hofmannsthal had initially intended these lines to be sung from the orchestra pit [Briefwechsel, Hofmannsthal to Strauss, 14. V. 1915], but Strauss opposed this and was apparently able to convince the poet to change his position.) The Spirits exit after having spoken to the Empress.	The lines of the Spirits are simply set, but the accompaniment, where the Bronze Door Motive and the Cavern Motive are being sounded in the brass section, will probably cover the words.
The text which Hofmannsthal wrote for the Empress for the Temple Scene is very carefully constructed. There are two major sections, each comprising fifty-three verse lines. The first fifty-three verse section contains two separate nineteen verse-line monologues framing a fifteen-verse segment. The second major section of fifty-three verse lines contains a thirty-eight line monologue (19 x 2) followed by a fifteen-line segment. Both of the nineteen verse-line speeches of the first major section fall into two parts, one which contains thirteen lines, the other six: Part I: Vater, bist dus? Drohest du mir aus dem Dunkel her? Hier siehe dein Kind! Mich hinzugeben hab ich gelernt, aber Schatten hab ich keinen mir erhandelt. Nun zeig mir den Platz, der mir gebührt inmitten derer, die Schatten werfen.		Strauss actually opened the Temple Scene after the departure of the Spirits, for only then does the key of E-flat major first sound, which is the key center for the first part of the scene. Following a brief introduction in the brass section which contains the Release from Prison Motive, a violin solo recapitulates the entire development of the Empress over an E-flat pedal point. During the solo the following motives are fused together to form a new entity: the Empress Motive, the Love Theme #1, the Marriage Theme, and the Sorrow Motive. (Consider in this context Hofmannsthal's comment to Strauss on December 28, 1913: "die tierhaft geisterhaften Elemente in der Kaiserin werden dann [im dritten Akt] in einem höheren Medium zu einer neuen Wesenheit verschmolzen erscheinen." Briefwechsel.) This new combination of elements becomes an introduction to the Empress' first four verse lines ("Vater bist dus" to "Hier siehe dein Kind!"), which are similar to a recitative in style. The lines are unaccompanied and the melody is simple; comprehension seems to be assured. Thereafter, a cantilene begins wherein the vocal line and a solo violin, later replaced by a solo horn, offer a duet. The important lines "aber Schatten / hab ich keinen" will probably be understood because here the violin

194

TABLE OF ANALYSIS (continued)

Text	Visual Effects	Music
Part II: Goldenen Trank, Wasser des Lebens, mich zu stärken, bedarf ich nicht! Liebe ist in mir, die ist mehr. (D III 232.) The division into two parts is based upon the Empress' reaction to the springing forth of the fountain. As a whole, the speech touches upon four different points: 1) the Empress addresses her father ("Vater, bist dus?"); 2) she confesses to her lack of a shadow ("aber Schatten / hab ich keinen!"); 3) she claims for herself a place among men (Nun zeig mir den Platz . . . inmitten derer / die Schatten werfen!"); 4) she denies a need for the "Water of Life" ("Wasser des Lebens . . . / bedarf ich nicht"). If the audience is to sympathize with the Empress' agony in this scene, some of the verse lines must be understood. A bare minimum would be the verse lines quoted in the immediately preceding analysis. The section which separates the two monologues of the Empress contains the following fifteen-line exchange which is primarily a temptation of the Empress by the Guardian of the Threshold: Stimme von oben: So trink, du Liebende, von diesem Wasser! Trink, und der Schatten, der des Weibes war, wird deiner sein, und du wirst sein wie sie! Kaiserin: Jedoch was will aus ihr? Die Stimme der Frau: Barak! Baraks Stimme: Wo bist du? Die Stimme der Frau: Wehe, wo? Baraks Stimme: Her zu mir! Die Stimme der Frau: Ach, vergebens! Baraks Stimme: Weh! Verloren! Kaiserin: Baraks Stimme! Baraks Blick! Meine Schuld hier wie dort, dort wie hier! (D III 233.) It is important that the audience comprehend that should the Empress drink of the water, the Wife's	A fountain of golden water springs up from the ground. When the Empress denies that she needs the "Water of Life," she steps away from the fountain. The score contains the following instruction: "Der Hüter der Schwelle wird zur Seite der verhängten Nische sichtbar." Hofmannsthal at one time expressed a desire that this was to be the method of staging this individual. (Briefwechsel, Hofmannsthal to Strauss, 14. V. 1915.) The pressures of war-time are perhaps responsible for the inconsistency between the score and the Steiner edition.	doubles the voice. The lines "Nun zeig mir den Platz . . . / inmitten derer / die Schatten werfen" may not, however, be comprehended because the two melodic lines of the duet tend to be independent of each other here. The play of the water from the fountain is programmatically portrayed by harp glissandi and a new motive played by a flute, the Temptation Motive. (See musical example #68.) Strauss also employed the Judgement Motive here. The Empress' verse lines dealing with the fountain are set in a florid style matching the programmatic portrayal of the fountain. The line where she denies any need for the "Water of Life" ("bedarf ich nicht") is again set syllabically. The florid style which was first employed for the Empress' acknowledgment of the existence of the fountain is employed for the setting of the Guardian's lines. Hofmannsthal had suggested that something extraordinary be employed for the setting of these lines: "Für die Hüter der Schwelle, welche trügerische Magier oder Dämonen, Verführer sind, denke ich mir eine höchst besondere Stimmführung, mannweiblich, verlockend und dabei abstossend, wie wenn eine Schlange singen würde. Vielleicht lässt sich eine männliche Stimme in besonders hoher Lage (Falsett) oder eine weibliche Stimme in seltsam tiefer verwenden oder noch weit Schöneres, als mir einfallen kann." (Briefwechsel, Hofmannsthal to Strauss 19. IX.1915.) Strauss's solution was to shift from the primarily syllabic setting of the text which he customarily used to a style employing melismas. Some of the words may be understood because they are syllabically set; most will not because of the florid style. Those which are set syllabically are: "trink"; "des Weibes war"; "du wirst sein wie sie." Perhaps these phrases will be sufficient to allow the audience to follow the plot. Additionally, the Empress' line

TABLE OF ANALYSIS (continued)

Text	Visual Effects	Music
shadow would become hers, presumably saving the Emperor. They should also be aware of the Empress' concern for the Wife (Jedoch was wird aus ihr?"¹) and for Barak ("Baraks Stimme!" "Meine Schuld / . . . dort wie hier!") Settings of these lines which would allow comprehension would help the audience to follow the plot.	The fountain slowly subsides.	"Jedoch was wird aus ihr?" is set in a declamatory style and her lines "Meine Schuld / dort wie hier" are doubled in the orchestra, probably allowing comprehension. Strauss did not set the line "hier wie dort", apparently preferring the more regular four-line speech for his musical design than the uneven-numbered five-line speech.

The counterpart to the Empress' opening nineteen-line speech is:

```
Part I:   Sternennamen
          rief ich an,
          rein zu bleiben
          von Menschenschuld!
          Blut ist in dem Wasser,
          ich trinke nicht!
Part II:  Doch welch ich nicht!
          Mein Platz ist hier
          in dieser Welt.
          Hier ward ich schuldig.
          hierher gehör ich.
          Wo immer du
          dich birgst im Dunkel--
          in meinem Herzen
          ist ein Licht,
          dich zu enthüllen!
          Ich will mein Gericht!
          Zeige dich, Vater!
          Mein Richter, hervor!
                 (D III 233-34.)
```

Strauss did not use an exact A B A musical form to set the first section of the Temple Scene; there are, however, suggestions of this form. The composer utilized harp glissandi to accompany part of the first six lines here, thus establishing a correspondence between these lines and the last six lines of the first nineteen-line speech. The Sorrow Motive, the Keikobad Motive and the Empress Motive occur in the settings of both thirteen-line sections of the monologues.

Like the first nineteen-line speech, this one breaks into two parts of six and thirteen verse lines each. The order is, however, reversed this time, the six line speech preceding instead of following. The interior order of the content is also reversed, giving here: 1) a refusal to drink the water ("Ich trinke nicht"); 2) a claim for a place for herself among men ("Mein Platz ist hier / in dieser Welt"); 3) an emphasis upon her internal brightness ("in meinem Herzen / ist ein Licht"); 4) a direct address to her father Keikobad ("Zeige dich, Vater! / mein Richter, hervor").

The structure of the first fifty-three-line section of the Temple Scene is, therefore,

```
A:  nineteen verses . .
    m: thirteen verses
    x: four verses
    y: five verses
    z: four verses
```

TABLE OF ANALYSIS (continued)

Text	Visual Effects	Music

B: n: six verses
     fifteen verses
A: nineteen verses
   n: six verses
   m: thirteen verses
     z: five verses
     y: five verses
     x: three verses
	The light behind the curtained niche becomes brighter, revealing the Emperor, rigid and stone-like, upon a rocky throne.	A short orchestral interlude depicts the growing intensification of light by means of an E-flat minor chord which begins pianissimo and crescendoes to a fortississimo playing of the Stone Motive. This intro-duction to the second fifty-three-verse section of the scene, like the first one, is characterized by a pedal point on E-flat. (E-flat minor designates a struggle with fate for Strauss.)

The next speech of the Empress encompasses thirty-eight verses, the total of the two preceding monologues: Ach! Weh mir! Mein Liebster starr! Lebendig begraben Im eigenen Leib! Erfüllt der Fluch! Meines Wesens unschuldige Schuld an ihm gestraft, weil er zu sehr mein Geheimnis geliebt, um das er mich wählte-- erbarmungslos dahingeopfert meinem Geheimnis sein liebendes Herz! Ungelöst meiner Seele Knoten von Menschenhand-- Starr nun die Hand, die ihn nicht löste-- Versteinert sein Herz von meiner Härte! Mein Geschick seine Schuld! Meine Schuld sein Geschick! Weh, ihr Sterne, also tut ihr an den Menschen!		Strauss wrote to Hofmannsthal on July 18, 1916, that he intended to treat the entire thirty-eight verses at this point, from the time when the Empress first glimpses the Emperor to her outcry "Ich kann nicht" as melodrama, spoken words with orchestral background. A pedal point on F-sharp, underlying most of the verse lines, binds the passage together. The Stone Motive provides the primary melodic material for the background of the first twenty-nine verses; a new motive, the Awaken Motive (see musical example #69), is dominant during the next six verses, and the Emperor as Lover Motive provides the background for the last three verses.

197

TABLE OF ANALYSIS (continued)

Text	Visual Effects	Music

Mit d r sterben,
auf, wach auf!
Aug in Aug,
Mund an Mund,
mit dir vereint,
lass mich sterben!
Nicht diesen Blick!
Ich kann nicht helfen,
ich kann nicht!
    (D III 234-36.)
 	
The first twenty-nine verses 1) establish that the Emperor has indeed turned to stone ("Mein Liebster starr"), 2) recapitulate the events which have led to this occurrence ("Ungelöst / meiner Seele Knoten"), and 3) indicate the Empress' acceptance of responsibility for the Emperor's fate ("Meine Schuld / sein Geschick"). The next six lines ("Mit dir sterben") give the Empress' response to the Emperor's fate; she wishes to die with him. In the last three lines ("Nicht diesen Blick! / Ich kann nicht helfen") the Empress denies to the Emperor that she has the ability to help him, indicating that she is unwilling to take the Wife's shadow because of the great unhappiness which it will bring to Barak and the Wife.
Hofmannsthal apparently had not originally intended these thirty-eight lines to be spoken, but readily agreed to Strauss' request that he handle them in this manner. (Briefwechsel, Hofmannsthal to Strauss, 24. VII. 1916.)
In these verses the external and internal conflict of the Empress reaches its most extreme point of development; here is the apex before the ultimate decision.
 	
A fifteen-verse section follows the thirty-eight spoken verses of the Empress:
 	
Unirdische Stimmen: Die Frau wirft keinen
    Schatten,
    der Kaiser muss versteinen!
Stimme von Oben: Sprich aus: Ich will! und
    jenes Weibes Schatten
    wird dein!
Und dieser stehet auf und wird lebendig
und geht mit dir!
Und des zum Zeichen neige dich und trink!
Kaiserin: Versuch mich nicht,
Keikobad!
Ich bin den Kind!
lass mich sterben,
	The Empress approaches the Emperor. She wishes to hold him in her arms, but dares not. The intense gaze of the Emperor causes her to retreat.
	
	The Empress sinks to the floor, covering her eyes with her hands. The statue glows in a very bright light.
	
	The statue darkens as the prophecy is intoned.
	
	The golden fountain springs forth and the Guardian of the Threshold appears a second line.
		The verse lines of the Falcon's prophecy are set to the familiar Falcon Cry Motive, but for basses instead of sopranoes; the high dynamic level and the sudden appearance of an easily recognized motive in an unexpectedly low register produce tension. This tension recedes somewhat as the Guardian of the Threshold tempts the Empress once again. Her verse lines are set in the same florid style and with the same motives as the first temptation by the Guardian. This time, however, they occur above a pedal point on G. Strauss altered the verses for Barak and the Wife, setting these lines:
		    Baraks Stimme: Weh uns Armen!
		    Stimme der Frau: Hab Erbarmen!
		    Baraks Stimme: Sterben!

198

TABLE OF ANALYSIS (continued)

Text	Visual Effects	Music
eh ich erliege! Baraks Stimme: Nirgend Hilfe! Der Frau Stimme: Wehe, sterben! Kaiserin: Ich--will--nicht! (D III 236-37.) This fifteen-line segment in combination with the preceding thirty-eight-line monologue gives the entire section fifty-three verse lines, exactly the same number as occurred in the immediately preceding section. The internal conflict of the Empress is pressed to an extreme by the voices urging conflicting solutions; finally the point is reached where she screams her rejection of the shadow.	The fountain becomes quiescent.	Stimme der Frau: Sterben! Baraks Stimme: Nirgend Hilfe! Stimme der Frau: Wehe! sterben! The Empress' five verses are set once again melodramatically; they occur against a background of harp glissandi, representing the flowing of the fountain, and the voices of the Dyer couple singing the verse lines given immediately above. Pedal points on C and D also underlie her words. Strauss utilized a brief orchestral interlude employing the Price Motive, the Traitor Motive, the Anger Motive, and the Nurse Motive to build up to one tremendous crash of dissension as the Empress screams her first scream. An E minor chord occurs in the bass register of the orchestra, above which are piled an A major chord and a B-flat major / minor chord. This chord subsides instantly, providing space for the Empress' final line "Ich--will--nicht!" The harp glissandi, representing the flow of the fountain, immediately stop as she forces this sentence over her lips. This concludes the E-flat major section of the scene.
	Complete darkness momentarily envelops the stage; then a light from above begins to illuminate the figures. A dark shadow falls from the Empress who has risen from the floor. The Emperor rises from the throne and begins to descend the steps toward the Empress.	A pause in the orchestra emphasizes the complete darkness on stage; then an orchestral interlude programmatically depicts the growing intensity of the light and the appearance of the Empress' shadow, whose arrival is portrayed by the Shadow Motive in a descending pattern. The Emperor as Hunter Motive accompanies the Emperor's first movements as he comes back to life. An inverted pedal point on F-sharp (G-flat) provides continuity to the interlude.
For the remainder of the Temple Scene dominance shifts from the Empress to the Emperor, who begins with a sixteen-line speech: "Wenn das Herz aus Kristall zerbricht in einem Schrei, die Ungebornen eilen wie Sternenglanz herbei. Die Gattin blickt zum Gatten, ihr fällt ein irdischer Schatten von Hüfte, Haupt und Haar. Der Tote darf sich heben aus eignen Leibes Gruft-- die Himmelsboten eilen herníeder aus der Luft!" So ward mit zugesungen,		The Emperor's "Awakening Song" consists of an amalgamation of many motives: the Empress Motive, the Shadow Motive, the Love Themes #1 and #2, the Stone Motive. The only new material occurs in a one-measure extension of the Children Motive. (See musical example #70.) Most of the motives sound from the orchestra, to which the vocal line is adjusted. The key center is A major. New musical interest is provided by the instrumentation: the celeste receives several arpeggiated chords to play.

Text	Visual Effects	Music
da ich im Sterben war. Nun darf ich wieder leben! Schon kommt die heilge Schar mit Singen und mit Schweben-- (D III 237.) The meaning of the lines is not important; their primary purpose is to express the return of vitality to the Emperor.		The Chorus of the Unborn Children utilizes the Children Motive and its one-measure extension.
Phrases only, not the complete text, of the Chorus of the Unborn Children occur at this point: Einzelne: Hört, wir wollen sagen: Vater! Andere: Hört, wir wollen "Mutter" rufen! Einige: Steiget auf! Andere: Nein, kommt herunter! Zu uns führen alle Stufen! (D III 238.) The words are unimportant; it is necessary, however, that an unearthly and ethereal joy be communicated through the setting of their lines.		
In an attempt to identify the voices singing from above, the Empress asks: Sind das die Cherubim, die ihre Stimmen heben? (D III 238.) The Empress answers her with the following twelve verses: Das sind die Nichtgeborenen nun stürzen sie ins Leben mit morgenroten Flügeln zu uns, den fast Verlorenen; uns eilen diese Starken wie Sternenglanz herbei. Du hast dich überwunden. den Vater und die Kinder, die Ungebornen, frei! Sie haben uns gefunden, nun eilen sie herbei! (D III 238.)	The Empress gestures toward the heavens.	Both the Empress' question and the Emperor's answer are set to previously established motives: the Price Motive, the Phoenix Motive, and the Sorrow Motive. The vocal lines are doubled in the orchestra; this simplification may allow these important lines to be comprehended. The key center is now B major.
Both the Empress' question ("Sind das die Cherubim?") and the Emperor's answer ("Das sind die Nichtgeborenen") need to be understood because they identify the singers of the following chorus, which sings off-stage. The remaining lines are important only as vehicles to express the joy of the Empress and the Emperor at their reunion.	The Emperor steps down from the last step. As the Empress starts to walk toward him, a short prelude to the Song of the Unborn Children sounds. This is accompanied by an ever increasing brightness from an overhead source.	

200

Text	Visual Effects	Music
The Chorus of the Unborn Children sings the following lines: Hört, wir gebieten euch: Ringet und traget, dass unser Lebenstag herrlich uns taget! Was ihr an Prüfungen standhaft durchleidet, uns ists zu strahlenden Kronen geschmeidet! (D III 239.) The words are important only as bearers of an emotional content, specifically as an expression of serene joy. The meaning is unimportant.	The Empress falls on her knees and is soon joined by the Emperor. As the chorus begins to sing, both the Emperor and the Empress cover their faces with their hands. Upon the completion of the chorus the Empress and the Emperor rise and gaze steadily upward toward the source of the sound. Their hands touch.	A short prelude to the Song of the Unborn Children consists primarily of arpeggiated chords on the celeste; this continues as the accompaniment to the chorus. The one-measure extension which has been added to the Children's Motive provides the primary melodic material for the Children's Chorus. The key is G major, which remains the key center for the rest of the scene. (G major is Strauss's key for the expression of childlikeness.)
The Empress and the Emperor respond to the joy which the Unborn Children have expressed by singing a duet of their own happiness: Kaiserin: Engel sinds, die von sich sagen! Ihre Stärke will uns tragen! Ungeboren, preisgegeben, ohne Anker, ohne Ziel! Wie sie rufend uns umschweben, bir ich, bin ich dir gegeben! Kaiser: Nirgend Ruhe, still zu liegen, nirgend Anker, nirgend Port, nichts ist da--nur aufzufliegen ist ein Ort an jedem Ort. Wie sie rufend uns umschweben, bist du, bist du mir gegeben! (D III 239-40.) As with most of the other ensemble numbers the specific meaning of the words need not be comprehended in order to follow the plot. Instead, the verses are vehicles for the expression of joy; this has been true of nearly all lines since the revitalization of the Emperor.		Strauss set the duet of the Emperor and the Empress with a complete chorus of the Unborn Children as background. The Children Motive with its one-measure extension, the Price Motive, the Phoenix Motive, and the Renunciation of Motherhood provide the musical materials.
	As the Empress and the Emperor embrace, clouds surround them so that they are no longer visible.	The orchestral interlude begins with the Love Themes and the Judgment Motive.

201

TABLE OF ANALYSIS (continued)

Text	Visual Effects	Music
	Act III scene iv	

Text	Visual Effects	Music
	A landscape becomes apparent which contains a sharply rising cliff, an abyss, and a waterfall. The Empress and the Emperor are above the waterfall, but descending.	As the landscape appears, the key center shifts to B-flat major and the musical material includes the Price Motive, the Phoenix Motive, the Phantom Motive, and the Freedom Motive. These motives anticipate the setting of the verse lines of Barak and the Wife, where the same motives are employed.

The reunion of the Wife and Barak takes place:
Frau: Trifft mich sein Lieben nicht,
   treffe mich das Gericht,
   er mit dem Schwerte!
Barak: Steh nur, ich finde dich.
   Schützend umwinde dich,
   ewig Gefährte!
   Schatten, dein Schatten,
   er trägt mich zu dir!
Frau: Gattin zum Gatten!
   Einziger mir!
Die Ungeborenen: Mutter, dein Schatten!
   Sieh wie schön!
   Sieh deinen Gatten
   zu dir gehn!
   (D III 240-41.)
This short fourteen-line section falls into three parts. The first part, the first six lines, consists of Wife's and Barak's attempts to find each other. The Wife's lines, because she mentions the sword, inject dramatic interest into the opera after the immediately preceding lyrical scene of the Empress, the Emperor, and the Unborn Children. The second section, the next four verses, consists of the recognition that the Wife has regained her shadow. The third section, the final four lines, consists of an expression of joy by the Unborn Children.
	The Wife appears on the left side of the abyss, while Barak becomes visible on the right side. The Wife sees Barak and reaches out to him. As she does this, her shadow falls across the abyss toward Barak.	The more dramatic of these lines which accompany the reunion of Barak and the Wife, the opening six verses, are set in an appropriately dramatic style, the Wife singing a high B during her last verse and Barak singing an F and a G above middle C during his solo. As the Wife reaches out to Barak, a short orchestral interlude depicts the arrival of her shadow. Strauss accomplished this in a manner similar to the one which he employed when the Empress received her shadow: highly pitched strings descend, utilizing the Joy Motive and the Desire for Children Motive, however, rather than the Shadow Motive.
		A key change from B major to D major accompanies the change in the verse lines from the first six verses, or part one, to the next four lines, or part two.
		The final four lines of this section, those sung by the Unborn Children, are set with the same motives and in the same key as the immediately preceding four lines by Barak and the Wife. The structural form of the music is, therefore, A B B, while the verse form is A B C.

	A golden bridge replaces the Wife's shadow and Barak and the Wife rush into each other's arms. The Empress and the Emperor stand together at the edge of the abyss and look down at the Dyer Pair who in turn look up toward the Imperial Couple.	An orchestral interlude provides the accompaniment for the pantomime on the stage. The Blessedness Motive gives way to the Judgment Motive and a variation on the Sword Motive; a prolonged G major chord resounds in preparation for the closing section of the opera, in C major.

TABLE OF ANALYSIS (continued)

Text	Visual Effects	Music
Hofmannsthal wrote the following verse lines to close the opera: Barak: Nun will ich jubeln, wie keiner gejubelt, nun will ich schaffen, wie keiner geschafft, denn durch mich hin strecken sich Hände, blitzende Augen, kindische Münder, und ich zerschwelle vor heiliger Kraft! Kaiser: Nur aus der Ferne war es verworren bang, hör es nun ganz genau, menschlich ist dieser Klang! Rührende Laute-- nimmst du sie ganz in dich. Brüder, Vertraute! Chor: Brüder! Vertraute! Die beiden Frauen: Schatten zu werfen, beide erwählt, beide in prüfenden Flammen gestänlt. Schwelle des Todes nah, gemordet zu morden, seligen Kindern Mütter geworden! (D III 241-42.) There is no indication in the Steiner edition that these verse lines were intended as an ensemble, but the location of the verses at the very end of the opera seems to require this assumption. The words are not important; they serve only as vehicles for the expression of joy, the robust joy of Barak with his four-beat verse line, the more quiet joy of the Emperor with his three-beat verse line, and the serene joy of the Empress and the Wife with their two-beat verse line.	A veil falls, allowing only the contours of the figures and of the landscape to be discerned.	Strauss began the finale with a solo for Barak, a solo for the Emperor, and a unison duet for the women; this occurs before the actual ensemble starts. During some of the women's lines, however, the chorus and the Emperor interject their comments as preparation for the ensemble. Barak's solo is by far the most striking melodic and rhythmic structure of the finale; it might be considered an independent song in itself. When the ensemble begins, it serves as its cantus firmus. (See musical example #71.) Eventually both Barak and the Emperor abandon their own verse lines and sing the verse lines of the women. The large ensemble ends shortly after the Chorus of the Unborn Children sings several repetitions of its single verse line. The dominant motives for the ensemble are the Price Motive, the Phoenix Motive, the Happiness Motive, which has been incorporated into Barak's solo, and the Extended Children Motive. A short orchestral interlude of considerable contrapuntal complexity--at one point the Joy Motive, the Phantom Motive, the Freedom Motive, the Emperor as Lover Motive, and the Sorrow Motive are all sounding at the same time--drops the dynamic level rapidly in preparation for the epilogue-like chorus of the Unborn Children.

TABLE OF ANALYSIS (continued)

Text	Visual Effects	Music
The final verses of the opera are hymn-like in style and intended to be sung from the orchestra pit: Die Stimmen der Ungeborenen: Vater, dir drohet nichts, siehe, es schwindet schon, Mutter, das Ängstliche, das euch beirrte. Wäre denn je ein Fest, wären nicht insgeheim wir die Geladenen, wir auch die Wirte! (D III 242.) Because these verses speak of danger overcome, a great sense of security and relief attends them. The audience will profit if they can comprehend them.	The curtain falls slowly.	A few bars in the orchestra which contain the Empress Motive and the Judgment Motive in ever slower rhythms complete the winding down of tension. The musical form of the ensemble and the final chorus is approximately A A B.

CHAPTER V

CONCLUSION

The final remarks of this study are divided into three parts. The first section determines which of the poet's desires for the musical setting of his text the composer was successful in fulfilling and which not. The analyses of Chapters III and IV provide the bases for the conclusions which are drawn. Part two of this chapter contains a discussion of the assessments of the opera. The final section discusses the probable future of the work.

Hofmannsthal's Desires for the Text: Fulfillment or Lack of Fulfillment by Strauss

Hofmannsthal desired, as the introduction to the Table of Analysis in Chapter IV enumerates them, four primary goals for the setting of his libretto, the Frau ohne Schatten. First, he expected, or at least hoped, that Strauss would perceive the forms of the speeches and set them with music appropriate for their structure.(1) Second, he expected Strauss to develop the musical characterizations of the figures in a manner which was consistent with the characterizations begun in the libretto. (2) Third, he desired that the musical setting of the text should allow comprehension of significant verse lines. (3) Fourth, he perceived an analogy between his Frau ohne Schatten and Mozart's Zauberflöte (4); by means of this analogy he envisioned a definite musical style as an appropriate setting for his libretto. Each of these desires is discussed below from the standpoint of the analyses contained in the two preceding chapters of this study.

Strauss's Realization of the Libretto Structures: Agreement and Disagreement

The analysis in Chapter IV documents many instances where Strauss perceived the libretto as Hofmannsthal wished, for the musical setting appropriately enhances the text. This occurred, for example, in Strauss's setting of the Emperor's lyrical verse lines:

> Denn meiner Seele
> und meinen Augen
> und meinen Händen
> und meinem Herzen
> ist sie die Beute
> aller Beuten
> ohn' Ende!

(D III 154-55.)

Hofmannsthal wrote these verses in a lyrical style, constructing them so that both the parallel grammatical forms of each succeeding line and also the delay of the subject of the sentence heightens the emotional intensity.

CONCLUSION

Strauss composed the lines so that emotional intensity increases with each verse and culminates in the final verse. (See page 108 of the analysis.)

Purely emotional outbursts, such as the Wife's scream when she perceives that the Nurse and the Empress are deserting her and leaving her alone with the Youth (Act II scene iii), were in every case given an appropriately highly-charged setting by Strauss. In this particular instance the Wife sings ''Ah!'' on the pitch level of high C. Another specific emotional outburst is the Empress' cry of dismay when she discovers that she must witness the Wife's disloyalty to Barak: ''Weh! Muss dies geschehen / vor meinen Augen?'' (D III 184.) The words are not important, for they do not convey essential information, but the emotional reaction is significant. Strauss set the verses so that the orchestra doubles the vocal line, thereby giving emphasis to the vocal melody; minor chords, a moderately high tessitura, and syncopation between the vocal line and the basic meter of the orchestra carry the emotional content.

The use by Strauss of a modified rondo form to set the following text with its ABCBA structure offers another example of close agreement between the text and its musical setting:

O Tag des Glücks, o Abend der Gnade!	A
Das war ein Einkauf!	B
Schlag ab, du Schlachter, ab vom Kalbe)	
und ab vom Hammel! Und her mit dem Hahn!)	
Du Bratenbrater, heraus mit dem Spiess!) C	
Heran, du Bäcker, mit dem Gebackenen,)	
und du, Verdächtiger, her mit dem Wein!)	
Wenn wir einkaufen, das ist ein Einkauf!	B
O Tag des Glücks, o Abend der Gnade!	A
	D III 187.)

Although Strauss did not utilize the traditional classical rondo form to set these verses, he did set the first two lines and the last two lines homophonically while setting the intervening lines polyphonically. The resulting effect is that of an ABA form.

Formally, Strauss also followed the structure which Hofmannsthal gave to part of the Empress' temple scene (Act III scene iii). The first fifty-three lines of the scene exhibit an ABA form. Although Strauss did not employ a classical rondo here either, the similarities in both ''A'' sections are great enough to justify calling the setting an ABA form. (See page 196.)

The analysis also documents cases where Strauss and Hofmannsthal differed in their conception of a particular speech or situation, for a divergence in their treatment is apparent. Identifiable musical bases underlie many of these differing interpretations. This is most obviously the case where Strauss altered a word

206

or syllable in order better to fit the text to the setting which he desired to use. This explains the change which he made in the verse line "Schweiget doch, ihr Stimmen" (D III 212) to "Schweigt doch, ihr Stimmen" (B&H Act III#4). (See page 173.) Strauss's major alteration of the text of Act II scene i also has a basis in music, for here he used a rondo form for the last half of the scene which was not inherent in the text. (See pages 144-45.)

Musically, this type of alteration can often be defended on the grounds that Strauss's genius created not something lesser for his deviation but rather something different. This is especially noticeable in the musical setting which the composer gave to the last part of the Wife's speech at the end of Act II scene iii:

> Denn es ist nicht von heute, dass du meine Stimme hörest
> und fassest sie nicht in deinem Sinn,
> und ist dir ferne, die du nahe glaubst,
> und wähnest, du hättest sie im Gehäuse
> wie einen gefangenen Vogel
> der dein ist,
> um wenig Münze
> gekauft auf dem Markt:
> die doch anderswo, anders daheim.
>
> (D III 200.)

The structure of verses six to eight here, where there is a sudden reduction in the number of accents and syllables per line, suggests that Hofmannsthal envisioned a relaxation of tension for the end of this speech. Strauss, however, gave these lines great dramatic interest, even setting the word "Markt" on the pitch level of a high B. The composer's apparent desire to write an effective exit for the Wife outweighed his concern for the text at this point. The result is that the text sounds forced and unnatural, but the Wife leaves with a flourish.

As far as differing conceptions of the opera are concerned, there is additionally the case of the third act which Strauss kept lengthening until Hofmannsthal finally protested:

> Aber dennoch: nun eine neue Verbreiterung der früheren Stelle!
> Mehr und immer mehr! Muss es sein? Lieber Dr. Strauss! Wenn
> auch der Einfall in Es-dur sicher machtvoll und schön - bedenken
> Sie's zweimal! Denken Sie vieler Gespräche! Des Gespräches im
> Park von Versailles, wo Sie das schlagende Gleichnis mit dem ver-
> grössernden Kuhauge gebrauchten!
> Ich lege den neuen Text bei. Aber bedenken Sie, dass der Anfang
> vom Ende immer da ist, wo der Einfall über die Szene, die Szene
> über den Akt herrschen will, statt umgekehrt. - Verzeihen Sie
> mir: es wird - vielleicht Sie selber eingeschlossen - kaum jemand
> geben, der es so wahrhaft gut mit Ihnen, Ihrer Produktion und
> deren Zukunftsschicksal meint! (5)

CONCLUSION

The opinions of many conductors and directors have justified Hofmannsthal's fears, for in productions today a large part of the third act is cut, specifically much of the argument between the Empress and the Nurse (III ii), much of the Nurse's banishment scene (III ii), and most of the Empress' melodrama lines in the Temple scene (III iii). (6) Although a desire to shorten a rather long opera probably influences these decisions, there are other, perhaps more convincing reasons for these specific omissions.

The Nurse's attempt to dissuade the Empress from entering the bronze door (III ii) consists of fifty lines of monologue. The words are unimportant, for gestures on stage will convey their meaning; their primary significance lies solely in their delay of the Empress' exit. Because the words are insignificant and because the action on stage at this time is a retarding one, the music must sustain the opera at this point. Strauss, however, has not previously characterized the Nurse with any beautiful melodies and to do so at this point would be inconsistent with the style of characterization which he has chosen. Nor does the music command attention by any grotesqueness or monumental intensity as often occurs in Elektra. As a result, neither text, nor actions, nor music are able to carry the opera at this time. Hofmannsthal may justifiably be criticized for consenting to write fifty verse lines of a retarding nature; half that number, which is what is usually performed, is almost too much. Strauss, on the other hand, is also at fault for having requested additional lines for this scene.

Approximately the same number of measures (115 as compared to variously, 75 or 125) are cut from the Nurse's banishment scene (III ii). This section of the third act contains both a part of the exchange between the Nurse and the Messenger and also the entirety of the quartet by the Nurse, the Messenger, the Wife, and Barak. The verses, having been written for ensemble, are unimportant; dramatically, the impending banishment of the Nurse is delayed. The situation, with its insignificant verse lines and retarding action, is much like the one discussed in the immediately preceding paragraph, where the Nurse attempts to persuade the Empress to leave the bronze door. The two scenes are differentiated musically, though, because Strauss this time provided a lyrical musical line by employing the Protection Theme (see musical example # 60). He placed, however, the theme in the orchestra or else gave it to Barak to sing, who throughout most of the scene, including the quartet, is absent from the stage. The lack of any purely vocal melody sung from the stage seems to be the reason why this section is omitted from performances.

A third major and customary omission in this act occurs in the melodrama section of the temple scene (III iii). Originally, Hofmannsthal had enthusiastically greeted Strauss's decision to write this section in melodrama:

> Der Erinnerung an die Szenen des III. Aktes (mit Ausnahme der
> ersten) haftet, ich kann mir nicht helfen, lieber Dr. Strauss,
> etwas Beschwerendes und Trübes an. Ich kann mir nicht helfen!
> Und ein so unerwartetes Urteil in mir selber, eine solche Be-

drückung, ganz wie wenn man in eigener Arbeit etwas nicht
ganz Geglücktes hinter sich liegen weiss - das ist, ich weiss
es, das ist kein Irrtum. Dass Sie den letzten Teil dieses schwe-
ren, dumpfen Werkes im Sprechrezitativ auflösen wollen, ist
mir eine wahre Erleichterung! (7)

Upon hearing the opera, however, he changed his mind and gave this opinion:

Sollten Sie aber daran gedacht haben, die Stelle [in der "Aegyp-
tischen Helena"] bei fortlaufendem farbigem Orchester über dem
Tönestrom sprechen zu lassen, so erscheint mir das noch unmö-
glicher [als unbegleitendes Sprechen]. Schon die paar Worte der
Kaiserin im letzten Akt [der "Frau ohne Schatten"], gesprochen,
während das Orchester fortströmt, erscheinen mir grässlich,
wahrhaft durchs Ohr ins Herz schneidend - aber das mag dort noch
entschuldbar sein, an dieser einzigen und dazu kurzen Stelle -
aber hier - und wo man noch dazu genau verstehen soll: denn es ist
ein Angelpunkt der Handlung! (8)

With unerring judgment Hofmannsthal seems to have discovered why this section of
the opera is cut as extensively as is possible: the change from a libretto which is
completely set to music (as contrasted to a Singspiel with its intermittent arias and
spoken dialogues) to melodrama seems to constitute a breach in style. The effect is
unpleasant, even jarring, to the aesthetic perception.

Although the responsibility for the excessive length of the third act and
hence for much of its weaknesses rests primarily with Strauss, these instances are
not the only ones where the opera was fundamentally changed, even weakened, because of a lack of concord between the librettist and the composer. The verse lines
of the Nurse which prepare for and give the terms of the pact, for example, exhibit
distortion of emphasis as they now stand in the opera. The exceedingly dramatic
Renunciation of Motherhood Motive (see musical example #28) gives extraordinary
impact to the verses which precede the statement of the pact itself. When the pact
does occur, even though it is set to a new motive which appears in the vocal line, it
is overshadowed by the previous lines. Contrary to the musical setting, Hofmannsthal's verses exhibit a dramatic intensity for the pact itself which is greater than
the lines which precede it and are preparatory to it. (See the Table of Analysis,
pages 128-30.)

Another instance of lack of unanimity between libretto and setting occurs
during Act II scene iv, the Empress' nightmare scene. The text exhibits a growing
intensity in meaning, progressing from point A, the Empress' awareness of her
guilt, through points B and C, her awareness of her inability to help the Emperor
and her awareness of the destruction which she has brought to Barak, to point D,
the fear that she brings death to others. The speech culminates in the Empress' desire to take the death and destruction which she has brought to others upon herself:

209

Weh, Amme, kannst du schlafen! -
Da und dort
alles ist
meine Schuld -
Ihm keine Hilfe,
dem andern Verderben -
Barak, wehe!
Was ich berühre,
töte ich!
Weh mir!
würde ich lieber
selber zu Stein!

(D III 203.)

Strauss' setting for these lines places the climax of the speech on the word ''Verderben,'' setting the second syllable of this word on a high D-flat, the highest vocal note
in the entire score. Although the solo is unquestionably effective dramatically as it
now stands, the divergence from Hofmannsthal's intent is also clear.

In spite of these differences in interpretation of various speeches in the
libretto, Strauss did follow the structural form of Hofmannsthal's verses most of
the time, as the analysis in Chapter IV documents.

Strauss's Realization of the Libretto
Characters: Agreement and Disagreement

There are a great number of correspondences between the characterizations begun by Hofmannsthal in the libretto and those completed by Strauss in the
opera. The portrayal of the Empress in the music of the first act, for example, so
beautifully stresses her lightness, her airiness, and her brilliance that Hofmannsthal's original conception, as expressed in the words alone, is by comparison lacking in life and contour. The brilliance of the accompaniment with its violin obligato
line, the brightness of the F-sharp major key, and the high soprano tessitura all
contribute to create an unforgettable fairy-being. When a clarinet replaces the violin in the orchestral characterization of the Empress and the high soprano tessitura
is dropped to a middle or even to a low range in the temple scene of the third act,
truly tangible evidence is given of her change from fairy-creature to human being.

In addition to this agreement between the librettist and the composer
about the general characterization of the Empress, Strauss fulfilled Hofmannsthal's
desire that the Empress' voice should dominate the final ensemble of Act II (9) by
the manner in which he constructed this section of the opera: the Empress initiates
the ensemble and sings at a high pitch level, which, being situated above all others
most of the time, commands the entire ensemble.

An exception to these close parallels between the librettist's and the com-

CONCLUSION

poser's characterizations of the Empress occurs in the finale of the third and final act. The Empress here lacks a melody which is truly expressive of the joy which is contained in the text. Perhaps the length of time required for the completion of the opera caused the composer to lose interest in her. Although this surmise may explain why the Empress' final musical lines are unsatisfying, it does not excuse Strauss for this major deficiency.

As for the Emperor, a study of the libretto reveals that Hofmannsthal envisioned the Emperor as the hunter and the lover. Strauss emphasized these qualities by the kind of motives which he wrote for this figure. A hunting call and a surge of passion are evident in the musical examples #7, #10, and #11. The "sweet voice," for which Hofmannsthal expressed a desire when he characterized the Emperor to Strauss in 1913 (10), came to reality in the long, flowing melodic lines which Strauss composed for the tenor voice of this figure. The poet himself praised Strauss's melodies for the Emperor, indicating his approval of this characterization. (11)

The difficulty which Strauss experienced in writing music for the Empress in the finale(12) is also apparent in the music which he wrote for the Emperor in the third act. The Emperor's aria upon re-awakening to life is a pastiche of motives from the first and second acts, noticeably lacking in new musical material. His vocal lines in the finale, like the Empress' are also lacking in emotional intensity.

Although the Empress remains the principal figure in the opera by virtue of her pivotal position in the plot, the dignity and simplicity of the motives with which Strauss surrounded the Dyer suggests that Barak was his favorite character. Indeed, the composer's identification with Barak may have been very great, considering that Hofmannsthal "discreetly," as he expressed it, spoke of the similarity of the Wife to Pauline de Ahna, Strauss's wife. (13)

The composer's affection for Barak did not mislead him, however, as he sought to bring this character to life in music. Barak's childlike nature is evident in the simplicity of melody and rhythm with which Strauss customarily characterized him, while his strength is expressed in the sturdiness of the folk-song "Trag ich die Ware." Strauss's characterization of Barak must have pleased Hofmannsthal, for the poet spoke approvingly of this character. (14) Barak's extreme goodness may later have struck both composer and poet as overdrawn, however, for the character of Mandryka in the later opera Arabella, originally much like Barak, was redrawn to give him a measure of guilt.

Although Strauss's characterizations of the Empress, the Emperor, and Barak generally parallel the outlines begun by Hofmannsthal in the libretto, the completed figure of the Wife exhibits areas not only of agreement but also of divergence. The collaborators apparently agreed with one another in planning to show the change of character which she undergoes. Her attainment of maturity, as reflected in her cessation both of her criticism of Barak and also of her day-dreaming, was expressed by Strauss in a fundamental change in the manner in which he set her verses.

CONCLUSION

Throughout the first two acts the composer set her nagging and even her dreaming to music which within the stylistic context of the entire opera is expressive of a negative emotional content: the melodic lines tend to be angular and to employ wide skips, the rhythm often necessitates a rapid declamation, and dissonances abound in the accompaniment. An especially appropriate musical interpretation of the Wife's dreamy vacillation between commitment to Barak and desertion of him occurs at the end of the second act where Strauss set the Wife's lines with a tonic which wavers between F minor (F major and F minor are keys closely associated with Barak) and F# minor (the Wife's day-dream of the Youth "Von wo der Strand" centers in F# major and the Youth Motive first appears in the Wife's vocal line in F# major). The lack of beauty in the Wife's vocal lines for the greater part of Acts I and II contrasts greatly with the resonant, flowing lines of her opening aria in Act III. The change in her being which is thus portrayed is very great, the music beautifully enhancing this aspect of the libretto.

Although both the strident aspects of the Wife's personality and also her fundamental change in character are given excellent expression in the music, her tendency to dream is not as apparent as Hofmannsthal may have intended. A study of the libretto reveals that the Wife displays dissatisfaction with her life not only by means of her bitter criticism of Barak, which is greatly in evidence throughout the first two acts of Strauss's setting, but also by means of her tendency to daydream and escape from the life which she leads. This quality does not receive as much emphasis in the completed opera as it does in the libretto alone. Comprehension of the line "O Welt in der Welt! O Traum im Wachen" (D III 173), for example, would have given the audience an insight into this escape-oriented aspect of her character. As Strauss composed the line, however, the words tend to be covered by a fairly dense contrapuntal accompaniment, thereby obscuring an important part of the Wife's personality.

Strauss, in characterizing the Wife, wrote music for her which often seems better suited for performance by an instrument rather than by a voice. This quality tends to oppose Hofmannsthal's desire that the figures of the opera be characterized by the vocal line. It would, however, be difficult to imagine a type of setting which would be more appropriate for characterizing the Wife than the one which Strauss employed. Perhaps the librettist's desire for characterization by means of the vocal line had to be compromised in this specific case.

As was the case with the Empress and the Emperor, the Wife's vocal line for the finale of the opera lacks new musical material. The cumulative effect of this deficiency in so many of the principal figures tends to cause a decrease in interest at a time when the engagement of the audience should be the greatest.

The rather close relationship which exists between Hofmannsthal's sketch of the four principal figures (the Empress, the Emperor, the Wife, and the Dyer) and Strauss's final realization of them does not seem to hold true for the figure of the Nurse. In a letter to Strauss which he did not mail, Hofmannsthal expressed concern

CONCLUSION

that they - librettist and composer - had not completed this figure as he had foreseen her:

> (. . . und auch in der neuen Oper fehlt es daran nicht [dass wir - Hofmannsthal und Strauss - auseinandergekommen sind], fürchte ich; bezieht sich auf die Figur der Amme, nehmen Sie es nicht schwer, es wird das Ganze nicht alterieren.)(15)

Although this letter does not suggest to what aspect of Strauss's characterization of the Nurse Hofmannsthal took exception, a study of the score reveals two likely possibilities. First, Strauss's intensely serious characterization of the Nurse resulted in a grotesque vocal line which tends to cover the humorous aspects of her personality. Lines such as "Schnell dreht sich der Wind / und wir rufen dich wieder" (D III 197), which reflect the Nurse's ready tongue and wit, lack the deftness and humor which a well-played Mephistopheles gives to Goethe's Faust. Second, the Nurse's characterization does not exist primarily in the vocal line, as Hofmannsthal might have desired it. Frequently the orchestral line assumes greater importance than the vocal line, as is the case in Act I scene ii, where the Nurse seeks to dazzle the Wife with promises of wealth and beauty, or in Act III scene ii, the Nurse's banishment scene, where the music takes the form of a scherzo for orchestra. Traditional cuts which are made in the opera at these points seem to justify the poet's prejudice against characterization by means of the orchestra.

In spite of these differences between vision and realization, there are specific instances where the characterization of the Nurse appears to be well-suited to the text. One of these cases occurs at the opening of the second scene of Act III where the wordy anxiety of the Nurse contrasts with the calm self-assurance of the Empress. Another instance occurs with the setting of the conjuration of the Youth in Act II scene i, where the Nurse's music is at such a variance from the general tenor of the scene. Although Strauss's characterization of the Nurse does not significantly alter the basic relationships of the text (see Hofmannsthal's comment quoted above), the frequent lack of primary musical interest in her vocal line tends to be detrimental to the opera as a whole.

One of the minor figures of the opera, the Youth, received distressed attention from Hofmannsthal after the poet first heard Strauss's characterization of him. The poet feared that the audience would accept the Youth as a real human being, for Strauss's original characterization had not indicated the Youth's essentially supernatural nature. Instead, Strauss had given this figure a vocal line in Act II which is at least the equal, if not the superior, of the vocal line which the Empress sings immediately before him. Hofmannsthal expressed his concern to Strauss in a letter dated May 14, 1915:

> . . . es war ein schwerer Fehler von mir, nur durch die Okkupation der Kriegszeit erklärlich, dass ich Sie nicht genug daran erinnerte, dass der "fremde Jüngling" ein Phantom ist,

von einem Mimiker zartest zu spielen - und mit geisterhafter
Stimme von irgendwoher (-aus dem Orchester) zu singen; nun
haben Sie ihn leider Gottes anders aufgefasst, das macht mir
schwere Sorgen, und ich bitte Sie herzlich, diesen Punkt nicht
leicht zu nehmen. Er ist ja eben durchaus nicht aus einer Welt
mit den Menschen, sondern ist aus einer Welt mit dem Falken
und mit den fünf Ungeborenen, die aus den Fischen singen - wo
Sie den Kontrast doch so wundervoll gefunden haben - so macht
es mich ganz unglücklich, dass es hier nicht stimmt . . . .
Darum wäre es meine innige Bitte, ob Sie nicht versuchen
könnten, in der einzigen Szene, wo das Phantom den Mund auf-
tut, doch - bei Wahrung des Motivs - die Führung der Stimmen
in eine einzigartige, nicht menschliche, geisterhafte umzubie-
gen. (16)

The opera is customarily presented as Hofmannsthal here suggested; a dancer
mimes the part on stage, while the individual who sings the role is placed in the orchestra pit with his back to the audience.

Viewed as a whole, Strauss's characterizations of the libretto's figures
exhibit consistency with Hofmannsthal's apparent intent. Where divergence does
occur, as with aspects of the Nurse and the Youth, the libretto is strong enough not
to be thereby destroyed.

Strauss's Realization of Verses
Significant for Comprehension

The analysis in Chapter IV reveals that Strauss tried diligently to set the
significant lines of the opera in a manner which would enable their comprehension,
thus attempting to fulfill one of Hofmannsthal's desires. His efforts toward this end
are particularly noticeable throughout Act I scene i where the Messenger and the
Nurse identify the major characters and foreshadow the development of the plot. The
low range and the subdued nature of the accompaniment for the line "Wirft sie einen
Schatten?" (D III 150), for example, offer evidence of Strauss's desire that lines
like this be comprehended. As the composer later conceded, his attempts to facili-
tate comprehension by the audience were only partially successful:

In ersterer [in der "Frau ohne Schatten"] ist der Versuch ge-
macht - besonders in der Partie der Amme - unter Begleitung
eines grossenteils solistischen, nur fein untermalenden
Orchesters den Stil und das Tempo des alten Seccorezitativs
neu zu beleben, bisher leider nicht mit dem Erfolg, dass der
gerade in diesen Szenen äusserst wichtige Dialog restlos zu
absoluter Deutlichkeit gebracht wurde.
    Sei es nun, dass infolge einer fehlerhaften Veranla-
gung meinerseits selbst dieses so ganz dünne und durchsichtige

CONCLUSION

Orchester sich immer noch zu polyphon gebärdet, zu un-
ruhig figuriert ist und das gesprochene Wort auf der Büh-
ne behindert, sei es, dass die mangelhafte Sprechtechnik
des Durchschnittes unserer Opernsänger oder die bei uns
Deutschen leider oft gaumige Tonbildung und zu starke
Tongebung auf unseren grossen Bühnen daran Schuld tra-
gen. (17)

Given Hofmannsthal's text, which is far more demanding of the listener than, for
example, the text of the Barber of Seville, this lack probably hinders acceptance of
the opera. On the other hand, a greater tendency in the direction of spoken recita-
tive, such as developed by Arnold Schoenberg for use in his Pierrot Lunaire, would
certainly have removed the work from the traditionally conceived genre of opera and
might possibly have been more detrimental to the work as a whole than the difficulty
which this lack of comprehension presents. The individual who desires to follow the
nuances of the opera text is, therefore, faced with the necessity of having considerable homework to do before he attends a performance.

One example of the problem which the listener faces occurs with the setting of the Empress's verse line "Zur Schwelle des Todes" (D III 219). Because
this line signifies the great danger which the Empress will have to face should she
enter the bronze door, comprehension would aid the audience's understanding of the
plot. The vocal setting, however, spanning the two octaves from high C to middle C,
will probably cover the words. The end result is an extremely dramatic vocal line
which probably cannot be understood. Whether or not the drama of the vocal line
compensates for the loss of comprehension is questionable. In any case, the listener
probably will have to be previously acquainted with the line in order to comprehend
it in performance.

Strauss's Lack of Achievement of
Lightness and Deftness of Style

As for Hofmannsthal's desire that the completed opera should exhibit similarity to Mozart's Zauberflöte in its transcendence of darkness and evil by means
of a stylistic unity characterized by lightness and deftness, the poet himself expressed dissatisfaction with the final result. He first sensed a divergence from his
original intention when Strauss played the third act for him in 1916:

Der Erinnerung an die Szenen des III. Aktes (mit Ausnahme der
ersten) haftet, ich kann mir nicht helfen, lieber Dr. Strauss,
etwas Beschwerendes und Trübes an. Ich kann mir nicht helfen!
Und ein so unerwartetes Urteil in mir selber, eine solche Be-
drückung, ganz wie wenn man in eigener Arbeit etwas nicht ganz
Geglücktes hinter sich liegen weiss - das ist, ich weiss es, das
ist kein Irrtum. (18)

215

CONCLUSION

The feeling which Hofmannsthal expressed here did not leave him, for he not infrequently referred to the "heaviness" of the Frau ohne Schatten. In his criticisms, however, he accepted for himself part of the responsibility for this ponderous quality:

> Für bestimmt schwebt mir dieses vor: dass alle drei [Opern-
> dichtungen, die Hofmannsthal plante], bei noch so grosser Ver-
> schiedenheit, Werke eines leichteren Genres werden sollen,
> nicht Riesenlasten auf Ihre Schultern, wie die "Frau ohne Schat-
> ten" eine gewesen sein muss - freilich haben Sie sie, wie spielend,
> den steilsten Berg hinaufgetragen. (19)

> Der Erfolg des grossen, ernsten Werkes [der "Frau ohne Schatten"]
> in Berlin freut mich recht sehr. Ich war über Dresden damals wirk-
> lich betrübt. Nun sind wir wohl für Deutschland überm Berg und kön-
> nen uns wieder Leichterem zuwenden. (20)

> Ueber der "Frau ohne Schatten" sind wir beide zu schwer gewor-
> den. (21)

Obviously, Hofmannsthal felt that he and Strauss were not as successful in finding a style characterized by lightness as he had desired. Another comment made by the poet suggests which aspect of the libretto he regarded as "heavy":

> Er [Dr. Paul Eger, ein Theaterdirektor, den Hofmannsthal
> kannte] sagte mir viel Angenehmes und Gescheites darüber
> [über den Text von "Helena"]. Es freut mich, dass er es so
> klar findet. Er sagte, das in der "Frau ohne Schatten" Ange-
> strebte sei hier völlig erreicht (im Dichterischen, namlich
> ein Geheimnis in Gestalten und Situationen symbolisch auszu-
> sprechen). Ich will hoffen, dass er recht hat. (22)

Apparently lying behind this comment is one of the basic tenets of Josef Nadler's Literaturgeschichte Oesterreichs, an idea for which Hofmannsthal expressed tacit approval by quoting. He included the following words from this work when he was writing about his Jedermann and Mozart's Don Giovanni:

> Verwandt sind sie beide durch und durch, denn beide sind sie
> ein wahres Theater, nicht aus der Rhetorik geboren, nicht aus
> dem Psychologischen, sondern aus jenem Urtrieb, "der das
> Uebermenschliche greifbar vor sich sehen will und tiefen Ab-
> scheu hegt vor jeder formlosen Abstraktion".
>   (P III 449.)

It may be that the "secret" (Geheimnis') of the Frau ohne Schatten which he found to be incompletely tangible was the moral aspect of the Empress' decision not to

216

CONCLUSION

harm Barak in Act III scene iii. Karl-Joachim Krüger pointed out this problem area
in 1935:

> . . . das Wort als Ethos- und Geistträger geht nicht mehr
> völlig in Musik auf: die melodramatische Tempelszene der
> Kaiserin! Wohl ist die "Frau ohne Schatten" als "Spiel" kon-
> zipiert, aber dieses geistig so hintergründige Märchenspiel
> ist <u>nicht mehr das Spiel der Oper.</u> Hier trennen sich Hof-
> mannsthals und Strauss' Arbeitssphären. (23)

It is obviously true that Strauss found this aspect of the opera difficult to compose.
Aside from the circumstantial evidence of the change to melodrama which points to
this problem, there also exists a letter to Hofmannsthal from Strauss criticizing in
detail the lack of realism in the Empress' actions throughout this scene:

> Hier vermisse ich, dass die Kaiserin sich gar nicht über <u>ihr</u>
> <u>Verhältnis zum Kaiser</u> mehr ausspricht . . . .
>
> . . . es berührt sehr unsympathisch, dass die Kaiserin nur
> von dem Gedanken an ihr eigenes Menschentum so erfüllt ist,
> dass sie nur der Leiden des Färberpaares gedenkt und den
> <u>Kaiser ganz vergessen hat.</u>
>
> Ich meine: der unlösbare Konflikt, in den die Kaiserin geraten
> ist, der nur durch höhere Geistermacht gelöst werden kann,
> müsste viel deutlicher und plastischer zum Ausdruck kommen.
> Die Kaiserin opfert doch, da sie den Schatten nicht durch Be-
> trug erwerben will und durch Zerstörung des Glückes des Ehe-
> paares Barak, ihren geliebten Gatten. Hierin liegt an sich
> etwas Unnatürliches und Unsympathisches. Darum müsste die
> Entsagung der Kaiserin auf Liebe, auf Errettung des Kaisers,
> der Entschluss des Büssenwollens viel eingehender motiviert
> werden. Sonst wird niemand begreifen, warum der Kaiserin
> das Glück Baraks näher steht, als ihr eigenes und das Leben
> des Kaisers. (24)

The scene was consequently rewritten according to the composer's desires, but the
difficulty which Strauss encountered in composing even this revision suggests that
the dramatic situation never acquired the degree of plasticity which both he and Hofmannsthal desired.

As the analysis in Chapter IV reveals, there is generally a very close relationship between the text and the music, with the music only occasionally diverging
from Hofmannsthal's apparent intent. When this does occur, as in the exit of the
Wife in Act II scene iii (see page 207), it is an instance noteworthy for its exception-
ality. Nor can a single case of this kind, even in combination with several minor

CONCLUSION

deviations, vitiate the entire work; there are far too many obvious parallels between Hofmannsthal's apparent intent and Strauss's realization of the vision. The
most serious deficiency in the opera, the lack of joyous energy which is apparent in
the majority of the vocal lines of the grand finale is far more a failure of musical
inspiration than one of lack of agreement between text and music. The composer's
fulfillment of the poet's intent in the vast majority of instances tends to exculpate
him from any mistreatment of this particular text.

Assessments of the Frau ohne Schatten

Hofmannsthal's Assessment of the Opera

Hofmannsthal's reaction to the opera, although essentially negative (see
pp. 215-16), was not entirely so. He approved enthusiastically of the first two acts,
as these comments to his close friend Eberhard von Bodenhausen indicate:

> Ende April war Strauss bei mir und spielte mir die Aufzüge
> I und II der "Frau ohne Schatten" - die ihm in einer ganz
> wundervollen Musik gelungen sind. Die Musik ist eine Syn-
> these des Besten und Wahrsten, das er zu geben hat. (25)

His basic reserve toward the opera as an entirety, however, is apparent throughout
the correspondence between Strauss and himself, receiving expression in comments
like this one: "Ich bin sicher, dass fast Ihre schönste Musik darin [in der "Frau
ohne Schatten"] steckt - aber -"(26)

One aspect of the opera which Hofmannsthal apparently disliked first sur-
faced in the correspondence between the poet and the composer in 1927, eight years
after the premiere:

> . . . als naives Theaterpublikum will ich immerfort etwas
> vorgehen sehen, wie in allen guten Opern, und die viele Mu-
> siziererei bei herabgelassenem Vorhang ist mir ein Greuel
> und, glauben Sie mir, Zehntausenden dümmerer Theaterbe-
> sucher mit mir, so schön diese einzelnen Konzertstücke, ge-
> nannt Zwischenspiele, auch sein mögen. (27)

Although this particular statement was written specifically to discourage Strauss's
suggestion that their next opera be written in scenes separated by orchestral inter-
ludes rather than in acts, the basic applicability to the Frau ohne Schatten still exists.

Even the most optimistic assessment which the poet made of the opera
lacks the enthusiasm which he expressed about Ariadne auf Naxos, as a comparison
of the following quotations reveals:

218

CONCLUSION

Trotzdem glaube ich, das Werk [die "Frau ohne Schatten"]
wird leben. Aber ich sage: glaube ich - bei der "Ariadne"
sage ich: weiss es. (28)

Alles in allem höre ich, immer aufs Neue, dies unser ge-
meinsames Werk ["Ariadne auf Naxos," zweite Fassung]
von allen aufs Liebste. Hier allein sind Sie ganz mit mir,
und hier - was geheimnisvoller ist - sind Sie auch ganz mit
sich selber gegangen. (29)

Strauss's Assessment of the Opera

Strauss, for his part, seemed to have less of a need to organize and express his thoughts about the Frau ohne Schatten than his collaborator. In any event
and for whatever reason, he was much more laconic in writing his assessments of
the opera. Like Hofmannsthal, he disliked the melodrama section of the third act,
for after he had completed the opera he described melodrama as "die unbeholfenste,
blödeste Kunstform, die ich kenne."(30) Moreover, he seemed very uncertain about
the quality of the entire third act:

Der III. Akt ist nun fertig: ich bin aber durch unsere sehr
wohltätige Unterhaltung so unsicher geworden, dass ich über-
haupt nicht mehr recht weiss, was gelungen, was schlecht
ist. (31)

Just as Hofmannsthal had his particular dissatisfaction with what he perceived as the "heaviness" of the opera, Strauss had his criticism of the libretto. He
found its romanticism a stumbling block:

Aber bei der "Frau ohne Schatten" den Stil anwenden, der
Ihnen sympathisch und auf den wir beide zusteuern müssen -
geht eben nicht. Da macht es nicht etwas mehr oder weniger
Musik oder Text, das liegt am Stoff selbst mit seiner Romantik,
seinen Symbolen - Figuren wie Kaiser und Kaiserin nebst Amme
sind nicht mit so roten Blutkörperchen zu füllen wie eine Marschallin, ein Octavian, ein Ochs. Da kann ich mein Hirn anstren-
gen, wie ich will, und ich plage mich redlich und siebe und siebe
durch, aber das Herz ist nur zur Hälfte dabei und sobald der
Kopf die grössere Hälfte der Arbeit leisten muss, wird ein Hauch
akademischer Kälte darin wehen (was meine Frau sehr richtig
"Musizieren" nennt), den kein Blasebalg zu wirklichem Feuer
anblasen wird. . . . Ich werde mir noch jede Mühe geben, den
III. Akt in Ihrem Sinne zu formen, aber wir wollen den Entschluss
fassen, die "Frau ohne Schatten" sei die letzte romantische
Oper. (32)

CONCLUSION

In spite of this criticism of the opera, Strauss was generally more optimistic in his assessment of it than was his librettist. Both of the following comments were included in letters which he wrote to Hofmannsthal:

> Die "Frau ohne Schatten" hat noch ihre Zukunft: seien Sie unbesorgt. (33)

> Trotz aller blöden Kritiken glaube ich auch heute noch, dass die "Frau ohne Schatten" nicht nur eine schöne Dichtung, sondern auch ein sehr bühnenwirksamer Operntext ist. Es gibt, auch heute schon Leute, die ihn sogar "verstehen"! (34)

Of a more general nature, but still complimentary of the opera were the following words written upon the occasion of Hofmannsthal's fiftieth birthday:

> Ich habe mich absichtlich an keiner literarischen Kundgebung zu Ehren Ihres 50. Geburtstages [1. Februar 1924] beteiligt, weil ich das Gefühl nicht bannen kann, dass alles, was ich Ihnen in Worten sagen könnte, banal wäre im Vergleich zu dem, was ich Ihnen als Komponist Ihrer herrlichen Dichtungen schon in Tönen gesagt habe. Dass es Ihre Worte waren, die aus mir das Schönste, was ich an Musik zu geben hatte, herausgeholt haben, darf Ihnen eine schöne Befriedigung gewähren, und so mögen denn Chrysothemis, die Marschallin, Ariadne, Zerbinetta, die Kaiserin und nicht zuletzt "bewundert viel und viel gescholten" H. [Helena] mit mir bei Ihnen eintreten und Ihnen vor allem danken, für alles, was Sie mir von der Arbeit Ihres Lebens gewidmet und in mir gefördert und zum Leben erweckt haben. (35)

There are even indications that Strauss felt this to be his best work. He commented in the article "Erinnerungen an die ersten Aufführungen meiner Opern" (1942): "gerade künstlerische Menschen halten es [die Frau ohne Schatten] für mein bedeutendstes Werk."(36) Perhaps it is not too much to presume that he included himself as one of these "artistic people."

Hofmannsthal's objection to a supposed "heaviness" and Strauss's objection to excessive romanticism aside, one other aspect of the opera received much distressed attention from the collaborators. The magic of the opera, upon which so much of the action pivots, was far more difficult to stage effectively than either of them had imagined when they first planned the libretto. Both of them tended initially to blame this difficulty upon the lack of imagination of Alfred Roller, who, as property and stage manager at the Vienna Opera, was in charge of the staging of the world premiere:

> Alle Zaubereien [für die Berliner Erstaufführung] werden kom-

CONCLUSION

men, sogar das Wasser und der Einsturz am Schluss des
II. Aktes. Das Schwert und die Verschiebung des Bettes auf
sinnige Weise gelöst, für alle unsichtbaren Stimmen auf und
hinter der Szene sind die besten Vorkehrungen getroffen, so
dass wir einen wesentlichen Fortschritt gegenüber Roller erwarten dürfen, der allzu resigniert im vornherein auf das
"Zauberstück" verzichtet hat. (37)

Ich danke Ihnen schön für das Freundliche und Gute, was Sie
mir über Berlin schreiben. Hier hat mich ja Roller mit den
Zaubersachen ganz im Stich gelassen. Das Phantastische ist
ihm halt nicht gegeben, vorher konnte ich das nicht so wissen.(38)

Strauss later ascribed the difficulties they encountered in trying to produce this opera successfully to the hardships of the immediate post-war period and
the restrictions on budgets which this tended to cause:

Die "Frau ohne Schatten" erlebte ihre glanzvolle Uraufführung
am 10. Oktober 1919 in Wien. Es folgten teils mehr oder weniger gelungene Aufführungen in Dresden, München, Berlin. In
mittleren und kleinern deutschen Bühnen, die das anfänglich
ziemlich missverstandene Werk brachten, erwies sich die Not
der Nachkriegsjahre der schwierigen Oper als besonders schäd-
lich, da ungenügende Ausstattung und mangelhafte Besetzung
dem Verständnis des Werkes hinderlich waren und den Erfolg
beeinträchtigten. (39)

Denn die " Frau ohne Schatten" krankt heute noch daran, dass
sie zu früh nach dem letzten Krieg auf die deutschen Theater
musste. Schon die zweite (damals) Dresdner Aufführung war
verunglückt. (40)

Whatever the reason, the fact is that the opera was not received enthusiastically, at
least in the sense that the Rosenkavalier was, whose success undoubtedly stood before the composer and the librettist - both as ideal and also as possibility.

Assessments of the Opera by Others

Reviews of the premiere in Vienna were mixed as the quotations below
reveal. The first was written by Ludwig Karpath, who had personal and artistic ties
to Strauss, the second by Paul Bekker, who, although highly regarded as a music
critic of that time, was distinctly antagonistic toward Strauss even before this opera
received its premiere (41):

Man kennt den dithyrambischen Schwung in Straussens Me-
lodiebildung, ein hymnenartiges Aufstreben, immer wieder

CONCLUSION

eine Steigerung, wo man längst ein Niedergleiten erwartet.
Alle Aktschlüsse sind wirkungsvoll, mit Raffinement so ge-
staltet. Ein Erschwerendes empfinden wir in diesem gross-
artigen Kunstwerk: zu wenig Harmlosigkeit. Im Märchen ver-
langen wir mehr Naivität. All der Zauberspuk will unbeschwert
genossen werden. Eine gewisse pathetische Breite nun sowohl
in der Dichtung wie in der Musik belastet einigermassen das
Werk, dem eine grössere Flüssigkeit zu wünschen wäre. Aber
was verschlägt's! Strauss hat mit der "Frau ohne Schatten"
sein Bestes gegeben, uns ein Werk geschenkt, das dem deutschen Genius zur höchsten Ehre gereicht. "Die Frau ohne
Schatten" ist ein Kunstwerk, geboren aus der kühnsten und
reichstbewegten Phantasie, ein hochragendes Denkmal deutschen Geistes und Könnens. (42)

Man pflegte früher in ähnlichen Fällen zu sagen: schade für
den Musiker, der ein dramatisch unergiebiges Buch vertont.
Dieses Bedauern ist falsch und unberechtigt. Es bezeugt eine
irrige Auffassung vom Wesen des musik-dramatischen Kunstwerkes und Schaffens. Man komponiert ein Buch nicht aufs Ge-
ratewohl, es ist auch kein Zufall, wenn ein Musiker gerade
diesen oder jenen Text für sich wählt. An solcher Auslese do-
kumentiert sich vielmehr die eigene Natur in ihren geheimsten
Absichten. Die Wahl des Werkes einer fremden Persönlichkeit
wird zur Selbstenthüllung. . . . . So sucht und findet auch
der Musiker sein Libretto - und so trägt er durch die Wahl die
Mitverantwortung.
Es wäre daher irrig, wollte man das Misslingen dieses Werkes
Hofmannsthal allein zur Last legen. Irrig nicht nur, weil die
Verbindung Strauss-Hofmannsthal schon so lange besteht, dass
beide einander zur Genüge erprobt haben. Irrig vor allem des-
wegen, weil jeder, der die Entwicklung von Richard Strauss seit
dem "Rosenkavalier" kritisch beobachtet, in der Musik der
"Frau ohne Schatten" nur das finden wird, was die vorangehen-
den Werke erwarten liessen: das Werk eines der ausserordent-
lichsten Talente, dem aber über das Talent hinaus das erlebnis-
fähige Menschentum, die Gabe der Wandlung fehlt, aus der erst
das Kunstschaffen grossen Stiles erwächst. (43)

Unlike the Rosenkavalier, which was extremely popular with the public in
spite of the mixed critical reviews which were given it, the Frau ohne Schatten did
not attract a large following. There were twelve additional performances in 1919
following the premiere on October 10, five in 1920, and four each in the years 1921-
1923. (44) Although the audiences of that time were not disposed to an eager acceptance of the work, many of Strauss's musician contemporaries were enthusiastic.

222

CONCLUSION

Franz Schalk, who directed the premiere, published these comments in a special issue of the Blätter des Operntheaters:

> Wollte man ein Paradoxon wagen, so könnte man sagen, dass diese Partitur keine Nebenstimmen, keine Füllstimmen kennt. Die melodische und harmonische Thematik füllt alles aus. Es ist nicht mehr Polyphonie im älteren Sinne, nicht mehr Stimme gegen Stimme, sondern ein Kontrapunktieren ganzer, oft thematischer Harmoniekomplexe, woraus sich polyrhythmische Gebilde von unerhörter Kühnheit mit einer gewissen Naturnotwendigkeit entwickeln.
>
> Die Kraft des musikalischen Gedankens zwingt alle widerstrebenden Gewalten zu einer organischen Einheit, deren Erfassung an den Zuhörer die letzten und höchsten Anforderungen stellt. Hier ist "Kunst"! Man muss sie nur verstehen lernen. . . .
>
> Harfen, Celesten, Pauken, Schlagwerk aller Art, chinesische Gongs und die aus der Frühzeit der deutschen Romantik wieder heraufbeschworene Glasharmonika vervollständigen den ungeheuren Klangapparat, dessen der Musiker, der Meister dieser Partitur bedurfte, um seine innere musikalische Gedankenwelt nach aussen hörbar zu machen. Deutlich geht aus diesem Werk wieder hervor, dass das Instrumentieren keine Kunst an und für sich ist. Sie ist durchaus abhängig von der Erfindung, von der Eingebung. Schlecht konzipierte Musik kann kein Gott gut instrumentieren, es sei denn, dass man müssige und kindisch-barbarische Klangspielereien für Instrumentationskunst nähme, wozu sich aber Professionisten nicht herbeilassen werden.
>
> Was die Strauss'schen Partituren so "gut" klingend macht, ist nicht das Raffinement in der Behandlung der einzelnen Instrumente und Instrumentalgruppen, sondern die Kunst seines musikalischen Satzes, der Reichtum und die Logik der Stimmführung. Diese Künste erscheinen in der neuen Partitur auf einer noch höheren Entwicklungsstufe als in den früheren Werken. (45)

Franz Schalk was not the only musician to appreciate the opera for the beauty of its music. Lotte Lehmann, who sang the part of the Wife for the premiere, was also partial to the music while at the same time she was very critical of the text:

> I must confess frankly that I never have been very fond of the tortuously elaborate libretto. To follow the intricate plot of this opera is impossible without considerable homework ahead of time. People have told me time and again that they find the music truly divine - "But what, in heaven's name, is the story all about?" That, in my opinion, is why Die Frau ohne Schatten will never enjoy great popularity.

> Still, the music is indescribably beautiful. It speaks
> a language all its own, simply overwhelming, and really re-
> quires no help from any medium other than itself. (46)

The beauty of the music is a constant in all of these reviews while the
text bears the brunt of the negative criticism. The rather constant approval of the
music in combination with the rather constant damnation of the libretto suggests both
the relative familiarity of the tonal language which Strauss employed and also the relative originality of Hofmannsthal's text. Edward Wright Murphy, in his statistical
analysis of three of Strauss's tone-poems – Don Juan, Ein Heldenleben, and Eine
Alpensinfonie, produces evidence again and again of Strauss's traditional use of the
tonal system:

> Almost one-third (31.4%) of Strauss' sonorities are major
> triads. He employs a slightly higher use of the major triad
> in each of the three works (27.6% in Don Juan, 30.3% in Ein
> Heldenleben, and 33.9% in Eine Alpensinfonie). . . . . There
> are twice as many major triads as minor triads (31.4% to 16.0%).
> Again, more minor triads are used in Eine Alpensinfonie than in
> the two earlier works (14.7% in Don Juan, 12.0% in Ein Helden-
> leben, and 19.4% in Eine Alpensinfonie) . . . . The major-mi-
> nor seventh is the most frequently occurring seventh chord
> (21.4%), and is second only to the major triad (31.4%) in number
> of occurrences. There is a decrease in use of the major-minor
> seventh from Don Juan to Eine Alpensinfonie (29.4% in Don Juan,
> 23.5% in Ein Heldenleben and 17.0% in Eine Alpensinfonie).
> Most of this decrease of 12.4% is made up by an increase in the
> use of the major and minor triad . . . . Three normal sonori-
> ties, the major and minor triad, and the major-minor seventh
> comprise over two-thirds (69.1%) of all sonorities. . . . In
> general, Strauss' sonorities are "conservative" and "traditional"
> (i.e., tertian in structure with the emphasis on the major and
> minor triad and the major-minor seventh chord). Exceptions to
> this are used for specific programmatic portrayals of stress,
> apprehension, conflict, and storm or tempest (i.e., the storm
> scene in Eine Alpensinfonie). (47)

Murphy's analysis documents not only Strauss's traditional use of the major-minor
tonal system, but also his slightly growing conservatism in the use of this system.
According to these statistics, Strauss stepped back somewhat from his position as a
leading exponent of the avant-garde, a position which he occupied in the decade 1890-
1900, when his tone-poems were the outrage of the music world. Perhaps he was
aware that a continued progression in the direction which he had begun led to atonality; he obviously rejected this path, choosing instead to retreat from it. He even
expressed his contempt for music written in this style by calling it "Bockmist." (48)
As a consequence when Arnold Schoenberg and others discarded the major-minor

CONCLUSION

tonal system, a step which Strauss refused to take, the avant-garde of the musical world not only passed him by but left him far behind. Strauss's conservatism with respect to atonality offers an explanation for his loss of pre-eminence in the musical world which is far more satisfactory than ascribing it to Hofmannsthal, which both Norman Del Mar (49) and Jakob Knaus (50) do. No matter how influential Hofmannsthal might have been upon Strauss, he certainly did not have the power over the composer to cause him to change his tonal resources. Strauss demonstrated too much individuality and independence during the period 1890-1905 for this type of assertion to be credible.

In contrast to Strauss's music for the Frau ohne Schatten, which by this period in the composer's life was fairly traditional when viewed within the context of concurrent developments within the musical world, Hofmannsthal's libretto is almost totally fresh and original. Although there are gossamer threads stretching from different aspects of it to different literary antecedents, the poet was here working primarily from his own imagination. He often did choose to write from specific literary antecedents, as demonstrated by his Jedermann, the Salzburger grosses Welttheater, Elektra, the Turm and others, but this did not occur with the Frau ohne Schatten. The one work which was well-known to German-speaking audiences at the time of the opera's premiere and which exhibited an obvious although tangential relationship to the poet's libretto was Adelbert von Chamisso's "Peter Schlemihls wundersame Geschichte" (1814). This tale, which tells of the exchange of a shadow for untold wealth, bears upon close study little resemblance to the Frau ohne Schatten. The close relationship in Hofmannsthal's tale of the principal figures to each other, which is demonstrated by the inability of the Empress in Act III either to renounce or to accept the shadow without causing repercussions in the lives of Barak, the Wife, and the Emperor, has no parallel in Chamisso's story. As a consequence, the audience at the premiere and throughout the first decade of the opera's life had no help from past literary or operatic experiences when it was confronted with the configurations and relationships of this opera. Ironically, the very originality of Hofmannsthal's tale apprears to have been a detriment to the opera; the audiences were simply taxed beyond their capacity to comprehend, as Lotte Lehmann's report above (see p. 223) indicates.

The Future of the Opera

In the final scene of the Frau ohne Schatten Hofmannsthal sought to portray life as a whole; the gauze veil which blurs spatial contours and the singing of the Unborn Children which unites generations are his means of expressing this unity. Space, which separates the Self from the Non-Self, and time, which separates the Now from Past and Future, are overcome; individual isolation is defeated. This oneness of time and space occurs as a personal experience only when the individual is least himself - when the Self exercises a broad responsibility for and commitment to others. Upon the fulfillment of this condition an overwhelming sense of immediacy attests that life's antinomies have been united. Reflection and analysis are temporarily banished. Nor is there a place for anticipation; like reflection, anticipation also destroys the possi-

bility of an eternally present unification of Self and Non-Self. Concurrent with the
coalescence of Self and Non-Self in an eternal present occurs the experiential merg-
ing of personal desires and external limitations. Total acceptance characterizes
the individual's attitude toward his life.

Although the society of the early twentieth century was characterized by
dichotomies, Hofmannsthal envisioned a world healed of its divisions, a community
to which beauty and righteousness were restored. Hofmannsthal's tale ends, therefore, with the unfolding of a utopia, for the world as experienced by the individual
has transcended itself and become perfect. The significance of the poet's vision of
utopia lies specifically in his assertion that no longer does man need to ascribe Par-
adise to a distant realm and time; it exists here and now and is available to everyone. The members of the audience, the "Zuschauer eines Schauspieles [als] Nach-
kommen des ursprünglichsten Chores" (A 328-29), also experience from Hofmannsthal's point of view this transcendence in the midst of life. The healing forces exhibited in the fairy-tale thus move into reality and begin their task of healing the world,
of molding the disparate elements of society into the wholeness of a community.

Hofmannsthal's libretto is so strongly oriented toward unification, toward
a coalescence of time and space, that there is a noticeable lack of dynamic movement
in the third act. Because the libretto of any opera is customarily the source of the
dramatic momentum toward the Future while the music provides the emphasis upon
the Now, this change of function requires an adjustment in the opera as a whole.
Either the music must carry the libretto forward by its dynamic movement or else
that section of the opera which is designed without dramatic impetus must be short.
If neither of these alternatives is realized, the opera is likely to become boring.

Unfortunately, nearly the entire third act of the libretto the Frau ohne
Schatten is incapable of sustaining dramatic interest. When the Empress refuses the
Wife's shadow during the finale of the second act, there is essentially no conflict to
be resolved during the third act. Nor is the audience, after having heard and seen
the Empress refuse the shadow once, likely to entertain seriously the propect that
she will accept it when it again becomes available to her in Act III scene iii.

One solution to this lack of dramatic conflict in the libretto would have
been the composition of an act which in brevity would have resembled a scene more
than an act. Perhaps this is what Hofmannsthal initially offered Strauss, but the
composer's desire to recapitulate the motivation of Acts I and II resulted in a last
act which is probably a third or a half again as long as had been originally written
by the poet. This length is excessive because its only function is to delay the final
coalescence of time and space which ends the opera. Perhaps the composer sensed
that the third act of the libretto consisted of a major divergence from traditional
operatic form; he may have been attempting to remedy what he sensed as a defect
when he requested change after change of Hofmannsthal, all of which lengthened the
libretto. The result, rather than improving the text, emphasizes its weakness, for
the delaying effect of the verbal recapitulations of Acts I and II only delay, and de-

CONCLUSION

lay excessively. Strauss is primarily responsible, therefore, for rejecting what might have been one possible solution to the lack of dramatic interest inherent in the third act.

One other possible solution of the problem presented by the text here might have been the composition of an extraordinarily fine musical setting. Had the music exhibited an even and high quality of inspiration, compensation would have been made for the lack of drama inherent in the libretto. Unfortunately, this did not occur. A steady decline in musically exciting material is apparent throughout the opera from the first scene to the last act. Perhaps the strain of war-time is evident here, for Strauss was more adversely affected by the war than appearances suggest. Certainly the protracted nature of the work on this act, reflected in a composition span of sixteen months, testifies to possible interruptions due to the war which interfered with the work. This excessive span of time may also give evidence of a growing lack of interest by Strauss in the opera, boredom being thus responsible for the poorer quality of the music. Perhaps too, the wholeness and health of the third act were not within Strauss's resources to command, for the pathological and the extraordinary had definitely shown itself to be his particular métier.

In spite of the weakness of the third act, the positive qualities in both the text and the music of the work certainly justify its inclusion within the standard operatic repertory. There are indications that this may be occurring. Within the last ten years the opera has been produced far more frequently than previously was the case. It was presented in San Francisco in 1976 and at the Metropolitan Opera in 1978. Other recent performances have taken place in Paris (1972), Berlin (1973), Salzburg (1974, 1975), and Hamburg (1977). The neglect of much of the past half-century is hopefully at an end.

The work certainly deserves to be performed more frequently than it has been in the past. This remains true in spite of the fact that Hofmannsthal later rejected the optimism expressed in the Frau ohne Schatten, the hope that Western man could integrate the shadow aspects and the light aspects of his personality into one being; the ultimate result would be a society healed of its diversions and molded into a community characterized by beauty and love. This hope, conceived before the beginning of World War I, Hofmannsthal reversed as a direct result of his experiences during the war. The poet's final drama, the Turm (1928), depicts the collapse of a society; here a wholly integrated man and the small tentative beginnings of a community are utterly crushed by the materialistic forces of the world. The only consolation offered is that wholeness in one person did exist - even though this integration was not recognized by the world.

Strauss, although he was apparently willing, was unable to take even the first step - the step which recognizes the need for healing and attempts to promote it. In dealing with the malevolent and the pathological, as in Salome and Elektra, he apparently extended himself to the limits of his being. To heal this illness was beyond his capability, as was the awesome reversal of this optimism, the dry-eyed

clairvoyance which foresaw the defeat of the ideal of community in the Turm.
Strauss thus stands as a true representative of the twentieth century; although cogni-
zant that the society of which he was a part was sick to the very core of its being, he
was incapable of the strength needed to help reverse its progression toward disaster.

Perhaps the current revival of interest in the Frau ohne Schatten attests,
in addition to a belated recognition of its artistic worth, to a nostalgia for a lost
ideal, a wistful desire for something that may never be, rather than a belief in its
healing power. For society today, rent by divisions as great as any of the period
1900-1925, has few illusions about the possibility of the establishment of a community characterized by love and beauty. The opera the Frau ohne Schatten thus stands
before the audiences of the last quarter of the twentieth century as the incarnation of
a lost innocence and the realization of a lost hope.

Footnotes

(1) Richard Strauss - Hugo von Hofmannsthal: Briefwechsel, ed. Willi Schuh,
4th ed., Gesamtausgabe (Zurich: Atlantis Verlag, 1964), Hofmannsthal to
Strauss, 24. IX. 1913.

(2) Ibid., 28. XII. 1913.

(3) Ibid., 22. IV. 1914.

(4) Ibid., 20. III. 1911.

(5) Briefwechsel, Hofmannsthal to Strauss, 24. VII. 1916.

(6) The recordings of the opera directed by Karl Böhm (London A4505) and Joseph
Keilbarth (Deutsche Grammaphon 2711 005) demonstrate the types of cuts made
in the work.

(7) Briefwechsel, Hofmannsthal to Strauss, 24. VII. 1916.

(8) Ibid., Hofmannsthal to Strauss, 12. II. 1925.

(9) Briefwechsel, Hofmannsthal to Strauss, 25. VII. 1914.

CONCLUSION

Footnotes

(10) Ibid., 28. XII. 1913.

(11) Ibid., Hofmannsthal to Strauss, 1. VIII. 1916.

(12) Ibid. Strauss to Hofmannsthal, 28. VII. 1916.

(13) Ibid., Hofmannsthal to Strauss, 20. III. 1911.

(14) Ibid., Hofmannsthal to Strauss.

(15) Briefwechsel, 11. VI. 1916.

(16) Briefwechsel.

(17) Richard Strauss, "Vorwort zu 'Intermezzo,'" Betrachtungen und Erinnerungen, ed. Willi Schuh (Zurich: Atlantis Verlag, 1949), p. 115.

(18) Briefwechsel, Hofmannsthal to Strauss, 24. VII. 1916.

(19) Ibid., 18. IX. 1919.

(20) Ibid., 30. IV. 1920.

(21) Ibid., 22. IX. 1923.

(22) Ibid., 30. VIII. 1926.

(23) Hugo von Hofmannsthal und Richard Strauss: Versuch einer Deutung des künstlerischen Weges Hugo von Hofmannsthals, Neue Deutsche Forschungen: Abteilung Neuere Deutsche Literaturgeschichte, vol. 3 (Berlin: Junker und Dünnhaupt, 1935), p. 171.

(24) Briefwechsel, 15. IV. 1915.

(25) Briefe der Freundschaft, Hugo von Hofmannsthal - Eberhard von Bodenhausen: ed. Dora von Bodenhausen (Düsseldorf: E. Diederichs, 1953), 31. V. 1915.

(26) Briefwechsel, Hofmannsthal to Strauss, 22. IX. 1923.

(27) Ibid., 22. XII. 1927.

(28) Ibid., 16. V. 1921.

(29) Ibid., 16. V. 1918.

CONCLUSION

Footnotes

(30)   Ibid., Strauss to Hofmannsthal, 10. VII. 1917.

(31)   Ibid., ca. 16. VIII. 1916.

(32)   Ibid., 28. VII. 1916.

(33)   Ibid., 29. I. 1925.

(34)   Ibid., 2. XI. 1927.

(35)   Ibid., 29. I. 1924. The quotation is from Goethe's Faust, II. Teil.

(36)   Betrachtungen, pp. 201-02.

(37)   Briefwechsel, Strauss to Hofmannsthal, 8. III. 1920.

(38)   Ibid., Hofmannsthal to Strauss, 10. III. 1920.

(39)   Richard Strauss: Briefwechsel mit Willi Schuh, ed. Willi Schuh (Zurich:
        Atlantis Verlag, 1969), p. 189 (Strauss to Schuh, 9. XII. 1946).

(40)   Richard Strauss - Clemens Krauss: Briefwechsel, 2nd ed., edited by Götz
        Klaus Kende and Willi Schuh (Munich: C. H. Beck, 1964), p. 220 (Strauss to
        Krauss, 20. IX. 1941).

(41)   Briefwechsel, Strauss to Hofmannsthal, 30. VI. 1919.

(42)   Neue Freie Presse (Vienna), 11. X. 1919, quoted in Franz Grasberger,
        Richard Strauss und die Wiener Oper (Tutzing: H. Schneider, 1969), p. 194.

(43)   Frankfurter Zeitung, n.d., quoted in Grasberger, Strauss und die Wiener
        Oper, pp. 191-92.

(44)   Grasberger, Strauss und die Wiener Oper, p. 191.

(45)   "Blicken eines Professionisten in die Partitur der 'Frau ohne Schatten,' "
        n.d., quoted from Grasberger, Strauss und die Wiener Oper, pp. 189, 190.

(46)   Five Operas and Richard Strauss, trans. Ernst Pawel (New York: Macmillan
        Co., 1964), p. 63.

(47)   "Harmony and Tonality in the Large Orchestral Works of Richard Strauss,"
        Diss. University of Indiana, 1963, pp. 268-71, passim.

(48)   Briefwechsel, Strauss to Hofmannsthal, 3. V. 1928.

230

CONCLUSION

Footnotes

(49)   Richard Strauss: A Critical Commentary on His Life and Works, 3 vols.
       (Philadelphia: Chilton Book Co., 1962), II:437.

(50)   Hofmannsthals Weg zur Oper "Die Frau ohne Schatten": Rücksichten und
       Einflüsse auf die Musik, Quellen und Forschungen zur Sprach- und Kulturge-
       schichte der germanischen Völker, Neue Folge (Berlin: Walter de Gruyter,
       1971), p. 11.

BIBLIOGRAPHY

232

SELECTED BIBLIOGRAPHY

Works and Letters by Hugo von Hofmannsthal

Briefe der Freundschaft: Hugo von Hofmannsthal - Eberhard von Bodenhausen. Edited by Dora von Bodenhausen. Düsseldorf: Eugen Diederichs Verlag, 1953.

Briefwechsel zwischen George und Hofmannsthal. Edited by Robert Boehringer. 2nd enlarged ed. Munich: Helmut Küpper, previously Georg Bondi, 1953.

Hofmannsthal, Hugo von. Gesammelte Werke in Einzelausgaben. Edited by Herbert Steiner.
 Aufzeichnungen. Frankfurt: Fischer Verlag, 1959.
 Dramen I. Frankfurt: Fischer Verlag, 1953.
 Dramen II. Frankfurt: Fischer Verlag, 1954.
 Dramen III. Frankfurt: Fischer Verlag, 1957.
 Dramen IV. Frankfurt: Fischer Verlag, 1958.
 Erzählungen, Die. Stockholm: Bermann-Fischer Verlag, 1946.
 Gedichte und lyrische Dramen. Stockholm: Bermann-Fischer Verlag, 1946.
 Lustspiele I. Stockholm: Bermann-Fischer Verlag, 1947.
 Lustspiele II. Stockholm: Bermann-Fischer Verlag, 1948.
 Lustspiele III. Frankfurt: Fischer Verlag, 1956.
 Lustspiele IV. Frankfurt: Fischer Verlag, 1956.
 Prosa I. Frankfurt: Fischer Verlag, 1950.
 Prosa II. Frankfurt: Fischer Verlag, 1951.
 Prosa III. Frankfurt: Fischer Verlag, 1952.
 Prosa IV. Frankfurt: Fischer Verlag, 1955.

Hugo von Hofmannsthal - Rudolf Borchardt: Briefwechsel. Edited by Marie Luise Borchardt and Herbert Steiner. Frankfurt: Fischer Verlag, 1954.

Hugo von Hofmannsthal - Carl J. Burckhardt: Briefwechsel. Edited by Carl J. Burckhardt. Frankfurt: Fischer Verlag, 1958.

Hugo von Hofmannsthal - Harry Graf Kessler: Briefwechsel 1898 - 1929. Edited by Hilde Burger. Frankfurt: Insel Verlag, 1968.

Richard Strauss - Hugo von Hofmannsthal: Briefwechsel. Edited by Willi Schuh; commissioned by Franz and Alice Strauss. 4th complete ed. Zurich: Atlantis Verlag, 1970.

SELECTED BIBLIOGRAPHY

Writings, Musical Compositions, and Letters by Richard Strauss.

Richard Strauss: Briefwechsel mit Willi Schuh. Edited by Willi Schuh. Zurich: Atlantis Verlag, 1969.

Richard Strauss - Clemens Krauss: Briefwechsel. Edited by Götz Klaus Kende and Willi Schuh. 2nd. ed. Munich: C. H. Beck, 1964.

Strauss, Richard. Betrachtungen und Erinnerungen. Edited by Willi Schuh. 2nd ed. Zurich: Atlantis Verlag, 1957.

_____. Elektra. Tragödie in einem Aufzug von Hugo von Hofmannsthal. Musik von Richard Strauss. Op. 58. N.p.: Adolph Fürstner, 1908, 1909, 1910; copyright assigned to Boosey & Hawkes Music Publishers Ltd., London, for all countries except Germany, Danzig, Italy, Portugal and the U.S.S.R., 1943.

_____. Die Frau ohne Schatten. Oper in drei Akten von Hugo Hofmannsthal [sic]. Musik von Richard Strauss. Op. 65. N.p.: Adolph Fürstner, 1916 and 1919; copyright, assigned to Boosey & Hawkes Music Publishers Ltd., London, for all countries except Germany, Danzig, Italy, Portugal and the U.S.S.R., 1943.

_____. Der Rosenkavalier. Comedy for Music in three Acts by Hugo von Hofmannsthal. Music by Richard Strauss. Op. 59. Paris: Adolph Fürstner, 1912; copyright assigned to Boosey & Hawkes Music Publishers Ltd., London, for all countries except Germany, Danzig, Italy, Portugal and the U.S.S.R., 1943.

Secondary Literature

Works Pertaining to Hugo von Hofmannsthal

Alewyn, Richard. Ueber Hugo von Hofmannsthal. 2nd ed. Göttingen: Vandenhoeck and Ruprecht, 1958.

Ascher, Gloria J. "Die Zauberflöte" und "Die Frau ohne Schatten": Ein Vergleich zwischen zwei Operndichtungen der Humanität. Bern: Francke Verlag, 1972.

Bauer, Sibylle, ed. Hugo von Hofmannsthal. Wege der Forschung, no. 183. Darmstadt: Wissenschaftliche Buchgesellschaft, 1968.

Block, Haskell M. "Hugo von Hofmannsthal and the Symbolist Drama." Wisconsin Academy of Sciences, Arts and Letters 48 (1959): 161-78.

SELECTED BIBLIOGRAPHY

Coghlan, Brian. Hofmannsthal's Festival Dramas: Jedermann; Das Salzburger
    grosse Welttheater; Der Turm. London: Cambridge University Press, 1964.

Erken, Günther. Hofmannsthals dramatischer Stil: Untersuchungen zur Symbolik und
    Dramaturgie. Hermaea: Germanistische Forschungen: Neue Folge, no. 20.
    Tübingen: Max Niemeyer Verlag, 1967.

Gundolf, Friedrich. Excerpts from "Das Bild Georges." Jahrbuch für die geistige
    Bewegung, 1 (1910): 19-48. Quoted in Hofmannsthal im Urteil seiner Kritiker:
    Dokumente zur Wirkungsgeschichte Hugo von Hofmannsthals in Deutschland.
    Edited by Gotthart Wunberg. Frankfurt: Athenäum, 1972.

Haas, Willy. Hugo von Hofmannsthal. Köpfe des XX. Jahrhunderts, no. 34. Berlin:
    Colloquium Verlag, 1964.

Hammelmann, H. A. Hugo von Hofmannsthal. London: Bowes and Bowes, 1957.

Hederer, Edgar. Hugo von Hofmannsthal. Frankfurt: Fischer Verlag, 1960.

Knaus, Jakob. Hofmannsthals Weg zur Oper "Die Frau ohne Schatten". Quellen und
    Forschungen zur Sprach- und Kulturgeschichte der germanischen Völker.
    Berlin: Walter de Gruyter and Co., 1971.

Kobel, Erwin. Hugo von Hofmannsthal. Berlin: Walter de Gruyter and Co., 1970.

Krüger, Karl-Joachim. Hugo von Hofmannsthal und Richard Strauss: Versuch einer
    Deutung des künstlerischen Weges Hugo von Hofmannsthals. Neue Deutsche
    Forschungen: Abteilung Neuere Deutsche Literaturgeschichte, no. 3. Berlin:
    Junker und Dünnhaupt, 1935.

Mach, Ernst. The Analysis of Sensations and the Relation of the Physical to the
    Psychical. Translated from the 1st ed. by C. M. Williams. Revised and
    translated from the 5th ed. by Sydney Waterlow. New Introduction by Thomas
    S. Szasz. New York: Dover Publications, Inc., 1959.

McKenzie, Margaret. "The Pilgrimage of Man: A Study of the Works of Hugo von
    Hofmannsthal." Ph.D. Dissertation, University of Chicago, 1958.

Miles, David H. Hofmannsthal's Novel "Andreas": Memory and Self. Princeton:
    Princeton University Press, 1972.

Naef, Karl J. Hugo von Hofmannsthals Wesen und Werk. Zurich: Max Niehans Verlag,
    1938.

Nehring, Wolfgang. Die Tat bei Hofmannsthal: Eine Untersuchung zu Hofmannsthals
    grossen Dramen. Germanistische Abhandlungen, no. 16. Stuttgart: J. B. Met-
    zlerische Verlagsbuchhandlung, 1966.

235

Norman, F. , ed. Hofmannsthal, Studies in Commemoration. London: Institute of
Germanic Studies, 1963.

Pautz, Barbara Garwig. ''The Salzburg Festival: In Theory and in Practice.''
Master Thesis, University of Colorado, 1967.

Schafer, Rudolf H. Hugo von Hofmannsthals ''Arabella.'' Bern: Verlag Herbert Lang,
1967.

Schmid, Martin Erich. Symbol und Funktion der Musik im Werk Hugo von Hofmannsthals. Heidelberg: Carl Winter-Universitätsverlag, 1968.

Schoolfield, George C. ''The Pool, the Bath, the Dive: the Water Image in Hofmannsthal.'' Monatshefte: A Journal Devoted to the Study of German
Language and Literature 45 (November 1953): 379-88.

Wunberg, Gotthart, ed. Hofmannsthal im Urteil seiner Kritiker: Dokumente zur
Wirkungsgeschichte Hugo von Hofmannsthals in Deutschland. Frankfurt:
Athenäum, 1972.

Works Pertaining to Richard Strauss

Baum, Günther. ''Hab' mir's gelobt, ihn lieb zu haben . . . '': Richard Strauss
und Hugo von Hofmannsthal, nach ihrem Briefwechsel dargestellt. Berlin-
Halensee: Max Hesses Verlag, 1962.

Del Mar, Norman. Richard Strauss: A Critical Commentary on His Life and Works.
3 vols. Philadelphia: Chilton Book Co. , 1962-1972.

Gerlach, Reinhard. ''Richard Strauss: Prinzipien seiner Kompositionstechnik (mit
einem Brief von Strauss). '' Archiv für Musikwissenschaft 23 (1966):277-88.

Grasberger, Franz. Richard Strauss und die Wiener Oper. Tutzing: H. Schneider,
1969.

Kralik, Heinrich. The Vienna Opera. Translated by Richard Rickett. London:
Methuen and Co. Ltd. , 1963.

Krause, Ernst. Richard Strauss: The Man and His Work. Translated by John Coombs.
London: Collet's, 1964.

Lehmann, Lotte. Five Operas and Richard Strauss. Translated by Ernst Pawel.
New York: The Macmillan Co. , 1964.

Mann, William S. Richard Strauss: A Critical Study of the Operas. London: Cassell,
1964.

SELECTED BIBLIOGRAPHY

Marek, George R. Richard Strauss: The Life of a Non-Hero. New York: Simon and Schuster, 1967.

Murphy, Edward Wright. "Harmony and Tonality in the Large Orchestral Works of Richard Strauss." Ph. D. Dissertation, University of Indiana, 1963.

Newman, Ernst. Richard Strauss. With a personal note by Alfred Kalisch. Select Bibliographies Reprint Series. New York: Books for Libraries Press, 1969.

Röttger, Heinz. Das Formproblem bei Richard Strauss: gezeigt an der Oper "Die Frau ohne Schatten" mit Einschluss von "Guntram" und Intermezzo". Neue Deutsche Forschungen: Abteilung Musikwissenschaft, no. 5. Berlin: Junker und Dünnhaupt, 1937.

Schuh, Willi. Hugo von Hofmannsthal und Richard Strauss: Legende und Wirklichkeit. Bayerische Akademie der Schönen Künste. Munich: C. Hanser, 1964.

_____. Kritiken und Essays. Vol. 1: Ueber Opern von Richard Strauss. Zurich: Atlantis, 1947.

Works Pertaining to Aesthetics

Barfield, Owen. Poetic Diction: A Study in Meaning. London: Faber and Gwyer Ltd., 1928: reprint ed. with an Introduction by Howard Nemerov, New York: McGraw-Hill Book Co., 1964.

Cassirer, Ernst. An Essay on Man: An Introduction to Philosophy of Human Culture. New Haven: Yale University Press, 1944.

Cone, Edward T. Musical Form and Musical Performance. New York: W. W. Norton and Co., 1968.

Hanslick, Eduard. The Beautiful in Music. Edited, with an introduction, by Morris Weitz. Translated by Gustav Cohen. Indianapolis: Bobbs-Merrill, 1957.

Kraussold, Max. "Musik und Mythus in ihrem Verhältnis." Die Musik 18 (1925-26): 176-87. Reprinted in translation in Reflections on Art: A Source Book of Writings by Artists, Critics, and Philosophers. Edited by Susanne K. Langer. Baltimore: Johns Hopkins Press, 1968.

Langer, Susanne K. Feeling and Form: A Theory of Art Developed from "Philosophy in a New Key". New York: Charles Scribner's Sons, 1953.

_____. Philosophy in a New Key: A Study in the Symbolism of Reason, Rite, and Art. 3rd ed. Cambridge: Harvard University Press, 1957.

SELECTED BIBLIOGRAPHY

Langer, Susanne K. Problems of Art: Ten Philosophical Lectures, New York: Charles Scribner's Sons, 1957.

_____. ed. Reflections on Art: A Source Book of Writings by Artists, Critics, and Philosophers. Baltimore: The Johns Hopkins Press, 1958.

Lorenz, Alfred. Das Geheimnis der Form bei Richard Wagner. Vol. III: Der Musikalische Aufbau von Richard Wagners " Die Meistersinger von Nürnberg". 2nd ed. Tutzing: Hans Schneider, 1966.

Meyer, Leonard B. Emotion and Meaning in Music. Chicago: University of Chicago Press, 1956.

_____. Music, the Arts and Ideas: Patterns and Predictions in Twentieth-Century Culture. Chicago: University of Chicago Press, 1967.

Nietzsche, Friedrich. Die Geburt der Tragödie oder Griechentum und Pessimismus in Werke in drei Bänden. Edited by Karl Schlechta. Munich: Carl Hanser Verlag, 1966. I:7-134.

Weisinger, Herbert. The Agony and the Triumph: Papers on the Use and Abuse of Myth. East Lansing: Michigan State University Press, 1964.

Wellesz, Egon. Essays on Opera. Translated by Patricia Kean. London: Dennis Dobson Ltd., 1950.

Wheelwright, Philip. Metaphor and Reality. Bloomington: Indiana University Press, 1962.

_____. The Burning Fountain: A Study in the Language of Symbolism. Bloomington: Indiana University Press, 1954.

APPENDIX

APPENDIX

List of Musical Examples(1)

1.	Keikobad	31.	Mistress
2.	Nurse	32.	Pact
3.	Messenger	33.	Fire Flickering
4.	Shadow	34.	Youth
5.	Empress	35.	Erotic Love
6.	Dissension	36.	Heart
7.	Emperor as Lover	37.	Deception
8.	Stone	38.	Hypocrisy
9.	Falcon Cry	39.	Sorrow
10.	Emperor as Hunter	40.	Youth Awakening
11.	Love Themes #1 and #2	41.	Generosity
12.	Talisman	42.	Anger
13.	Tears	43.	Bitterness
14.	Falcon	44.	Magic
15.	Traitor	45.	Animal
16.	Beating	46.	Lack of Commitment
17.	Descent to Mankind	47.	Freedom
18.	New Day	48.	Servant
19.	Activity	49.	Judgment
20.	Irritability	50.	Cavern
21.	Work	51.	Guilt
22.	Children	52.	Fear
23.	Desire for Children	53.	Stupidity
24.	Happiness	54.	No Blood
25.	Joy	55.	Sword
26.	Blessedness	56.	Denial
27.	Market Song	57.	Transformation
28.	Renunciation of Motherhood	58.	Vision
29.	Flattery	59.	Countenance
30.	Secret	60.	Protection

APPENDIX

61. Release from Prison

62. Bronze Door

63. Marriage Theme

64. Answer

65. Price

66. Phoenix

67. Agitation

68. Temptation

69. Awaken

70. Extended Children

71. Jubilation

Footnote

(1) All musical examples are taken from: Richard Strauss, <u>Die Frau ohne Schat-</u>
<u>ten,</u> Oper in drei Akten von Hugo Hofmannsthal, Musik von Richard Strauss,
Op. 65. (Copyright 1919 by Adolph Fürstner: copyright assigned 1943 to
Boosey & Hawkes Music Publishers Ltd. , London, for all countries except
Germany, Danzig, Italy, Portugal and the U.S.S.R.) The examples are cited
according to act, scene and rehearsal number in this manner: I i: 50.

1. Keikobad (I i: 0)

2. Nurse (I i: 0)

3. Messenger (I i: 1)

4. Shadow (I i: 6)

5. Empress (I i: 7)

6. Dissension (I i: 10)

7. Emperor as Lover (I i:12)

8. Stone (I i:19)

9. Falcon Cry (I i:28)

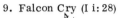

10. Emperor as Hunter (I i:32)

11. Love Themes #1 and #2 (I i:43)

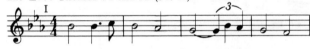
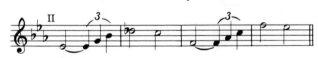

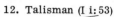
12. Talisman (I i: 53)

13. Tears (I i: 62)

14. Falcon (I i: 60)

15. Traitor (I i: 89)

16. Beating (I ii: 0)

17. Descent to Mankind (I i: 83)

18. New Day (I i: 86)

19. Activity (I ii: 11)

20. Irritability (I ii: 8)

21. Work (I ii: 12)

22. Children (I ii: 17)

23. Desire for Children (I ii: 21)

24. Happiness (I ii: 30)

sehr ruhig

246

25. Joy (I ii: 31)

26. Blessedness (I ii: 39-40)

pp subito

27. Market Song (I ii: 50)

(Vocal)

(Horn)

28. Renunciation of Motherhood (I ii: 101)

*

29. Flattery (I ii: 54)

(Violin) *p*

*See the Children Motive, #22.

30. Secret (I ii: 66)

kennt   das   Ge - heim   -   nis.

31. Mistress (I ii: 89-90)

32. Pact (I ii: 106)

3

33. Fire Flickering (I ii: 115)

pp

34. Youth (II i: 0)

f

35. Erotic Love (II i: 0)

p espr.

36. Heart (II i: 0)

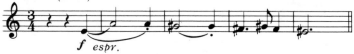

f espr.

37. Deception (II i: 1)

p

38. Hypocrisy (II i: 2)

p

39. Sorrow (II i: 22)

f

249

40. Youth Awakening (II i: 28)

41. Generosity (II i: 47)

pp ben sostenuto

42. Anger (II i: 49)

sf

43. Bitterness (II iii: 137)

p

3

44. Magic (II iii: 112)

ff *sf*

45. Animal (II iii: 130)

p

46. Lack of Commitment (II iii: 136-37)

47. Freedom (II iii: 138)

48. Servant (II iii: 148)

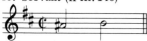

49. Judgment (II iv: 172)

50. Cavern (II iv: 169)

51. Guilt (II iv: 178)

52. Fear (II v: 193)

53. Stupidity (II v: 201)

54. No Blood (II v: 221)

55. Sword (II v: 227)

56. Denial (II v: 228-29)

57. Transformation (II v: 228)

58. Vision (III i: 9)

*

59. Countenance (III i: 11)

60. Protection (III i: 19)

61. Release from Prison (III i: 30)

* See the Stupidity Motive, #53.

62. Bronze Door (III ii: 48)

f marc.   *dim.*   *p*

63. Marriage Theme (III ii: 61)

64. Answer (III ii: 70)

65. Price (III ii: 91)

66. Phoenix (III ii: 92)

67. Agitation (III ii: 98)

p agitato

68. Temptation (III iii: 142)

69. Awaken (III iii: 158)

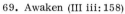

ff con moto

70. Extended Children (III iii: 174)

71. Jubilation (III iv: 212)

*See the Happiness Motive, #24.

255

STUDIENREIHE ZUR GERMANISTIK

German Studies in America:

Bd. 1 Nordmeyer, Rubaijat von Omar Chajjam. 2. Aufl. 104 S., brosch. und Lwd., 1969.

Bd. 2 Richards, The German Bestseller in the 20th Century. A complete Bibliography and Analysis. 276 S., Lwd., 1968.

Bd. 3 Germer, The German Novel of Education 1792–1805. A complete Bibliography and Analysis. 280 S., Lwd., 1968.

Bd. 4 Gerlitzki, Die Bedeutung der Minne in "Moriz von Craun". 132 S., Lwd., 1970.

Bd. 5 Bowman, Life into Autobiography. A Study of Goethe's "Dichtung und Wahrheit". 162 S., Lwd., 1971.

Bd. 6 Putzel, Letters to Immanuel Bekker from Henriette Herz, S. Pobenheim and Anna Horkel. 108 S., Lwd., 1972.

Bd. 7 Geldrich, Heine und der spanisch-amerikanische Modernismo. 304 S., Lwd., 1971.

Bd. 8 Friesen, The German Panoramic Novel in the 19th Century. 232 S., Lwd., 1972.

Bd. 9 Novak, Wilhelm von Humboldt as a Literary Critic. 142 S., Lwd., 1972.

Bd. 10 Shelton, The Young Hölderlin. 282 S., Lwd., 1973.

Bd. 11 Milstein, Eight Eighteenth Century Reading Societies. A Sociological Contribution to the History of German Literature. 312 S., Lwd., 1972.

Bd. 12 Schatzberg, Scientific Themes in the Popular Literature and the Poetry of the German Enlightenment, 1720–1760. 350 S., Lwd., 1973.

Bd. 13 Dimler, Friedrich Spee's "Trutznachtigall". 158 S., Lwd., 1973.

Bd. 14 McCort, Perspectives on Music in German Fiction. The Music-Fiction of Wilhelm Heinrich Riehl. 154 S., Lwd., 1974.

Bd. 15 Motsch, Die poetische Epistel. Ein Beitrag zur Geschichte der deutschen Literatur und Literaturkritik des achtzehnten Jahrhunderts. 218 S., Lwd., 1974.

Bd. 16 Zipser, Edward Bulwer-Lytton and Germany. 232 S., Lwd., 1974.

Bd. 17 Rutledge John, The Dialogue of the Dead in Eighteenth-Century Germany. 186 S., Lwd., 1974.

Bd. 18 Rutledge Joyce S., Johann Adolph Schlegel. 322 S., Lwd., 1974.

Bd. 19 Gutzkow, Wally the Skeptic. Novel. A translation from the German with an Introduction and Notes by Ruth-Ellen Boetcher Joeres. 130 S., Lwd., 1974.

Bd. 20 Keck, Renaissance and Romanticism: Tieck's Conception of Cultural Decline as Portrayed in his "Vittoria Accorombona". 120 S., Lwd., 1976.

Bd. 21 Scholl, The Bildungsdrama of the Age of Goethe. 80 S., Lwd., 1976.

Bd. 22 Bartel, German Literary History 1777–1835. An Annotated Bibliography. 230 S., Lwd., 1976.

Bd. 23 Littell, Jeremias Gotthelf's "Die Käserei in der Vehfreude". A Didactic Satire. 122 S., Lwd., 1977.

Bd. 24 Carels, The Satiric Treatise in Eighteenth-Century Germany. 168 S., Lwd., 1976.

Bd. 25 Lensing, Narrative Structure and the Reader in Wilhelm Raabe's "Im alten Eisen". 118 S., Lwd., 1977.

Bd. 26 Profit, Interpretations of Iwan Goll's late Poetry with a comprehensive and annotated Bibliography of the Writings by and about Iwan Goll. 202 S., Lwd., 1977.

Bd. 27 Hollyday, Anti-Americanism in the German Novel 1841–1862. 212 S., Lwd., 1977.

Bd. 28 Horwath, Der Kampf gegen die religiösen Traditionen: Die Kulturkampfliteratur Oesterreichs, 1780–1918. 242 S., Lwd., 1977.